Café Crème Guide
to the
Cafés of Europe

Thanks are due to our hard-working team of researchers, who have travelled through Europe seeking out the best cafés for this fourth edition of the Guide: Roderic Lowe, Philip and Ana Diment, Nick Scade, Marcus Ackerman, Chris Eveleigh, Helena Baker and many others.

Thanks also to all those connected with organising the ceremonies for the 2000 award-winners, in particular Café Nicola, Lisbon; Café Comercial, Madrid; Le Metro, London; and the overall European winner Les Deux Magots, Paris. Congratulations to them and to all the other award-winners - a full list appears on pages 19-20. Thanks to all the readers who entered our competition and everyone who wrote to us about their favourite cafés.

Last, but certainly not least, thanks are due to Leigh Simpson for his brilliant work behind the camera and to Nicole Keogan and Peter Long for their sterling work in and out of the office.

Roy Ackerman

Published by Compendium
43 Frith Street, London W1D 4SA

Edited by Peter Long
Art Direction and selection
by Roy Ackerman

© 2001
Tadema Studios
35 Tadema Road
London SW10 0PZ

Designed by Frank Ainscough
Photography by Leigh Simpson
Printed and Bound in Hong Kong throught Printworks Int. Ltd.

ISBN 1 902579 37 2

Contents

CAFÉ CRÈME

Foreword

The fourth edition of the Café Crème Guide to the Cafés of Europe features over 800 cafés in 90 towns and cities in 16 countries throughout Europe. Our team of researchers covered thousands of miles, sipped gallons of coffee and nibbled on tons of snacks to ensure that the Guide offers a complete cross-section of cafés which together reflect the ever-increasing interest in café culture, led by the desire to relax, take a break and socialise in informal surroundings. The boom that cafés have been enjoying in recent years has often been at the expense of the pubs and wine bars, but restaurants, too, have had to look to their laurels at a time when value for money is a major factor in the choice of where to eat. The range and scope of cafés has vastly increased in the past decade, but the criteria remain the same: a place where you can feel at home when alone or relaxed and happy in a crowd; a place where you can linger at your leisure over a coffee and a newspaper; a place where you can eat but are not obliged to. Each of the 800 entries has something else to add: it could be the location, the decor, the history or some other special feature. And whatever its qualities, a café is nothing without its staff and its customers: the staff, whose job it is to provide a warm, genuine welcome for friends and strangers alike; the customers, who can feel happy and relaxed in the knowledge that they are welcome visitors whose custom is appreciated.

How to use this Guide

Aims and Ethics
The Guide does not try to be comprehensive in any of the towns and cities included. Every one of the 800 cafés featured has been visited at least once by our researchers, but there are inevitably many more which could be worthy of inclusion. We would always like to hear from owners who think their cafés deserve an entry in future editions and from readers telling us about their favourite cafés (see the 'Write Your Own Review' section for a chance to win a great prize).

Information by Country
Countries are listed alphabetically. Each begins with a title page showing the international dialling code from the UK. The country's capital city heads the entries, followed by other towns and cities in alphabetical order. In the UK the order is England, Scotland, Wales, Northern Ireland.

Entries
Recommended establishments are listed alphabetically in each town or city. Prefixes such as Bar, Café, The and La are usually ignored; thus Café Rose appears under 'R' and Le Central under 'C'.

Café Crème Awards

The Café Crème Awards were initiated to recognise and honour the outstanding contributions that the winning cafés have made to their own environments and to society in general by providing the best in ambience, service and style - places to relax with a drink and a snack and reflect on the good things in life.

The Café Crème Café of the Year Awards were created to recognise and reward cafés which are outstanding in every aspect of their business: quality of food and drink, welcome, service, decor.

The Café Crème Special Awards acknowledge all the above and also recognise individuality, personality, history and tradition - attributes that can turn a good café into a very special one.

The Café Crème Awards are recognised throughout Europe as the supreme awards for café-owners, adding greatly to the prestige and standing of their establishments. Some of the winners for 2000 are pictured at the ceremonies where they were presented with their awards (see 2000 'Award Ceremonies' section). These events invariably generated great acclaim and considerable local and national media interest, and all the winning cafés thoroughly deserved their recognition.

Top of the Awards is the Grand Award European Café of the Year. All Café of the Year winners receive a Café Crème plaque, a certificate recording their achievement and the opportunity to host a reception celebrating their award.

All cafés featured in the Guide receive a copy of the Guide and stickers to display in the windows of their cafés.

CAFÉ CRÈME

2001

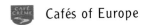
2001 Grand Award Europe

Café Landtmann

Vienna, Austria

In a city famed throughout the world for its cafés and café culture, Café Landtmann is truly outstanding. Grand, elegant and rich in refined, old-world charm, it first opened its doors in 1873, since when generations of artists, actors, theatregoers and politicians have been loyal customers, and Freud was a regular. They all came, as they still do, to enjoy the civilised ambience and the mouthwatering cakes and pastries.

CAFÉ CRÈME

2001

2001 Country Awards

Austria

Café of the Year
Café Landtmann, Vienna
Old-world charm and scrumptious patisserie in one of Vienna's most renowned cafés

Special Award
Niemetz, Salzburg
Lovely cakes and pastries in a venerable little patisserie palace

Benelux

Café of the Year
Le Falstaff, Brussels
Residents and tourists both love this splendid art nouveau café, patisserie and ice cream parlour

Special Award
Café Americain, Amsterdam
An outpost of 1930s America, with splendid original light fittings, tile murals and stained glass

Denmark

Café of the Year
Opera Cafeen, Copenhagen
Busy bar and restaurant near the Opera, with striking wall hangings

Special Award
Café Gertrud, Odense
A little piece of Paris, right down to the zinc bar counter. Good French wines

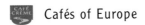

2001 Country Awards

France

Café of the Year
Bouillon Racine, Paris
Belgian cooking and Belgian beer in a vast, splendid dining hall in art nouveau style

Special Award
Excelsior, Nancy
Wonderful art nouveau surroundings and furniture by Majorelle. Quite a setting for a coffee and a snack!

Germany

Café of the Year
Hollandische Kakaostube, Hanover
More than just a place of refreshment, a step back to gentler, more civilised times

Special Award
Et Kaduffke, Dusseldorf
A family-run old-timer, long favoured by the more mature tipplers of Dusseldorf

Ireland

Café of the Year
Clancy's, Cork
One of Cork's oldest and best-loved café-bistro-bars

Special Award
Kaffé Moka, Dublin
Popular coffee houses with late hours and regular music and poetry events

2001 Country Awards

Italy

Café of the Year
Quadri, Venice
Renowned, elegant café-restaurant with gilded mirrors and painted panels....and its own orchestra

Special Award
Antico Caffè della Pace, Rome
A favourite of film stars, this is one of the most fashionable cafés in fashionable Trastevere

Portugal

Café of the Year
A Brasileira, Lisbon
The most renowned of Lisbon's old coffee houses, with elaborate art nouveau decor. Pavement tables are a must for people-watching

Special Award
Gambrinus, Lisbon
An exclusive, happening bar that's long been a favourite with the Lisbon smart set

Scandinavia

Café of the Year
Operabaren, Stockholm
Clubby bar, wine cellar, café with a spectacular ceiling painting. Haunt of royalty and stars of stage, screen and sports arenas

Special Award
Grand Café, Hotel Driftselskap, Oslo
Famous café in a venerable hotel, with a giant mural of notable habitués and a mouthwatering central buffet

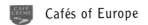 Cafés of Europe

2001 Country Awards

Spain

Café of the Year
Café de Oriente, Madrid
Grand and stylish café in a grand and stylish setting opposite the Royal Palace. Popular throughout long opening hours

Special Award
El Quatro Gats, Barcelona
Haunt of artists down the years, a great place to meet for a coffee or a glass of wine

United Kingdom

Café of the Year
Browns, Bristol
Great choice of eating and drinking in a grand building designed in 1783 in the style of the Doges Palace in Venice

Special Award
Arches, London
Splendid little wine bar-cum-café with a full house of bric-a-brac and a super selection of well-priced wines

Write your own review

and win a weekend break in Vienna

The Café Crème Guide to the Cafés of Europe is offering you the chance to have your very own café review published in the next edition of the Guide, with the added incentive of a weekend break in Vienna for the best review. All you have to do is write a review of your favourite café in no more than 100 words. The café can be anywhere in a European town or city and should not be featured in this edition of the Guide. Please try to include all the essential statistics of the establishment (address, telephone, opening times) as well as your own address and telephone number.

Please send your review to:
Café Crème Guide
35 Tadema Road, London SW10 0PZ
or fax it to 020 7352 2041
or e-mail it to
tadstudios@ukgateway.net

Entires must be submitted by 30 November 2001 and winners will be notified by the end of the year. Entries will not be returned and copyright for published reviews will remain the property of the Café Crème Guide.

For the Overall Winner
A published review with acknowledgement in the next edition of the Café Crème Guide to the Cafés of Europe, and a free copy of the Guide.
A three-night weekend break for two in Vienna, including flights, transfers and Bed & Breakfast accommodation in a four-star hotel, a meal in Café Landtmann, our Grand Award winner, and £250 spending money.

For five runners-up
A published review with acknowledgement in the next edition of the Café Crème Guide to the Cafés of Europe, and a free copy of the next Guide.

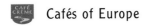

2000 Europe Award

Grand Award European Café of the Year 2000

Les Deux Magots, Paris, France

Jacques Mathivat, Director General of Les Deux Magots, is shown here receiving the Guide's most coveted and prestigious award from Roy Ackerman. The reception, which took place at the café on June 7, 2000, was attended by a large number of well-known French journalists and media people. Both the event and the book received wide coverage in the French press, from specialist publications like *Cuisine Actuelle* to the leading national newspaper *Le Figaro*, and also featured in several television programmes. The award recognised the history and tradition associated with one of the best-known cafés in the world, a café which in its 125 years' life has been almost a second home to many of the greatest French and American literary and artistic figures. A truly outstanding café, and a worthy successor to our previous winners, El Pabellon del Espejo in Madrid and Caffè Florian in Venice.

2000 Country winners

Café Nicola, Lisbon, Portugal

On a sunny day in July 2000 the local and national press of Portugal gathered at Café Nicola for the presentation of the Café of the Year Award for Portugal to Paulo Batista da Costa, the café's General Manager (on the right). In the lovely art deco surroundings of the Café, Mr da Costa expressed his delight at receiving this prestigious award. At the same ceremony the manager of Pavilhao Chines, Luiz Pinto Coelho, seen here on the left, received a Special Award. The event attracted considerable interest in newspapers, both regional and national, in magazines and in tourist publications, as well as on local and national radio.

2000 Country winners

Café Comercial, Madrid, Spain

June 29 was a red-letter day for the owners of Café Comercial, chosen as Café of the Year for Spain. Olga Maria Ramos sang a song written specially for the occasion and Roy Ackerman presented the Café's owners, Isabel Contreras and Isabel Serratacó, with their award. Mr Ackerman praised the quality of the food and drink, the friendly service and the delightful ambience of this most inviting of cafés. The event, which was well reported in the press, concluded with a discussion on café culture and its influence down the centuries. The participants included figures from the artistic and cultural worlds as well as those directly concerned with cafés.

2000 Country winners

Pavilhao Chines, Lisbon, Portugal

Luiz Pinto Coelho, seen here with Roy Ackerman, received his Special Award during the ceremony at Café Nicola (see page 16). Mr Coelho has had a distinguished career in interior design, and his unerring sense of style is evident in his wonderfully ornate bar-café, which also houses his private collection of art, antiques and memorabilia assembled over 50 years.

Le Metro, London, United Kingdom

Le Metro, a shoppers' haven between Harrods and Harvey Nichols, won the UK Café of the Year Award for the year 2000. In the words of Roy Ackerman: 'Le Metro extends a warm welcome to visitors from all over the world who want somewhere to recover from their shopping exploits. At the same time, the place is home to locals who like to chat with friends, read the papers or simply savour the cosmopolitan atmosphere. Local residents and staff from neighbouring offices and shops use Le Metro all the time. Some call in up to four times a day.' Joseph Levin, Managing Director of Le Metro's owners the Capital Group, was delighted with the award. He said: 'The Café Crème Guide is extremely prestigious and is known throughout Europe. We are thrilled to be involved.'

All the winners

Europe
1998 Caffé Florian, Venice
1999 El Pabellon del Espejo, Madrid
2000 Les Deux Magots, Paris
2001 Café Landtmann, Vienna

Austria
1998 *Café of the Year:* Café Sperl, Vienna
Special Award: Hawelka, Vienna
1999 *Café of the Year:* Hotel Sacher, Vienna
Special Award: Valena, Vienna
2000 *Café of the Year:* Tomaselli, Salzburg
Special Award: Café Diglas, Vienna
2001 *Café of the Year:* Café Landtmann, Vienna
Special Award: Niemetz, Salzburg

Benelux
1998 *Café of the Year:*
Café Luxembourg, Amsterdam
Special Award: Café in den Vogelstruys, Maastricht
1999 *Café of the Year:* De Groote Witte Arend, Antwerp
Special Award: De Ultimatie Hallucinatie, Brussels
2000 *Café of the Year:* Amadeus, Brussels
Special Award: Tomas, Eindhoven
2001 *Café of the Year:*
Le Falstaff, Brussels
Special Award:
Café Americain, Amsterdam

Denmark
2000 *Café of the Year:* Victor, Copenhagen
Special Award: Franck A, Odense
2001 *Café of the Year:* Opera Cafeen, Copenhagen
Special Award: Café Gertrud, Odense

France
1998 *Café of the Year:* Café Marly, Paris
Special Award: Les Pipos, Paris
1999 *Café of the Year:* La Cigale, Nantes
Special Award: Pause Café, Paris
2000 *Café of the Year:* Les Deux Magots, Paris
Special Award: Les Flots Bleus, Marseilles
2001 *Café of the Year:* Bouillon Racine, Paris
Special Award: Excelsior, Nancy

Germany
1998 *Café of the Year:* Café Einstein, Berlin
Special Award: Luigi Tambosi am Hofgarten, Munich
1999 *Café of the Year:* Wintergarten im Literaturhaus, Berlin
Special Award: Café Reitschule, Hamburg
2000 *Café of the Year:* Café Adler, Berlin
Special Award: Bobby Reich, Hamburg
2001 *Café of the Year:* Hollandische, Hanover
Special Award: Et Kaduffke, Dusseldorf

Ireland
1998 No award
1999 *Café of the Year:* Bodega, Cork
Special Award: Bridge Café Bar
(Bewley), Dublin
2000 *Café of the Year:* Thomas Read,
Dublin
Special Award: The Palace, Dublin
2001 *Café of the Year:* Clancy's, Cork
Special Award: Kaffé Moka, Dublin

Italy
1998 *Café of the Year:* Caffè Florian,
Venice
Special Award: Antico Caffè Greco,
Rome
1999 *Café of the Year:* Osteria Caffè
Italiano, Florence
Special Award: LaTega, Verona
2000 *Café of the Year:* Babington's,
Rome
Special Award: Giubbe Rosse, Florence
2001 *Café of the Year:* Quadri, Venice
Special Award: Antica Caffè della Pace,
Rome

Portugal
1999 *Café of the Year:* Martinho da
Arcada, Lisbon
Special Award: Majestic Café, Oporto
2000 *Café of the Year:* Café Nicola,
Lisbon
Special Award: Pavilhao Chines, Lisbon
2001 *Café of the Year:* A Brasileira,
Lisbon
Special Award: Gambrinus, Lisbon

Scandinavia
2000 *Café of the Year:* Fazer, Helsinki
Special Award: Theatercaféen, Oslo
2001 *Café of the Year:* Operabaren,
Stockholm
Special Award: Grand Café, Hotel
Driftselskap, Oslo

Spain
1998 *Café of the Year:* Café Gijon,
Madrid
Special Award: Café de l'Opera,
Barcelona
1999 *Café of the Year:* El Pabellon del
Espejo, Madrid
Special Award: Pilar del Toro, Granada
2000 *Café of the Year:* Café Comercial,
Madrid
Special Award: Café Iruña, Bilbao
2001 *Café of the Year:* Café de Oriente,
Madrid
Special Award: El Quatro Gats,
Barcelona

United Kingdom
1998 *Café of the Year:* Mud Dock Café,
Bristol
Special Award: Picasso, London
1999 *Café of the Year:* The Troubadour,
London
Special Award: Madisons, Belfast
2000 *Café of the Year:* Le Metro,
London
Special Award: Café Concerto, York
2001 *Café of the Year:* Browns, Bristol
Special Award: Arches, London

Austria

A land of enchanting scenery, of mountains, rivers, glorious lakes, peaceful little villages, castles and vineyards. Music is everywhere, from bands of violins and guitars and accordions in the country inns to events of world stature in Vienna and Salzburg. In Imperial days there were hundreds of Austrian choirs - the Vienna Boys Choir was instituted in the court of the Emperor Maximilian. Hand in hand with the music goes the dance, and the waltz is as delightfully fresh and light today as when it first thrilled the nation in the early years of the 19th century, and the famous Viennese Balls have always been a highlight of the social season. If the summer season is filled with music, song and church bells, the whole year is filled, in the cities at least, with the tinkle of delicate cups meeting delicate saucers in the famous coffee shops. Turkish invasions gave the Austrians a taste for coffee, which they traditionally enjoy with superb pastries, and this delectable duo is a favourite with the whole of society in a variety of surroundings, from the simplest student café to the grandest and most glamorous coffee house. The most famous of the pastries is the *Sachertorte*, created by a 16-year-old apprentice who was to become the owner of the Sacher Hotel in Vienna, but close behind come apple strudel, Linzertorte and fruit dumplings.

Vienna

Vienna's history dates back to around 100AD, when it was founded as a military outpost of the Roman Empire. It later became a bastion of Christianity against the Turks and as an imperial city was the base of the Hapsburg rulers of the Austro-Hungarian empire. It now plays a major role in the modern world: it's been the seat of OPEC since 1967, several UN agencies have their headquarters there and in 1998 Austria had a spell at the helm of the European Community. It has sufficient elegant buildings, museums, theatres, shops and parks to keep tourists happy for many a long day, and in the evenings confirms its status as one of the world's leading centres of classical music. The Vienna Boys Choir sings on Sunday at the Hofburg, the Imperial Palace that was the winter home of the Hapsburgs. Vienna is also renowned for its coffee shops, bars and cafés, and its night life teems with clubs and cabaret.

Kaffee Alt Wien

Bäckerstrasse 9
Tel: 1 512 5222
Open: 10.00-02.00 (Fri & Sat till 04.00)
Tucked away in narrow Baker Street, this is more for locals during the day, the smarter jobs for visitors being two streets away. A 'brown' café in many ways: the walls are covered in posters, there are lots of newspapers, and the nicotine-stained paintwork may well have been cream once, now it's certainly brown. The atmosphere is the main draw to this typical old Viennese café dimly lit with globe lighting. At night it comes to life with a younger crowd.

Bränerhof

Stallburggasse 2
Tel: 1 5 12 38 93
Open: 07.30-20.30 (Sat till 18.30, Sun 10.00-18.30)
Bränerhof is near the Imperial Palace, the Treasury, and the famous Spanish Riding School, and the Dorotheum auction house is around the corner, along with lots of antique shops. It offers a relaxed coffee house atmosphere, with excellent waiter service and fine cakes and pastries, and on Saturday and Sunday between 15.00 and 18.00 the Schelz Trio (violin, piano and cello), led by Professor Schelz, play gentle music. The cream interior and globe lighting are classic. Inside the tables are marble-topped, outside flowers and green planting enclose a terrace visible through the wide box sash windows, where you can enjoy an excellent apple strudel and coffee with a newspaper, including the foreign press.

Café Central

Herrengasse 14
Tel: 1 533 37 63 26
Open: 08.00-20.00 (Sun 10.00-18.00)
Located in the very centre, in the architecturally important Ferstel Palace, and recently refurbished in Venetian style, this was an important rendezvous for some of the literary giants at the end of the 19th century. Occupying a point on the fork with Strachgasse, in front of the tall arched windows either side of the entrance are terrace tables secluded from the pavement by potted shrubs. A concert café, with live music every weekday. Smart, and popular with both locals and tourists.

Demel

Kohlmarkt 14, 1010
Tel: 1 535 17 17-0
Open: 10.00-19.00
In the beginning, 1786, it was Ludwig Dehne who opened his patisserie in St Michael's Square. In 1857 his eldest son passed it on to his chef-patissier Christoph Demel, and it was renamed in his honour by a later generation in 1911. Meanwhile it acquired the patronage of Emperor Franz Josef I. It is still frightfully grand today, with elaborate ceilings and plaster-work, mirrored walls, smart furniture, and, towards the back, a winter garden: elegance at every turn. It prides itself on its excellent hand-made delights, and its old-fashioned politeness. On the list are hors d'œuvre, soup, snacks and pastries, among which Demeltorte, filled with glacé fruit, is a speciality. Wines by the glass, and good coffee with cream.

Café Diglas

Wollzeile 10, 1010
Tel: 1 5 12 57 65-0
Open: 07.00-23.30 (Thur-Sat till 01.00)

Associated with gastronomy since 1875, Franz Diglas senior successfully opened restaurants and a casino in Vienna. It was in 1918 that he persuaded his sons Hans and Franz back from America, and in 1923 they opened this café. It's located right behind St Stephen's Cathedral in the centre of the city. After WWII, artisans, composers and cabaret artists were frequent guests. It then lost its way for a while, and it was not until the fifth-generation Hans renovated the café in 1988 that the original concept was restored. Serving typical Viennese cuisine and excellent cakes from its own pastry shop, it attracts the young crowd in considerable numbers. Waltz melodies are played on Fridays and Saturdays.

Café Dommayer

Auhofstrasse 2, 1130
Tel: 1 877 54 65
Open: 07.00-24.00

Ever since the mid-19th century, Johann Strauss, cafés and the waltz have been a winning combination, and it was at Casino Dommayer in 1844 that Strauss made his debut as a conductor. Here in the 13th district close by the Schönbrunn Palace, you can sit on the pretty terrace at the front, in the elegant interior, or in the even prettier garden at the back, where Saturday afternoons host small concerts - a trio, a piano, perhaps some waltzing - from May to September at 14.00. The speciality is five kinds of sausage with sauté potatoes and the highly esteemed sauerkraut.

Café Drechsler

Linke Wienzeile 22, 1060
Tel: 1 5 87 85 80
Open: 03.00-20.00

The lively and popular foodie district of the Naschmarkt, selling fruit, vegetables, meat and fish, is where you'll find Café Drechsler, very much a locals and market bar. Popular with students, the lower room has two billiard tables. The food is fresh and simple, and good value for money: soups, main dishes, apple strudel.

Frauenhuber

Himmelfortgasse 6
Tel: 1 512 8383
Open: 08.00-23.30
Closed: Sun

It's just off the main pedestrian shopping street, but the granite-topped tables with burgundy velvet upholstered armchairs, the oak parquet flooring, and the general air of peace and relaxation will transport you miles away from TGIF, MacD and the hordes. This has claims to be Vienna's oldest restaurant, and the homeliness and the aroma of coffee are delightfully welcoming.

Café Gloriette

Schönbrunner Schlosspark
Tel: 1 879 13 11
Open: 08.00-17.00

A café with a panoramic view, offering brunch on Saturdays and Sundays to live music. The setting is the park of Schönbrunn castle. Originally merely an ornate entrance to a grander palace, this café has, as a result, the most impressively ornate plasterwork and huge arched windows. The speciality is the produce of their in-house patisserie which can be enjoyed at their smart tables and armchairs inside, or looking at the gardens from the terrace.

Hawelka

Dorotheerstrasse 6
Tel: 1 512 82 30
Open: 08.00-02.00 (Sun from 16.00)
Closed: Tue

An archetypal Viennese art-conscious coffee-house, indeed a rendezvous for artists, and steeped in legend. The poster-decorated walls bear the record. The speciality is the Bucheln, a square brioche-like bun, served hot either with a vanilla custard, or filled with jam, and available from 22.00.

Korb

Brandstätte 9/corner of Tuchlauben
Tel: 1 5 33 72 15
Open: 08.00-24.00 (Sun 12.00-21.00)

Near St Stephen's Cathedral and St Peter's Church, this elegant café, haunt of many of Vienna's famous literary figures, is run by proprietress Susanne Widl. Korb, which means basket, has a 1960s interior, loads of newspapers, and a cabinet of cakes, including their excellent apple strudel. Inside there's a hushed atmosphere, away from the skittle alley, but for noise and bustle there are the terrace tables outside. Live classical music plays from 20.00 to 22.00.

Im Kunst Haus

Weissgerberlände 14
Tel: 1 712 0497
Open: 10.00-24.00

Located on the bank of the Danube to the east of the city centre, the Friedensreich Hundertwasser Art Gallery houses a café bestrewn with plants. Cloth-covered tables on a black and white tiled floor look out through tall french windows on to a pretty terrace and a wonderful garden. The typical coffee-house fare is delightfully enhanced by creative and imaginative cuisine. Live classical music is played from 19.00 to 22.00.

Café Landtmann

Dr Karl-Lueger-Ring 4
Tel: 1 532 0621
Open: 08.00-24.00

Entertaining customers now for over 125 years since it was first opened by Franz Landtmann, it was one of the most elegant places to go to in its time, and it is still at the centre of city life. It lies opposite the City Hall, with the National Theatre to one side and the University across the road, so it regularly plays host to politicians and students, theatre audiences and their stars. It's well-known for its traditional fare and excellent coffee and pastries, particularly the *marmorgugelhupf* - a circular yeast cake with a hole in the middle dusted liberally with vanilla sugar, and with a marbled appearance from the chocolate flavouring added before baking. Live classical music is played here Wednesday and Sunday from 14.30 to 17.30.

With its long and distinguished history, elegant ambience and top-notch food and service, Café Landtmann is a worthy winner of our Grand Award European Café of the Year for 2001.

Café Mozart

Albertinaplatz 2
Tel: 1 513 0881
Open: 08.00-24.00

This elegant café has been going for some 200 years, but it came to real fame some 50 years ago when it was used as a location in the cult movie *The Third Man*. It's right behind the Vienna State Opera, as any tourist will tell you, and is renowned for its in-house pastries, and its traditional and international cuisine. It's comfortable and spacious inside, but the best spot of all is a table under the awning along the terrace. Classical waltz melodies are played here regularly on Wednesdays and Sundays from 14.30 to 17.30.

Café Museum

Friedrichstrasse 6
Tel: 1 586 5202
Open: 08.00-24.00

On the corner of Karlsplatz, the café's design by the Austrian architect Adolf Loos is typical of the plain austere style of his middle years. The minimalist interior, with its half-panelled walls, is lit with bright globe lights. A little worse for wear, the white marble coffee tables have been chipped over the years; outside, the terrace tables under their permanent awning are more popular. It's a regulars' haunt, a rendezvous for poets and intellectuals, who come to read the piles of newspapers and magazines. The L-shaped room wraps around the kitchen, which produces excellent cakes - a speciality of the house. Espresso and more exotic coffees.

Oberlaa Konditorei Stadthaus

Neumarkt 16
Tel: 1 5 13 29 36
Open: 08.00-23.30 (till 20.00 in winter)

One of four in the city, this is Vienna's original cake emporium. It has a secluded terrace, surrounded by green planting. It's managed by Trixi Böck, who offers a 125ml glass of wine from 23sch, espresso at 29sch, and lots of cakes to take home.

Café Prückel

Stubenring 24
Tel: 1 512 6115
Open: 09.00-22.00

This is a large classic Viennese café with a 1950s interior, on a corner of the ring road, and opposite the Museum of Applied Arts and Vienna's City Park. It is also just two shakes from the heart of old Vienna. It serves super home-made cakes, and good snacks - the mushrooms and potato dish looks and tastes great. Lots of newspapers, including the foreign press, attract a cosmopolitan crowd, and if you're staying or living nearby and feeling lazy, it's a great place to spend a Sunday afternoon (the popular long terrace is in the quiet side street). Card playing is popular, and on Mondays, Wednesdays and Fridays there's live classical music from 19.00 to 22.00.

Raimann

Schönbrunnerstrasse 285, 1120
Tel: 1 813 5767
Open: 07.00-02.00 (Mon from 18.00, Thur-Sat till 04.00)

A suburban café in 1950s style with lots of local charm. Donauwelle (Danube Wave) on Saturday and Sunday is a cabaret with local Viennese artistes, including the opera diva, Frau Maria, reciting poetry. When the music stops you can amuse yourselves with a game of billiards or chess, or a snack - little eats include a selection of soups (goulash is a favourite), and ham and eggs.

Café Sacher

Philharmonikerstrasse 4
Tel: 1 51 4560
Open: 06.30-23.30

Around the corner from Café Mozart is the Sacher Hotel, where the famous Sachertorte is sold in the Café to an elegant, appreciative clientele. It was created in the absence of the head pastry chef by the 16-year-old second-year apprentice Franz Sacher for Prince Metternich in 1832, at the time when the British were debating the Reform Bill. Today's Sacher pastry chefs use more than 800,000 eggs, 50 tons of chocolate and 40 tons of sugar each year in making the sachertorten, which are exported all over the world. The café's beautifully preserved 19th-century decor, with chandeliers, antiques and portraits of the royal family, cannot fail to impress the visitor, who is pampered by the smartly dressed waitresses in their frilly aprons. Classical music is played from 17.00 till closing time in the hall and the red bar. In fine weather the terrace is a popular spot.

Sailer's Gulaschmuseum

Schulerstrasse 20
Tel: 1 512 1018
Open: 09.00-24.00 (Sat & Sun from 10.00)
Proprietor Herbert Svatunek sports a moustache and grey ponytail, and here offers, as the name suggests, a wide range of goulash - at least seven of them are always available! At the marble bar counter, with matching tiled floor, you can enjoy a range of five red wines to go with it, or on their own. Tucked away in a narrow street not far from the Cathedral, it's well worth a visit.

Savoy (Café Linke Wienzeile)

Linke Wienzeile 36
Tel: 1 586 7348
Open: 17.00-02.00 (Sat 09.00-18.00 & 21.00-02.00)
Closed: Sun
Opposite the Naschmarkt, a vegetable and meat market in the week, but increasingly a flea market especially at the weekend. Its rather pompous interior seems incongruous with the area, but it has a soul and drive of its own - many is the famous visitor who's come here, but the thrust of the clientele is from the bourgeoisie, the well-off in their casual clothes, mixing with the local residents and students. The robust and ornate facade and finely glazed windows lead to the elaborate interior of mirrors, trompe l'œil ceiling, marble table-tops and imperial style decor. Savoy is also called Linke Wienzeile Café, which is embossed over the revolving door on the corner of Köstlergasse; the ivy growing up the front gives it a timeless appeal.

Café Sperl

Grumpendorferstrasse 11, 1060
Tel: 1 586 41 58
Open: 07.00-23.00 (Sun from 15.00)
Established in 1880, Café Sperl truly maintains its 19th-century appeal - old oak parquet floor; billiard tables to the right; marble-topped tables in all the windows, with the better light to read the papers by; brass chandeliers; a mouthwatering display of cakes; outside tables under a mature leafy oak. This is old Vienna, but is much appreciated by modern Viennese and a much further flung clientele. Herr Staub, third generation of the current owners, keeps a careful watch on proceedings from behind his desk. Coffees, wine, snacks and main meals.

Valena

Zirkusgasse 36
Tel: 1 214 5577
Open: 06.00-18.30 (Sat till 13.00)
Closed: Sun

Founded in 1860 as an Imperial Court patisserie, now a very friendly café, run in charming style by Kurt Valena and his wife. Small and out of the way, it is situated in the traditional Jewish area of the city. It still has Hapsburg blue walls and floor tiles and in the cellar, still working away hard, is a steam baking oven of 1924 – practically the last of its kind in Vienna. This is a very unusual little café and bakery, complete with armchairs to sit in while you're waiting to be served in the shop. It's a real treat to choose from the vast array of pastries, cakes and bread and then settle snugly into an armchair to enjoy a pot of coffee and one or two tasty delights.

Café Weimar

Währingerstrasse 68/corner of Wilhelm Exnergasse
Tel: 1 317 12 06
Open: 08.00-24.00 (Fri & Sat till 04.00, Sun from 10.00)

A shiny black Bösendorfer upright piano has pride of place in the centre of the café, because, on Wednesday and Saturday from 19.30 to 22.30 and on Sunday at 16.30 it's concert time. A visit here makes it clear why Danish pastry is called Viennoiserie everywhere else (even in Denmark!) - it's absolutely delicious! Established in 1900, and lit by crystal chandeliers, Weimar is particularly popular in the evenings with artists and audiences of the nearby Volksoper. But it's equally in demand during the day - those breakfasts, and the imaginative Viennese cuisine at lunchtime!

Salzburg

The birthplace of Mozart is a city of music - everything from drinking songs and folk tunes to church choirs, from The Sound of Music to the great symphonies. The Summer Festival, one of the leading music festivals in the world, runs from late July to the end of August and attracts the very best musicians and singers in works by Mozart and many other great composers. The house where Mozart was born in 1756 is now a small museum, whose exhibits include his violin and spinet. Towards the other end of the scale, thousands of tourists arrive each year to show their love for the 1964 classic The Sound of Music, which was filmed in and around Salzburg, and many of them take advantage of a guided tour complete with taped music. Salzburg has many other treasures than its music, including the coffee shops, the green onion domes, the vast baroque cathedral, the ancient abbey, the lovely gardens and the marvellous puppet theatre.

Fidelen Affen

Priesterhausgasse 8
Open: 17.00-24.00
Closed: Sun
Tel: 662 877361

'Fidelen Affen' means 'The Jolly Monkey', and the walls of this jolly place are covered with cartoon pictures of monkeys up to their monkey tricks. Locals of all ages gather to enjoy a beer or two, either at terrace tables in the pedestrianised street or inside, where there are wooden tables and chairs, solid stone pillars, a brick-paved floor and a central copper-topped bar under a vaulted ceiling, all adding up to a very Austrian feel. Business is particularly brisk on music nights, when customers slake their thirsts and discuss the entertainment. Staff are all in blue and cheerfully hurry about their business.

Glochenspiel Café

Mozartplatz
Tel: 662 841403
Open: 09.00-23.00 (winter till 19.00)
Closed: last 3 weeks Jan

A popular spot on the Mozart tourist trail, located in 'his' square. After a hard stint of sightseeing, what better than a glorious ice cream or perhaps a cake and a drink. The interior has something of an art deco look, and *the* place to be is sitting on the first-floor veranda watching the world go by and hearing it as well when there's a live music performance. Full restaurant menu.

Hagenauerstube

Universitatsplatz 14
Tel: 662 842657
Open: 09.00-24.00 (Sun in summer from 15.00)
Closed: Sun in winter

A splendid bierstube/café in University Square opposite the University Church, with tables and chairs set out under parasols among the market stalls. This is part of the building where Mozart was born. On draught are a pils and an excellent fraziskaner weiss beer, and four wines are available by the glass. You can make a wish at the wishing well and set your watch by the sundial, whose steel gnomon (bar) above the water casts its shadow on to brass Roman numerals on the pavement. In the same ownership is Bazillus, a little place with some tables out on the bank of the broad Salzach River that divides the old city.

Humboldt Stuben

Anton Neumayerplatz 4, A-5202
Tel: 662 843171
Open: 16.30-02.00 (Fri, Sat & Sun from 11.00)

You couldn't guess it from the name, but this is actually a tapas bar, with around 40 little dishes displayed on the white marble bar counter and a good range of alcoholic and non-alcoholic beverages to accompany them. Bigger dishes, also with a Spanish flavour, cater for more serious appetites, including a very good paella. Outside, on the sloping square, are five planked levels of folding tables and chairs, Spanish pottery ashtrays and a statue of the Madonna and Child dated 1692.

Café Konditorei Fürst

Brodgasse 13, A-5020
Tel: 662 843759
Open: 08.00-20.00 (Sun & Bank Holidays from 09.00)
The place for the sweet of tooth, and the birthplace of Salzburg's very own *Mozartkugel*, a toothsome trio of marzipan, nougat cream and bittersweet chocolate. The renowned *Salzburger Nockerl* is another speciality, and the goodies are accompanied by an excellent range of teas and coffees, and even a few wines.

Niemetz

Herbert-von Karajan-Platz 11, A-5020
Tel: 662 843367
Open: 09.30-18.00 (later during the Music Festival)
Closed: Sun (except during the Music Festival)
A favourite place of refreshment for singers from the Festspielhaus opposite. Edmund Niemetz opened a pastry shop here in 1890, and in 1930 his son Walter founded the now famous chocolate factory, where the *Schwedenbombe*, known worldwide as Vienna Delights, was developed. This recently refurbished, chintzy little patisserie palace, formerly an archbishop's home, has pink marble floor tiles, marbled pillars supporting the low ceiling, and at the end a small set of organ pipes. Outside, a row of terrace tables stands in a decoratively cobbled courtyard away from the bustle of the square with its famous Horse Fountain. The cakes, the pastries and the speciality hot chocolate all slip down a treat.
Special Award 2001

Café Streif

Getreidegasse 50
Tel: 662 843181
Open: 10.30-01.00 (Sun, Bank Holidays & during the Music Festival 11.00-24.00)
A split-level café that's heavy on oak, but the sombre feel is alleviated somewhat by mirrors and plenty of lighting. The bar is at the back, with leather banquette sharing the seating with bentwood cane chairs. There is a small terrace outside in the pedestrianised street. Soups, steaks, sausages and sauerkraut head the menu. To drink: PS Bichlhof, Baron di Pauli 1996 südtirol; Kalterersee, auslese DOC Josef Brigl.

Café Tomaselli

Altermarkt 9
Tel: 662 844 4880
Open: 07.00-21.00 (Sun from 08.00, Jul & Aug till 24.00)
A renowned café approaching its tercentenary, with wonderful marquetry wall panelling, chandeliers, polished oak-block floor, cane-backed chairs, and brass hat and coat and umbrella stands. A girl circulates with cakes on a tray, constantly replenished from the display, which in turn is restocked by their own patissier. Tourists and townsfolk love the ambience and the cakes, which they can enjoy out on the terrace in fine weather. One of the favourite drinks is weizen gold from a private Salzburg brewery. Established as a coffee house, and bestowed with its magnificent coat of arms in 1753, it was taken over by Karl Tomaselli in the mid-19th century. His father, originally from Milan, had been a tenor in Salzburg before moving to Vienna in 1807, and it was Karl who renamed the place after his family.

Café Wernbacher

Franz Josefstrasse 5, A-5020
Tel: 662 871460
Open: 08.30-24.00 (Sun till 18.00)
A handsome café (note the brass-panelled 'glass' ceiling) that used to specialise in Italian cuisine but now concentrates on Austria. Pasta is still on the menu, and the wine list includes Italy as well as Austria and France. Snacks take in soups, sausages, egg dishes and wiener schnitzel. Outside is a terrace of tables under the trees.

Winkeler Café

Mönchsberg 32, A-5020
Tel: 662 847738/9
Open: 11.00-23.00
Closed: Monday except in tourist season
Visitors to Salzburg should leave time for the 20-minute walk up Mönchsberg, or they can let the public lift from Anton Neumayerplatz do the donkey work. The view is superb, and the reward for the climb lies in a rest for refreshment at Winkeler Café with its delightful terrace and tempting ice creams. It's licensed and also has a full restaurant menu, and one of its specialities that alone makes the effort worthwhile is a spectacular *Salzburger Nockerl* soufflé.

Viennese walk

Austrians drink more coffee than any other beverage, with only Finland, Sweden and Denmark consuming more coffee per person. Vienna may be famous for its waltzes, but have you heard of the Viennese walk? According to an old tradition, the city's inhabitants consider it perfectly acceptable to walk out of a café without paying if the waiter fails to provide the bill after three requests.

Belgium

A country of 10 million souls with more than its fair share of imposing castles, pageants and parades, a jealously guarded artistic and cultural heritage, and three regional governments - Flanders, Wallonia and the bilingual city of Brussels. The country packs diverse attractions into its borders: holiday resorts with extensive beaches and dunes; the plains and lakes and marshes of the central area; the forests and rolling hills of the Ardennes; the history and architecture of Brussels, Antwerp, Bruges and Ghent. These cities in particular offer a great range of bars and cafés, some grand and prim, others more down to earth. Between them they're open more or less round the clock, so the early bird and the night owl will both find somewhere congenial to perch.

Brussels

A city of considerable contrasts, the thoroughly modern home of more than 850 international organisations but at the same time the proud protector of its heritage and traditions. The Grand'Place (Grote Markt to the Flemings) is one of Europe's most majestic squares and the various museums and galleries contain treasures from all periods of history and all parts of the globe. North of the city, and well worth a visit, stands the 330ft Atomium, a reminder of the 1958 World Fair.

Gambrinus, king of beer, is the city's patron saint, and the inner man will find refreshment of all kinds, at all prices and at almost all hours.

Café Amadeus

13 rue Veydt
Tel: 2 538 3427
Open: 18.30-01.00, also Sunday brunch 10.00-15.00
Closed: Mon

A wine bar and resturant in a former framemaker's workshop, reputedly used by Rodin. The candle-lit rooms are a mixture of baroque, Greek statues, Venetian chandeliers, lacquer-painted walls, cluttered period furniture (a haberdasher's counter displays the pastries) and a trompe l'oeil of an entire street. Beyond the large double doors is the glass-covered courtyard, where there are two main eating areas, one for snacking, the other for formal meals, and a bar area with high stools lined up against a long marble counter. Casked raspberry beer is a speciality, and there's a good wine list. Eat as much as you like Sunday brunch. Produce fresh from the market is used in the cooking - Argentine steaks a speciality; oysters in season.

L'Amour Fou

185 chaussée d'Ixelles (on pl Fernand Cocq)
Tel: 2 514 2709
Open: 09.00-03.00 (Sat & Sun from 10.00)

A long, narrow bar with a handsome parquet floor and rich wooden counter, its walls hung with works of local painters. A good place to relax in the daytime with a drink, a snack and a look through the newspapers on sticks. Sandwich bar at lunchtime. Good cocktails later on. Passiflore, a tea room in the same ownership as L'Amour Fou, is at 97 rue du Bailly, Tel: 2 538 4210.

A la Bécasse

11 rue de Tabora
Tel: 2 511 0006
Open: 10.00-00.30 (Fri & Sat till 02.00, Sun 11.00-24.00)

An 'ancient drinking hall' down a narrow alley, with a spartan bar reminiscent of a German Bierkeller: with long tables of scalloped oak, a low beamed ceiling and the bar loaded with glass steins and stone jugs. The draught beers (*gueuze, lambic*) are served in earthenware jugs. Good salads.

Le Corbeau

18 rue St Michel
Tel: 2 219 5246
Open: 10.00-01.00 (Fri & Sat till 03.00)
Closed: Sun

A classic Belgian tavern near Place des Martyrs, with an amazing variety of glasses - the most spectacular (and potentially the most awkward to use) is the 50cm high *chevalier*. Food is served until midnight except on Friday and Saturday, when the eating stop two hours earlier and the singing and dancing take over the room and often the tabletops - it gets very lively!
Music festival early September

L'Entrée des Artistes

42 pl du Grand Sablon
Tel: 2 502 3161
Open: 08.00-02.00

One of the many bars on the Place du Grand Sablon, which also has numerous antique shops and a Saturday flea market. L'Entrée is a favourite spot for people-watching - particularly at one of the outside tables. Inside, there's a long oak bar and two floors of wooden tables and chairs. The walls are covered with photographs of actors and other celebrities. Le Patron is a Harley-Davidson fan and organises the occasional HD night, when the street outside is stacked with the machines. Food is served noon till midnight.

Le Falstaff

19-25 rue Henri Maus
Tel: 2 511 8789/511 9877
Open: 09.00-03.00 (Sat & Sun 09.30-05.00)

Café, restaurant, patisserie, ice cream parlour, banqueting hall - the renowned Falstaff is all these, and is also classified as a Historical Monument, so no alterations can be made for 500 years. Its location two minutes from the Grand'Place and close to the Bourse makes it a popular choice for both Brussels residents and tourists. The café part alone, done out in splendid art nouveau and art deco styles with dark wood and huge mirrors, covers several rooms, and there's a covered terrace at the front. The house tipple is half and half - Gancia with sparkling Luxembourg wine – and there's also a good choice of beers (5 draught, 20 bottled) and a Brittany cider to go with the Belgian cuisine - anything from a snack to a full meal.
Benelux Café of the Year 2001

La Fleur en Papier Doré

55 rue des Alexiens
Tel: 2 511 1659
Open: 11.00-01.00 (Fri & Sat till 03.00)

A dark old bar in a 17th-century building, its walls covered with pictures and writings and doodles of the Belgian surrealists and Dadaists who once frequented the place. Join the entertainingly mixed clientele and guzzle your *gueuze* with a salad, spaghetti or croque monsieur.

Le Greenwich

7 rue des Chartreux
Tel: 2 511 4167
Open: 10.30-01.30

A large, bright, old-fashioned bar with art nouveau decor, marble tables and wood panelling. The atmosphere (in the daytime at least) is quiet and intense, partly because many of the customers are playing chess or Go. Cold snacks keep the brains sharp.

Hallowe'en

10 rue des Grands Carmes
Tel: 2 514 1256
Open: 12.00-01.00 (Fri & Sat till 02.00)
Closed: Mon

The name of this city-centre bar tells you what to expect: the decorations are mainly depictions of scary monsters and the like (two evil-looking bats stand on guard at either end of the bar) and the ceiling is covered with Hallowe'en bunting. Tables with candles in skulls are named after Jekyll and Hyde, Dracula and so on. Waiters wear a cassock and hood, but service comes with a smile, and not a fang in sight. On Saturday evenings actors entertain, performing anything from horror stories to love stories. Food is served till 23.00.

t'Kelderke

15 Grand'Place
Tel: 2 513 7344
Open: 12.00-02.00

A cellar restaurant in a splendid position on the stunning Grand'Place. The menu encompasses Belgian specialities including mussels and carbonnade à la flamande. Le Cerf, on the same premises, offers lighter snacks and live music.

Café Métropole

31 pl de Brouckère
Tel: 2 219 2384
Open: 09.00-01.00

A comfortable, stylish and civilised spot in the turn-of-the-century Hotel Métropole, with lofty ceilings and marble decorations on the walls and tinted mirrors. There's also a terrace on the pavement. A good place to sit in plush-upholstered comfort for a quiet drink and a light bite after meeting, as all Brussels does, in the splendid lobby. The house cocktail is L'Italiano, made with grancia.

Pablo's

51 rue de Namur
Tel: 2 502 4135
Open: 12.00-00.30 (later Fri & Sat)
Closed: L Sun

There's usually a party atmosphere at this glass-fronted restaurant, café and cocktail bar serving all things Mexican, including the background music (they participate in the Brussels jazz rally on the last weekend of May). The usual mix of tacos, enchiladas and quesadillas is on offer plus pitchers of Margarita, a bucket of six beers and a variety of cocktails. Meals are served from 12.00 to 15.00 and from 18.00 to 24.00

Poechenellekelder

5 rue du Chêne
Tel: 2 511 9262
Open: 11.00-24.00 (Fri & Sat till 02.00)

Owner Michel de Triest's amazing collection of over 600 puppets and mannequins, along with various collector's pieces connected with the history of Brussels, still leaves space for customers at Poechenellekelder, a café on three levels with the bar tucked away at the back. He stocks a good range of snacks, including cheese, tartines and croques, spaghetti and the very popular tete pressée (brawn). For liquid refreshment, the impressive choice runs to some 40 beers (the strongest is the bottled Bush Beer at 12%), plus fruit juices and genievres (schnapps) with ten fruit flavours. 70 seats inside, with a further 50 on the pavement in the summer.

Au Soleil

86 rue du Marché au Charbon
Tel: 2 513 3430
Open: 10.00-02.00

Once a men's clothing shop, now well suited for a pause for a drink and a snack, particularly in the summer at an outside table in the traffic-free cobbled side street. Outside are some original signs; inside, some splendid old ads and wooden fittings.

Sounds

28 rue de la Tulipe
Tel: 2 512 9250
Open: 11.30-04.00 (Sat from 19.00)
Closed: Sun & midsummer

A well-loved bar behind Place Fernand Cocq, with live jazz several nights a week and a cosmopolitan crowd of regulars. Note that the café is closed in mid-summer, traditionally re-opening on October 1st with a major jazz event. Sounds is owned by an Italian from Umbria, so specials include Italian dishes. If the summer is hot they stay open later, bringing the large garden into use. If the weather's bad, they go on holiday!

> "The great thing about making cognac is that it teaches you above everything else to wait – man proposes, but time and God and the seasons have got to be on your side."
>
> **Jean Monnet**

De Ultieme Hallucinatie

316 rue Royale
Tel: 2 217 0614
Open: 11.00-02.00 (Sat from 16.00, Sun from 15.00)
Closed: Sun
The area is not the most exclusive in the city, but this is certainly one of its most famous addresses, with marvellous ornate art nouveau decor in a well-preserved period house. It scores on several levels - a tavern for classic Belgian snacks and Belgian beers, a more formal restaurant, a night club in the converted stables. It's a favourite business person's rendezvous at lunchtime, while early in the evening a different crowd stops for refreshment en route to the Opera House.

Antwerp

Belgium's second largest city, and its grandest, is one of the world's biggest ports, despite lying more than 50 miles from the sea, and the harbour is well worth a visit. Antwerp is known as the Diamond Town, and the expertise perfected in the 16th century has kept it as the world's leader in the industry. Another gem is the magnificent Cathedral - the largest public building in Belgium, covering an area of 2½ acres. The painter Rubens is the city's most famous son and his works may be seen in the Cathedral and in his handsome town house on the Wapper Rubenstraat. Antwerp offers a good selection of cafés and bars, some of which stock literally hundreds of varieties of beer.

De Arme Duivel

1 Arme Duivelstraat
Tel: 3 232 2698
Open: 12.00-02.00 (Sat till 20.00)
Closed: Sun
Busy corner café for weekday shoppers in an area of designer outlets. It sells light snacks and seasonal Belgian cuisine, but mostly beer, wine, aperitifs and coffee.

Den Bengel

5 Grote Markt
Tel: 3 233 3290
Open: 09.00-03.00
This large bar is one of the oldest in the Grote Market (Grand-Place), with an unusual and amusing feature of cameo portraits of the customers when they were babies! Known as the chatterbox bar or chattering café, Bengel means 'rascal' and indeed some of the rascals' rascal children have grown to be customers and their photos are also on the walls. On the first floor is a big room for parties.

Café Beveren

2 Vlasmarkt
Tel: 3 231 2225
Open: 12.00-late (Fri & Sat *very* late!)
Closed: Tue
The place where music fans congregate for a spot of nostalgia and a glass or two of beer - the speciality is their own Bolleke Koninck. There's an amazing 60-year-old pipe organ here - for 20BF you get two tunes out of the repertoire of 37, but there's no choice because they play in strict rotation. In the front are a piano accordion, a saxophone, drums and lights - a fully working piece of inter-war music technology in this funny little bar with a terrace on the corner of the quay (Van Dijckkai). At the other end is an old juke box with songs from the '50s and '60s.

La Cirque Belge

13-14 Van Dijckkai
Tel: 3 232 9439
Open: 10.00-02.00 (Sat & Sun till 05.00 or 06.00)
A long-established bar, recently renovated but retaining its character, and also a restaurant specialising in mussels, waffles and pancakes. It also boasts 85 of Belgium's best beers behind its spacious horseshoe-shaped counter. And on Thursday, Friday, Saturday and Monday there's live music, the space vanishes and the place is packed.

Corsendonk Stadscafé

1 Suikerrui
Tel: 3 226 1391
Open: 10.00-24.00
A spacious corner café looking out across the quay to the Scholde river. The beer comes from their own brewery and snackers have a good choice that includes bread and cheese, croques, pasta dishes and salads. There's also a full à la carte menu and a decent choice of wines.

Den Engel

3 Grote Markt
Tel: 3 233 1252
Open: 09.00-02.00
A bright, friendly bar, one of the oldest in the square. The prices are very reasonable for such an address and note they are open quite early. This is not least because couples taking their marriage vows at the Town Hall opposite come here to celebrate in advance.

De Groote Witte Arend

18 Reyndersstraat
Tel: 3 226 3190
Open: 11.30-24.00 (Fri & Sat till 02.00)
Closed: Tue (also Wed in winter)
The name means 'Great White Eagle' and visitors can fly far away from the bustle of the city outside while listening to opera in this bar and tea rooms around a cloistered courtyard. The speciality here is the Arend cocktail - a concoction of apple and cherry juice mixed with a 25cl bottle of Duvel beer and topped with a drop of draught white beer. The tea shop serves teas and terrific coffees, and packets to take home, between 12.00 and 20.00, while the bar has on offer ten draught beers and a big range of laced coffees. Non-alcoholic drinks include teas and freshly squeezed fruit juices. For snacks, there's an amazing selection of AOC cheeses from France - better than in most cheese shops – and croques, pasta and club sandwiches.

"Happiness? A good cigar, a good meal, a good cigar and a good woman – or a bad woman; it depends on how much happiness you can handle."

George Burns

Jan Zonder Vrees

2 Krabbenstraat/8 Palingbrug
Tel: 3 232 9080
Open: 09.00-01.00 (Fri & Sat till 03.00)

'Fearless John' is a popular place just two steps from the Grote Markt in Old Antwerp. Snacks include prawns, scampi and the special Jan Zonder Vrees omelette, and there's a well-priced menu of the day. Good coffees, five beers on draought, 30 bottled. The 14th-century story goes that one day, to test his fearlessness, John's cousin dressed up as a ghost. Fearless John ran him through with his sword and immediately saw what he had done. Not knowing what to do, he ran away. On his journey he took up many just causes, made a good name for himself and returned a hero to the people of Flanders.

Kathedraal

17 Handschoenmarkt
Tel: 3 232 4014
Open: 11.00-24.00 (Sat & Sun till 01.00 or 02.00)
Closed: Wed in winter

A small modern bar next to its restaurant. It has a simple lunch menu - fish soup, croques, salads of speck/chicken/smoked fish, prawns, croquettes, baguette sandwiches, omelettes. The pleasant pavement terrace is typical of the cafés found in squares all over Europe, but still sadly rare in the UK.

Kulminator

32-34 Vleminckveld
Tel: 3 232 4538
Open: 11.00-24.00 (Sat from 17.00, Mon from 20.00)
Closed: Sun, New Year & early Aug

In a side street a little way from the historic centre, Kulminator is the HQ of OBP, a beer consumers' organisation, and the list of beers is of epic length: there are 600 of them! Some of the bottled beers (*gueuze*) are served in a basket as with an old Burgundy; indeed, there are vintages going back to 1979. Behind the bar is a hotchpotch of stacked beer crates of all different kinds, and shelves loaded with ranks of bottled beers lined up like soldiers. Classical music plays gently in the background, and people sit reading the newspapers at scrubbed wooden tables. Cold snacks of bread and cheese or sausage are always available. Outside seating.

De Muze

15 Melkmarkt
Tel: 3 226 0126
Open: 12.00-04.00

A well-known jazz café - the music starts at 22.00 every day except Sunday - but even then there's music if the players feel in the mood. De Muze is on four levels; the ground floor has bare red brickwork with a broad oak bar and cane chairs, while in the open-plan upper levels the chairs are bentwood. Drinks include six draught beers and a big choice of bottled beers and genevers, and there's a variety of snacks and light meals (croque monsieur, chili con carne, moussaka, apple tart).

Paeters Vaetje

1 Blauwmoezelstraat
Tel: 3 231 8476
Open: 11.00-02.00 (Fri & Sat till 05.00)
The 100 beers served at this small split-level bar all have their own particular serving glass, complete with imprinted logo! The glass shelves behind the old marble-topped mahogany bar are stacked with them. Two narrow spiral staircases lead up to the mezzanine and upper-floor levels, where the tables are old four-seater marble-topped mahogany types and the ceiling's exposed mahogany beams reflect the early trading days with the Far East. An old stove heats the place in winter, and the excellent home-made soups provide further warmth. The snack menu is supplemented by blackboard specials.

Pelgrom

15 Pelgrimstraat
Tel: 3 234 0809
Open: 12.00-01.00
The entrance leads from the cobbled street down some stairs to vaulted cellars which for many centuries were used by merchants to store their wares for the two annual fairs held in Antwerp. There is a private museum (open weekends) where you can see how the burghers lived in the 16th century. Service at Pelgrom is by waiters dressed in costumes that could have been painted by Brueghel. Specialities: food is Belgian-French cuisine; beers include Poorters and Pelgrom Grand Cru; excellent coffees.

De Plaisante Hof

25-27 Vlasmarkt
Tel: 3 213 1146
Open: 10.00-late
Pleasant indeed! Built in 1827, it's tucked away beyond a courtyard with hanging plants and garden tables and chairs. The main room is spacious, quiet and cool. Mussels are the speciality on the daily carte and there's a good, reasonably-priced wine list - all French - from Alsace, Rhone, Loire and Bordeaux.

Quinten Matsijs

17 Moriaanstraat
Tel: 3 225 0170
Open: 12.00-24.00 (Fri & Sat till 03.00, Sun till 20.00)
Quinten Matsijs, a pupil of Rubens, gives his name to one of the oldest bars in Flanders and probably in all the Low Countries, starting as a beer house in 1565. Matsijs was a frequent customer here along with other notables such as Willem Elschot, Werumeus Buning, Paul van Ostaijen and other Flanders writers and intellectuals. Specialities include typical Flanders food and beers.

't Tafeltje Rond

10 Gildekamersstraat
Tel: 3 233 4200
Open: 10.00-06.00
Next door to its restaurant (and indeed this is where the waiters come to get the drinks) the café is open almost round the clock and serves really excellent Illy coffee and local beers. The bar itself is a small, timber-topped, tile-panelled affair with a stout bar rail and in the back part of the room is the eponymous round table. There's a nice little pavement terrace.

De Vagant

25 Reyndersstraat
Tel: 3 233 1538
Open: 11.00-02.00 (Sun from 12.00)
In business for 460 years, this prestigious bar is very proud of its stock of 220 Belgian gins. In a side street close to the Cathedral, it is a serious place, where classical music plays and, sitting at long wooden tables on wooden chairs, you can read the daily and weekly papers and drink genevers (or beer or other spirits). The house cocktail is a mixture of white and lemon genevers, boosted by other liqueurs and fruit juices. Next to the bar, and at the entrance, are a shop and a restaurant in the same ownership.

Bruges

The birthplace of Flemish painting has kept the look of the Middle Ages, with atmospheric old buildings clustered by the canals and plenty for the visitor to discover in the historic town centre. Works by van Eyck, van der Goes and David hang in the Groeninge gallery, and the Memling Museum contains some of the most notable works of Hans Memling, who was born in 1433 and spent most of his working life in Bruges. In the last week of August, the Reiefest is celebrated along the canals, with music, singing and dancing evoking scenes from the Middle Ages to the Baroque. Bruges is sometimes known as 'the Venice of Flanders' or 'the Venice of the North'.

't Hof van Rembrandt

10 Eiermarkt
Tel: 50 33 7450
Open: 11.00-02.00

In the Eiermarkt (egg market) just behind the main market square, Rembrandt caters for all generations and all thirsts and appetites. The speciality is Belgian beer on tap with a guest beer of the month. There's a comfortable lounge seating area with a large open fireplace and leather-bound chairs in which to relax and read the papers or have a quiet chat, and a busy bar area with a small wall-mounted TV in the corner, where the younger generation meet to watch soccer and other sports. Outside, there's plenty of space on the terrace, which is partly covered by a retractable awning.

Taverne Curiosa

22 Vlamingstraat
Tel: 50 34 2334
Open: 10.00-01.00 (Sat till 02.00, Sun 12.00-24.00)

A stairway just off the main market square leads down to a medieval cellar with an oak bar and leather-bound straight-backed chairs at oak tables. It's a spacious bar-restaurant in two rooms with low, vaulted ceilings and a stone-flagged floor. They serve some 60 beers, five on tap; grills are a popular choice at lunchtime, after which tea is served; snacks are available up to 30 minutes before closing. Seasonal mussels are always worth ordering.

't Zwart Huis

23 Kuiperstraat
Tel: 50 34 1516
Open: 18.00-02.00 (later Fri & Sat)
Closed: Sun

When the soot-black brickwork was given a major clean and the whole premises refurbished some years ago, the name (The Black House) stuck. Steps lead into the principal room, which has, in the far corner, a long oak bar set with bar stools. The high beamed ceiling also looks down on another very spacious room with stout wooden tables and chairs on a solid wooden floor. Food is served in one part, and on Monday there's salsa dancing upstairs. The bar is a popular spot with the cast after the show is over at the theatre next door.

Ghent

Belgium's second largest port, the capital of East Flanders, stands at the confluence of the Lys and the Scheldt rivers. The prosperity of Ghent through the ages can be seen in its tall, elegant and well-maintained architecture - the familiar stepped gable frontages, beautifully kept stone and brick facades - and in its churches and the Cathedral. It was here that Wellington made his HQ on his way to Waterloo, for Ghent is a city that has always played fast and loose with the English and the French, playing one off against the other for its own political and commercial interest. Much in the way of Bruges, it can be investigated on foot, by horse-drawn carriage or by boat. If you see only one thing here it must be Jan van Eyck's amazing polyptich The Adoration of the Mystic Lamb in the Cathedral St-Bavon

Dreupelkot

13 Groentenmarkt
Tel: 9 224 2120
Open: 11.00-02.00 (or even later)

A genevers bar pure and simple, with an extensive list for the enthusiast. There are more than 180 Belgian gins with a multitude of flavourings (orange, lemon, passion fruit....) and strengths (30%-54% abv). This is where the owner serves; his restaurant is next door and there's a beer bar at the end. You can see a caricature of him on the arch over the side passage entrance to the place. The simple room has bare brick walls, a shelf down one side and plain wooden bar across the end, and an upturned barrel in the middle to rest your drink, unless you do the right thing and knock it back in one!

't Galgenhuis

5 Groentenmarkt
Tel: 9 233 4251
Open: 12.00-03.00
Closed: Mon

Probably the oldest and smallest café in Ghent; its name means 'the gallows', and it was the 17th-century gallows house in the vegetable market. Today's visitors hang around for snacks served in the pretty little bar, while those in search of a full meal head downstairs into the basement where, below the level of the River Lys, the restaurant is open lunchtime and evening. On the beams are some bon mots such as 'Don't talk too much or you'll hang yourself'. Outside terrace.

Waterhuis

9 Groentenmarkt
Tel: 9 225 0680
Open: 11.00-02.00 (Fri & Sat till 03.00 or 04.00)

A pretty bar down a cobbled terrace by the River Lys. It stocks 160 beers, with lots on tap, so the students who frequent the place have plenty of choice. Sandwiches and snacks and nourishing soups are available here, while for a bigger meal the sister restaurant is just next door.

Liège

A French-speaking major port with a population of some 200,000, standing close to the German and Dutch borders at the confluence of the Meuse and Ourthe rivers. It's a busy student centre, full of life, with a good choice of cafés, bars and restaurants. Waffles are a speciality. The area for café society and its associated restaurants is called L'Isle, opposite the Cathédrale St Paul et Trésor. The liveliest place of all on a Sunday morning is the mile-long La Batte street market selling just about everything that can be sold. Georges Simenon, creator of *Maigret*, was a Liégeois and many of the characters in his novels were drawn from the city.

La Brasserie Cathédrale

pl de la Cathédrale
Tel: 04 222 1386
Open: 08.00-24.00 (Fri & Sat till 02.00)

A classic French-style brasserie with tables set out under plastered beams. Outside there are lots of wicker chairs and tables where people take breakfast or a coffee or aperitif in the evening sunshine. The terrace is heated, and in December parents can watch their children ice-skating in the square from there or from the upstairs room. To eat: sandwiches, salads, grilled sausages, kebabs, crêpes, omelettes. To drink: five draught beers, 30 bottled, lots of spirits, French wines.

Bruit Qui Court

142 bd de la Sauvenière
Tel: 04 232 1818
Open: 11.00-24.00

An air of civilised calm prevails in the lofty mid 19th-century Grande Salle with vaulted ceiling, large ferns, subtle lighting, soothing Latin-American music and charming service. There's a good choice on the menu, and a very good French wine list. A comprehensive range of beers, too, and coffee from Colombia, Kenya, Ethiopia and Jamaica. The coffee is served with a dish of whipped cream, salt, condensed or evaporated milk and a piece of chocolate.

Les Carmes

2 rue Saint-Gilles
Tel: 04 223 6435
Open: 24 hours

However late the party ends, Les Carmes is ready for the survivors: it's open 24 hours a day, every day of the year. Their breakfasts are legendary, with eggs fricassee providing the sort of early morning sustenance that's just what the doctor ordered after a night's merrymaking. Later perhaps a glass of Rivaner from the Mosel, a beer or a coffee - all served with a welcome smile.

Danish Tavern

1 rue Pont d'Avroy
Tel: 04 222 3343
Open: 08.30-24.00 (Fri till 01.00, Sat till 02.00)

There are naturally some Danish specialities on the menu in this tavern, while among the drinks the influence is wider: French, with lots of Burgundian liqueurs and marcs; Scottish, with beer and 15 Scotch whiskies; Irish, with beer sold by le half and le pint. But in the morning it's time for breakfast and here they're ready to serve you coffee and offer a newspaper to read. A lot of oak is used in the tavern (floor, staircase, bar top) and decorative features include Bergerac blue glass bottles on the shelves.

> "Yes, social friend, I love thee well,
> In learned doctors' spite;
> Thy clouds all other clouds dispel,
> And lap me in delight."
> **Charles Sprague**, *To My Cigar*.

L'Elysée

153 bd de la Sauvenière
Tel: 04 222 2393
Open: 09.00-24.00 (Sun from 10.00, Sat 10.00-02.00)

They dub themselves 'un coin de Paris à Liège' - a corner of Paris in Liège. The brasserie is at the junction with Rue Pont d'Avroy, a main shopping street leading from the Cathedral. It is on two floors, ground and basement, with floor-to-ceiling windows at street level giving a great feeling of space. A long oak bar with the patina of age is set with leather-upholstered bar stools, and there's a heated terrace on the boulevard. Here the best-dressed Liégeois come for refreshment - wines, beers and their speciality, *café liégeois*, a dessert of coffee, ice cream and whipped cream. They have coffee from Sumatra, Columbia, Kenya and Ethiopia! Friday night is music night.

A Pilori

7 pl du Marché
Tel: 04 222 1857
Open: 09.00-23.00 (Sat 10.00-24.00, Sun 10.00-20.00)

In a building dating from 1632, this is one of the city's best known and best loved cafés. It stands in the old market place right opposite the Town Hall and has been at the centre of political life through the ages; it's also a favourite with legal people from the nearby Palais de Justice. The bar front is made of carved oak, and there are small oak tables and chairs sitting on a flagstoned floor; the ceiling has seriously old exposed beams and posts to support them. A covered terrace is used in summer. Snacks include croques and baguettes, and at lunchtime soup, omelettes, pasta and steaks.

La Taverne St Paul

8 rue Saint Paul
Tel: 04 223 7217
Closed: Sun
Open: 10.00-02.00 (or even till 05.00!)

Perhaps the oldest bar in Liège, certainly the oldest in its original state. Here's where the bourgeois start their evenings with a beer before going on to the main entertainment – or perhaps staying here, as this is a place with bags of character: beautiful rose aurore French marble fireplaces, handsome wood panelling and furniture, marble-topped tables, delightful staff Satuday night piano bar.

Czech Republic

Telephone Code: 00 420

Alandlocked country right in the heart of Europe, bordered by mountain ranges, with fine rolling fields, woods and river valleys, and a treasury of castles, palaces, churches and monasteries. Besides the beautiful capital city of Prague, the country's best-known tourist spots include the Bohemian spa resorts formerly known as Carlsbad, Marienbad and Franzenbad (now respectively Karlovy Vary, Mariánske Lázne and Frantiskovy Lázne); Brno, the regional capital of Moravia, famous for its bold modern architecture and known in the 19th century, because of its thriving textile industry, as the Manchester of Austria (the borders have changed); and Pilsen (now Plzen), renowned for its beer and home to several breweries and a beer museum.

Prague

With a population of about a million, 'Golden Prague' is a glorious city whose architectural heritage spans Gothic, Baroque, Art Nouveau and Cubist. The original part of the city, high above a bend in the River Vltava, a tributary of the Elbe, is the Slav fortress of Hradcany, containing the Castle (Hrad), St Vitus Cathedral, begun in 1344 and not completed until the 20th century, and the Basilica of St George - see St George slaying the dragon in a carving above the doorway of the south portal. This compact area is a must on the visitor's list of places to see, along with the magnificent medieval Charles Bridge, the superbly ornate Church of St Nicholas and the melancholy memorials in the Jewish quarter. An old waterworks in neo-Renaissance style on the riverfront is now a museum dedicated to the life of Bedrich Smetana, father of Czech music. Also not to be missed are the wonderful Tyn church with its chimes, a great statue in Wenceslas Square where Jan Palach set fire to himself in 1969, and the street called Parishská which is straight out of Paris's Left Bank. Prague has plenty of places of refreshment (notably for the consumption of beer, with the odd shot of a mind-blasting absinthe), though not many of the grand cafés of the glamorous inter-war years have stayed the course.

Café Archa

Na Porící 26, Prague 1
Tel: 2 23 24 149
Open: 09.00-21.00 (Sun from 13.00)
The tall ground floor of this modern building allows Café Archa to maximise its space by putting in a second level. Serving the office worker and local residents, it's a café in the modern style offering cakes, coffees and snacks. Theatrical pictures and posters.

Grand Hotel Europa Kavárna

Václavské nam 25, Prague 1
Tel: 2 2422 8117
Open: 07.00-24.00
Hotel Europa dates from 1889, when it was called the Archduke Stephan. However, between 1903 and 1905 it was completely renovated in the art nouveau style by well-known architects Bendelmeyer Hüschmann & Letzel, a firm which exists to this day. One of the most outstanding buildings in Wenceslas Square, the upper part is a hotel, while the ground floor is occupied by the spacious café with its oval gallery. The chandeliers and wall lights are now fed by electricity, but the light is subdued, keeping the warm glow that it always had. More substantial meals can be had in the art nouveau and Old Czech restaurant rooms. Outside, on either side of the entrance, there are raised terraces with smart brass chairs and tables where you can watch the elegant passers-by.

Café Franz Kafka

Siroká 12, Prague 1
Tel: 2 231 8945
Open: 09.00-21.00 (Fri & Sat 10.00-22.00)
This is another celebration of the Jewish Czech writer, who was born in Prague in 1883, when the city was in Bohemia. The café is located in the Jewish quarter - there's a High Jewish Synagogue just around the corner - and its grained panelled walls and booths with their dim lighting somehow reflect the writer's dark humour. The floor is tiled, the bar stands to the right, and there are some outside tables. Around the walls are some of Kafka's bons mots, some in German, his chosen language, some translated into Czech. A 20cl glass of wine is very reasonably priced at 50Kc (about £1); traditional fare includes goulash soup, chicken stew and rice. A place for the young intellectuals if ever you saw one.

The Globe Bookstore & Coffee House

Pstrossova 6, Prague 1
Tel: 24 91 62 64
Open: 10.00-24.00

The long-established bookstore-cum-coffee shop recently moved to premises in the centre of town. The same friendly atmosphere still prevails, as does the large selection of English-language books, while the café still serves home-made sandwiches, bagels, cheesecake, apple pie and other goodies. New is free use of the internet. Bring your own laptop or simply relax with a newspaper or listen to one of the monthly readings by budding authors.
Review submitted by Helena Baker

Café Imperial

Na Porící 15, Prague 1
Tel: 2 231 60 12
Open: 08.00-01.00

Built in 1914, the café occupies the ground floor of the hotel. It was particularly innovative at the time, the high walls and ceiling decorated in pierced ceramic, depicting hunting scenes and the flora and fauna in Eastern Europe. Immediately after the Second World War, it was commandeered by the upper communist echelons as their own refreshment venue and to entertain like-minded foreign dignitaries, and closed to the public. After the fall of the communist regime in 1989 there was a dispute as to its ownership, and until April 2000 it remained entirely closed. While its ownership is still in doubt in many people's minds, it would now seem once again to be permanently open, and flourishing as a café (though the hotel part still needs a lot done to bring it up to western standards, comfortable and very reasonably priced as it is). The huge L-shaped room has a stage at the far end where visiting musicians entertain. The prices are kind and the fare traditional - and the atmosphere is very special.

James Joyce

Liliová 10, Prague 1
Tel: 2 24 24 87 93
Open: 10.00-00.30

An Irish Pub with an interior from an old Belfast church, located in the Old Town Square. Pricy draught beers, including Guinness and Kilkenny, cause floods of nostalgia among expats. Snacks like potato skins and chicken wings accompany.

Café Louvre

Národní trída 20, Prague 1
Tel: 2 29 72 23/29 76 65
Open: 08.00-late

Café Louvre was established in 1902, but was closed between 1948 and 1992 when the socialists regarded it as being bourgeois and therefore unsuitable, so it was used as offices. Today it has been restored to its former elegant condition and offers a broad choice of breakfasts and coffees, and a wide selection of other dishes during the day, including some for vegetarians. A parlour is available for hire, with a non-smoking room, and there's also a seven table billiard club. The symbol of the Café is Ganymede (cupbearer to the Gods) offering refreshment to Zeus in the form of an eagle. The café is located on the first floor, with a view from the tall windows of the busy street below. At night it becomes a rock café

Kavárna Meduza

Belgicka 17, Prague 2
Tel: 2 225 15 107
Open: 11.00-01.00 (Sat & Sun from 12.00)

Outside the centre in a pretty, quiet, residential, tree-lined street, Meduza is well known among Prague café society. The unobtrusive entrance gives way to a spacious old-style café with a mixture of styles of furniture. It's a bit like the reception room of a large residence, which it once was. Charming, relaxed and comfortable, this is an ideal spot to read a book or newspaper in peace, or to play a game of chess.

Café Milena

Staromestske námestí 22, Prague 1
Tel: 2 260 843
Open: 10.00-20.00

Standing in the Old Town Square, this is the home of the Franz Kafka Society, and is named after his lover Milena Jesenka, a light in his otherwise gloomy life. The building also houses an art gallery where publications on his life and works are available. Decorated in 1930s style, the café is on the first floor, with the famous Astronomical Clock at eye-level through the window. The black chairs and pillars contrast with the white ceiling, walls and marble-topped tables, lit with art deco wall uplighters. Live music is played on the upright piano daily between 16.00 and 18.00. Besides all sorts of coffees and teas, there's a big selection of cakes, strudels, filled pancakes and ice creams.

Kavárna Obecni Dum

námestí Republiky 5, Prague 1
Tel: 2 200 27 63
Open: 07.00-23.00 (kitchen 12.00-16.00 & 18.00-23.00)
The huge windows of this stately building are double-hung sashes, which, when opened, allow the panelling below to fold away to give access to the vast, lofty room with its grand chandeliers. To the right of the imposing entrance, facing out onto Republic Square, is the grand restaurant, while to the left is the café. Built in the last period of the Austro-Hungarian Empire, between 1903 and 1912, its style is largely art nouveau, with neo-renaissance and neo-baroque bits thrown in. The building was intended to satisfy many of the social and cultural activities of the city folk and includes the Smetana Concert Hall. Popular with both residents and visitors to Prague, it has a constant flow of customers relaxing inside or sitting out on the terrace that stretches the length of the café front. Coffees, aperitifs, beers and wines are served by smartly dressed waiters throughout the day, along with snacks and brasserie-type dishes.

Café de Paris at Hotel Paríz

U Obecního domu 1, Prague 1
Tel: 2 422 2151
Open: 10.00-24.00
Situated next door to the extravagant art nouveau Municipal House (Obecní dum), from where Czechoslovakia declared its independence from the Austro-Hungarian Empire in 1918, the Café de Paris and its adjacent Sarah Bernhardt restaurant have been immortalised by the nation's most illustrious author Bohumil Hrabal in his *I Served the King of England*. This classy café in the foyer of Hotel Paríz, which starts the day with a variety of breakfast menus, still speaks of the golden age of almost a century ago, the time when café society reached its pinnacle, led mainly by such luminaries of the country's German-Jewish community as Franz Kafka and his tireless editor Max Brod, who seemed to spend most of their time in one café or another. *Review submitted by Helena Baker*

Premiera Caffé

Parízská 18, Prague 1
Tel: 2 231 03 67
Open: 08.30-01.00
An elegant café that spreads out on to the pavement under the trees in the smart street leading away from The Old Town Square towards the river. Baguettes and breakfasts are offered between 08.30 and 11.00, giving way to brasserie snacks - goulash soup, pasta, salads, pancakes and pastries. The local red and white wines are served in 20cl glasses, imported varieties in 10cl glasses.

Café Patio

Národní 22, Prague 1
Tel: 2 491 8072
Open: 08.00-23.00 (Sat & Sun from 10.00)
This establishment is found in the centre of town, halfway between Wenceslas Square and the River Vltava, and ambitious plans are afoot from the new owners of Le Patio group. Apart from expanding into major European cities, they are preparing exciting new projects such as delicatessens with home delivery service, a takeaway and a travel bureau aimed at exotic locations. Prague's Café Patio has been designed on several levels with interconnecting rooms. Exotic music, a stylish interior with an assortment of lanterns hanging from the ceiling, a ship of the line steaming towards the main entrance and a pagoda on the way to the basement antique shop are just a few elements to catch the eye and ear. The very reasonably priced salad bar menu changes daily and you can enjoy a grand array of freshly-made pastries washed down with fine Illy coffee served by friendly staff. A selection of local and foreign newspapers for browsing is available. Kafka did not visit Café Patio, but never mind - the café's motto is: *L'Art de Vivre*!
Review submitted by Helena Baker

La Provence

Stupartská 9, Prague 1
Tel: 2 900 54 510-512
Open: 11.00-02.00

La Provence is tucked away in a quiet street between the Old Town and Republic Squares, and its aspect is of a Languedoc timber-framed shop-cum-café. Inside is more rustic, with timber furnishings and bare brick walls. Incorporating all things Mediterranean, it offers snacks and meals, drinks and entertainment, with origins in France, Italy and Spain - salad mistral or niçoise, carpaccio or linguine, gazpacho or pinchitos along with many others. A restaurant, a café and a tapas bar, on two floors; the entertainment swings from jazz on Mondays, French songs to the piano on Tuesdays, dancing on Wednesdays, and so on. The upstairs part is called Banana Café.

Radost FX Café

Belehradská 120, Prague 2
Tel: 2 25 12 10 (office)
Open: 11.00-06.00

This vegetarian café goes on as before, the building housing a shop and a gallery, the café occupying a neat section inside on the right. Somewhat narrow and a bit cramped, it relies on a quick turnover. Sunday brunch and poetry readings.

Café Relax

Soukenická 7, Prague 1
Tel: 2 248 18 892
Open: 10.00-23.00 (Sat & Sun from 13.00)

In the north-east of the city centre, a short step from the River Vltava, a tributary of the Elbe, lies this comfortable, welcoming student café, offering well-spaced tables and a random selection of chairs, even a central rug to make it feel more homely. The high ceiling and full height windows enhance the feeling of spaciousness. Serving the excellent Illy coffee, with an espresso a mere 50p a cup, this well-named café attracts the young, who come during the day to read the papers or their current study book, or to play board games; the evenings are more boisterous.

Slavia Kavárna

Smetanovo nábrezí, Prague 1
Tel: 2 24 22 09 57
Open: 08.00-24.00

In a neo-classical building on the banks of the Vltava is this Slav Café, offering a service much as it was during the socialist times, a reminiscence of those fifty post-war years. Approached up a broad but austere staircase, a glass wall separates the stairwell from the reception, from which you are shown to your table. The café area stretches along the first floor, looking out at the National Theatre. Traditional filter coffee, and national dishes are offered and served by formally dressed staff, and the clientele are mostly residents of Prague and customers of long standing.

U Prince

Staromestske námestí, Prague 1
Tel: 2 242 138 07
Open: 10.00-01.00

In the corner of the Old Town Square is a robust building with a vaulted ground floor. The solid stone walls and paved floor are furnished with robust wooden tables and chairs. Many's the local family and tourist visitor who've refreshed themselves here, the speciality drink is the now popular everywhere Staropramen lager. Outside, under an extending canopy, is a formal terrace of tables in the square with comfortable basket-weave armchairs, secluded by green planting on either side. Here you can get a range of traditional Czech dishes, and some of the more familiar western European ones, served professionally by smartly dressed waiting staff. It's nice to be pampered.

Valmont Café

Parízská, Prague 1
Tel: 2 232 72 60
Open: 10.00-23.00/24.00

On the edge of the Jewish quarter, Valmont Café-Bar is a modern, smart corner establishment, presented in the traditional Parisian brasserie style. Tubular chairs with basket-weave seats and backs spread around outside on the patterned cobbled pavement. A stone's throw from the river Vltava, it is not far from Rudolfinum, an imposing building built 1876-1884 in neo-classical style, housing the Antonin Dvorak concert hall. The tall arched openings have french windows that open on to the street. A smart set choose to come after a stroll from their hotel or a cultural visit to the concert hall.

Velryba

Opatovická 24, Prague 1
Tel: 2 24 91 23 91
Open: 11.00-02.00

A just-below-street-level café with club and art gallery; the name means whale but it's not clear why. The popularity however, is obvious, especially among the intellectual crowd, and the reason for that is the very reasonable prices.

Denmark

The Jutland Peninsula and an archipelago of more than 400 islands, the majority of them tiny and uninhabited, make up the smallest and most southerly of the Scandinavian countries, a country where neither nuclear power plants nor the euro have a place. The country is fairly flat, very fresh and green, composed mainly of farmland and the occasional picturesque village. The best known Danes are Hans Christian Andersen, the composer Karl Nielsen and the philosopher Søren Kirkegaard. Fish, meat and cheese are staples of the Danish diet, and the favourite snack is the generous array of open sandwiches called smørrebrød. On the sweet side, but generally not too sweet, are the renowned Danish pastries. To drink, it's lager and aquavit, the one sometimes chasing then other. Coffee has found a niche, especially since the introduction of the European-style café-bars.

Copenhagen

Sculpted in 1913 by Edvard Eriksen and twice decapitated, the bronze statue of the Little Mermaid is Copenhagen's best-known sight. But this clean, pleasant city of some 600,000 souls on the eastern edge of the large island of Zealand has many other attractions. The magical Tivoli Gardens are among the most famous in the world, bringing in 4 million visitors every year, and also high on the tourist trial are the Danish National Museum, with its marvellously preserved 'bog people', the Carlsberg Brewery and the house on the north side of the harbour where Hans Andersen lived between 1845 and 1865. Copenhagen swings like nowhere else in Denmark.

Alex
Radhusplasden 77 (Farvergade)
Tel: 33 12 09 99
Open: 11.00-24.00 (Fri till 03.00, Sat 12.00-05.00)
Cosed: Sun
A convivial café opened in March 1999 by a Chinese restaurateur trying something Danish. It occupies a corner site, and clever use of sunny decor and mirrors achieves a very light, cheerful effect. A good espresso coffee is produced by a spectacular domed brass Italian machine holding pride of place on the corner of the L-shaped bar. Snacks and salads are served during the day, hot food in the evening. Thursday, Friday and Saturday are karaoke nights, starting at 23.00.

Café Restaurant Amadeus
Store Kongensgade 62, 1264 Kbh K
Tel: 33 32 35 11/ 33 32 46 03
Open: 07.30-23.00
A fun place just round the corner from the Royal Castle, with its own bakery open till 17.30, last dinner orders 22.00, and excellent Illy coffee to follow. All the baking is done on the premises by Denmark's acclaimed chef Allan Otto, and a mouthwatering display is on view as you enter. There's a quiet terrace at the back with tables under canvas 'gazebos'.

Hotel d'Angleterre Restaurant/Bar
Kongens Nytorv 34, 1021 K
Tel: 33 12 00 95
Open: 11.30-01.00
This recently renovated, luxurious and imposing 17th-century hotel across the square from the Opera and Nyhavn shows how the top and bottom of society used to rub along side by side. The bar leads to the restaurant, a classy venue for afternoon tea or a light supper before the opera, which is impressive not least for the ceramics designed in faux-Oriental style by the owner, Danish artist Bjorn Wiinblad. Special menus for special occasions such as Christmas and Easter.

Bang & Jensen Café
Istedgade 130
Tel: 33 25 53 18/40 32 02 42
Open: 08.00-02.00 (Sat from 10.00, Sun 10.00-24.00)
Home-made lemonade, filter coffee with a free refill, or Illy coffee for espresso. A café in the so-called red light district (gets redder further back towards the station) offering a meeting place for the young singles who have moved into the area for the economy of the rent. Cheerful girl staff work the bar, which is light and airy, with tables spilling out on to the pavement and more space up some steps behind the bar. Early bird breakfast 08.00-10.00; cocktail bar Saturday evenings.

Cap Horn
Nyhavn 21, 1051 Kbh K
Tel: 33 12 85 04
Open: 10.00-01.00
Once, perhaps 100 years ago, this was a hotel for ladies of the night, in what used to be a red light district. Now largely a restaurant, it also welcomes visitors for a coffee at the bar (espresso 17dk) or a beer on the terrace outside, served with a smile. It's a great place for watching sailing ships coming and going, or for watching the people walking up and down the quayside. Good range of bottled beers.

> "Sublime tobacco! . . .
> Yet thy true lovers more admire by far
> Thy naked beauties – give me a cigar!"
> **Lord Byron,** *The Island.*

Chit Chat Café

Sankt Peders Straede 24a, 1453 Kbh K
Tel: 33 33 93 39
Open: 11.00-23.00 (Fri & Sat till 01.00, Sun 10.00-17.00)

What was previously SMASH Café has a new owner in professional chef Christopher Howard. Located in the swanky/yuppie area east of the Royal Library and north of the City Hall Square, it has been smartly refurbished, with eyecatching use of steel, lovely flowers and clever lighting. Home-made luxury sandwiches, hamburgers and brasserie food - the menu changes weekly.

Café Dan Turell

Stor Regnegade 3-5, 1110 Kbh K
Tel: 33 14 10 47
Open: 10.00-24.00 (Fri & Sat till 02.00)
Closed: Sun

Opened in 1977, this was the second new-wave European-style café/bar in Copenhagen, the first being *Sommersko* (*qv*). Leatherette bench seating and a plain zinc bar top with formica back-bar suggest that the decor hasn't changed much since. It's named after a famous Danish literary figure who had fingers in many pies and was a prolific author. He died in the early 1990s and bar staff remember him as a regular visitor in the 1980s, smoking a little pipe of 'pot'. Brasserie-style snacks are available throughout the day, including salads, omelettes, pasta and bruschette - a mix of Italian and French, and daily specials add to the choice.

Drop Inn

Kompagnistraede 34, 1208 Kbh K
Tel: 33 11 24 04
Open: 11.00-04.00/05.00

Air-conditioning is welcome here, a music café established in the 30s when jazz was king; nowadays it's more rock and blues, with live music every night. During the day it's a peaceful café with the cheapest beer in town and a rack of newspapers to read outside under the awning or inside at the roomy teak-topped bar or sitting at a wooden tables on a bentwood chair.

Europa

Amagertorv 1
Tel: 33 14 28 89
Open: 09.00-24.00 (Fri & Sat till 01.00, Sun 10.00-19.00)

Modern and glass-fronted, spreading down into the square with its bronze fountain with three storks, under upside-down umbrellas (all the spines are on top) and opposite *Café Norden*. Come here for a tea or a coffee or a beer, a snack or a light lunch, to rest your weary feet after shopping, to enjoy the sun in the morning, or to avoid it in the afternoon.

Los Flamencos

Admiralgade 25, 1066 Kbh K
Tel: 33 16 34 35
Open: 17.00-24.00 (Fri & Sat from 13.00)
Closed: Sun

Owner Antonio opened here in 1996 and has received non-stop plaudits from his Danish critics - a tribute to his maintaining consistently high standards. He imports everything he can from Spain and the dishes - tapas and main meals - are produced as they would there, so it's all authentically Spanish, with nothing tailored to Danish tastes. Step down into the cantina - perhaps eight steps - to be greeted by soft Spanish music, and take a drink at the bar or sit in one of the capacious basket-weave armchairs set at square marble tables. If you order a bottle of house wine you only pay for what you drink.

Grand Teatret Foyer Caféen

Mikkel Bryggers Gade 8, 1460 Kbh K
Tel: 33 15 16 11
Open: 11.30-21.30

In the foyer of a once-grand theatre, now a complex of three cinemas, is this cool café spilling out on to the pavement. Classical music plays and you can have a drink, an ice cream, a sandwich or a cake before or after the film (first showing noon and then every two hours). But many people come here to relax with a newspaper in the very peaceful surroundings.

Kong Kursen
(Amalie Dorothea & Co's Restauration)

Kompagnistraede 4, 1208 Kbh K
Tel: 33 14 46 01
Open: 11.00-22.00 (winter till 18.00)
Closed: Sun

Chess and backgammon are played here at on marquetry boards inlaid in the tops of tables set on a cool herringbone brick-paved floor. The ceiling is decorated with old enamelled Danish advertisements, and outside there are aluminium tables and chairs for balmy days. A great selection of Danish open sandwiches and imaginative salads, meat snacks and lots of herring dishes await the hungry. Espresso coffee, Tuborg beers and house wines for liquid refreshment

Kafé Kys

Laederstraede 7
Tel: 33 93 85 94
Open: 10.00-01.00 (Fri & Sat till 02.00, Sun 12.00-24.00)

Young, beautiful staff serve excellent Illy coffee, draught beer and house wines, sandwiches and salads to young, beautiful customers sitting at pavement tables in a more-or-less pedestrianised street one away from the main shopping street. The music depends on the mood, and the mood is generally cool. Each month different artists display their paintings, which are for sale.

Langelinie Pavillonen

Langelinie, 2100 Kbh O
Tel: 33 12 12 14
Open: 12.00-24.00

Walk along the quayside towards the famous bronze of the little mermaid by Edvard Eriksen (twice restored after losing her head to vandals); just before you reach her is this spacious terrace restaurant-café serving a large selection of coffees, beers and snacks. It's set on three levels, two outside and the indoor restaurant atop, and provides a great vantage point for watching the comings and goings of all the wonderful craft, from small sailing dinghies to three-masters, speedboats to ocean-going ferries and liners and the new breed of Seacat. The Danes have the sea in their blood - it really is part of their lives. And the mermaid is worth seeing - it's her wistful look, so beguiling, even though she's pushing 90.

Lapostolle Café Bar

Gothersgade 11, 1123 Kbh K

Tel: 33 14 54 72

Open: 10.00-24.00 (Thur 10.00-02.00, Fri & Sat till 05.00)

An informal café-bar open for some years, with a frieze of a collage of posters and a background of bossa nova and other Latin music; old bentwood chairs stand at small cast-iron base tables by a simple zinc bar; newspapers lie in the rack for you to browse over a coffee or draught beer. The dark parquet floor gives way to two narrow raised pavement terraces outside under bright yellow awnings. Snacks, salads, fish dishes and Mexican food.

Mei Chiang

Tordenskjoldsgade 1,1055 Kbh K

Tel: 33 93 03 65

Open: 12.00-01.00 (Sun till 23.00)

Once a bakery, then a lunch shop, the two back rooms are now an elegant Chinese restaurant acquired some four years ago; the bar in front has a view of the street and a glance across the front of the Opera. Behind the bar are an elaborately carved piece of pine depicting the fruits of the field and vine and mirror-backed shelving, now holding liquor bottles but once doing duty in a Spanish apothecary. Always popular in the Opera season. Really good coffee.

Café Norden

Ostergade 61

Tel: 33 11 77 91

Open: 09.00-24.00 (Sun from 10.00)

A very popular modern café in the Hojbroplads (Hojbrohus), a pedestrian area with a fountain. Service on two floors and outside under large green awnings covers a selection of brownies, cookies, ices, soups, toasted and club sandwiches, tuna baps, salads, crêpes, nachos, peanuts and loads of coffees, juices, beers, wine and spirits. This is catering for the masses who flock here for refreshment, respite from shopping, to read the newspaper or to scour a thesis.

Café Nyhavn 17

Nyhavn 17

Tel: 33 12 54 19

Open: 10.00-02.00 (Fri & Sat till 03.00)

Closed: 10 days at Christmas

Traditional Danish snacks of open sandwiches and a lunch menu are served until 16.30, including the special 'platte' of seven types of food (meat, fish, cheese etc) served with bread. Later it becomes a bar, sometimes with live music. It retains its Scandinavian wood feel with a mahogany bar counter, a chunky brass rail held up by brass mermaid brackets, and matching tables and bentwood chairs. The other artefacts, although old, are antique-shop purchases. True to its past as a liquor store for sailors tradition, it has a big range of single malts both Scotch and Irish.

Palace Bar, Palace Hotel

Radhuspladsen 57, 1550 Kbh V
Tel: 33 14 40 50
Open: 12.00-02.00 (winter 15.00-01.00)
Opening on to the City Hall Square, with cane chairs at the pavement tables and comfortable tartan-upholstered chairs within, the bar offers a good sideways view of the facade of the Seat of the City Council. In the top row are the symbols of the officials, the town crier, the lamplighters and the guard. Below is the golden figure of the 13th-century Archbishop Absalon, in charge of the two dioceses of Roskilde and Lund (now in modern Sweden), each 35km away in opposite directions - hence his setting up shop here. The Palace Hotel, once a coaching inn, was started in 1907 (two years after the completion of the town hall) and finished in 1910. Speak to the jolly, knowledgeable bar manager (Jacob Glud) who will regale you with an interesting potted history. Good cocktails, plenty of eating choice in the Brasserie on the Square. Mainstream jazz is a regular feature.

Café Sommersko

Kronprinsengade 6, 1114 Kbh K
Tel: 33 14 81 89
Open: 08.00-24.00 (Sun from 10.00, Thur till 01.00, Fri till 02.00, Sat 09.00-02.00)
Established in 1976, this is part of a small group of café-bars with tables for lunches and dinners. Located just west of Nyhavn (the old port near the ferry terminals), it's a friendly place, with newspapers to read and young people whiling away a Saturday afternoon playing backgammon. It offers a good selection of traditional Danish beers on draught, Italian coffees and wine by the glass.

Opera Caféen

Gothersgade 2, 1123 Kbh K
Tel: 33 12 65 83
Open: 12.00-24.00 (Fri & Sat till 02.00, Mon till 22.00)
An eyecatching feature here is the series of oil-on-canvas wall hangings depicting Italian scenes; they could be originals from the café's first (1900) location nearer the Opera, but they certainly date from its opening here in 1934. At first it was just a bar used by many of the performers and stage staff as well as the opera-goers. It still remains busy in that role, but is now a restaurant in addition. Those wishing to dine (it now offers a lunchtime menu that is also available after the dinner menu has finished at 21.00) and see the Opera are strongly advised to book.
Denmark Café of the Year 2001

Victor Café/Brasserie

Hovedvagtsgade/Ny Ostergade 8, 1103 Kbh K
Tel: 33 13 36 13
Open: 08.00-01.00 (Thur, Fri & Sat till 02.00, Sun 11.00-23.00)
A busy, successful place on a corner site, with smartly clad staff and a clientele of all ages. Striking features include the ceiling, composed of opaque glass panels held in a diamond lattice in brass, and paintings by 15 different artists. From the two elaborate zinc-topped bar counters are served a good range of cocktails, draught and bottled beers, coffees Italian style and wines leading with their own-label house brand. A snack menu is printed on a long laminated card, Danish on one side, English on the other. The cooking on the main menu is French.

Odense

Little known before a canal was opened in the early 19th century linking it to the sea, Odense, on the fruit-producing island of Funen, is the birthplace of Hans Christian Andersen, though he spent little of his adult life here. His story is told in the Hans Christian Andersen Museum and his tiny Childhood Home.

Franck A

Jernbanegade 4, 5000 C
Tel: 66 12 27 57
Open: 09.00-01.00 (Sun 11.00-23.00)
Located in the city's pedestrian centre, Franck A serves all kinds of coffee and a range of cakes and light snacks. Sipping Illy coffee, browsing through the papers, listening to popular music, it easy to be content here. The friendly staff wear a distinctive uniform of grey shirts with Franck A, Illy and Martell logos, and black aprons with the Becks logo. There is a long wooden bar, with a separate dining area, and a mixture of low-volt modern and large half-globe lighting. Outside there are pavement tables. Good wines by the glass and some excellent draught beers.

Froggies

Vestergade 68, 5000 C
Tel: 65 90 74 47
Open: 11.00-02.00 (Fri & Sat till 05.00)
On the corner of Odense's pedestrianised shopping high street, Froggies is a daytime meeting and snacking place for shoppers and business people, and has a few pavement tables under awnings. Brasserie snacks and meals are on offer for shoppers and visitors here on business, and in the evening a lively young crowd takes over, making full use of the generous opening hours and enjoying the live music on Friday and Saturday.

Café Gertrud

Jernbanegade 8, 5000 C
Tel: 65 91 33 02
Open: 09.00-01.00 (Thur-Sat till 02.00, Sun from 10.00)
A little piece of Paris in Odense, and indeed the lovely decorative zinc bar top was made in Rue de Charonne in Paris (no.74: it's stamped on the counter). Posters abound and the globe lighting and the 'wicker' chairs outside add to the Paris effect. It is set on three levels - the street, the corner entrance and four steps up to the bar. Plats du jour are offered on Thursday, Friday and Saturday: starters, sandwiches, mains, salads, desserts and gateaux all at reasonable bistro/brasserie prices . As well as the draught beers there's a good wine list that's almost all French.
Special Award 2001

Ryan's Irish Bar

Fesketorvet 12
Tel: 65 91 53 00
Open: 11.00-02.00 (Thur till 03.00, Fri & Sat till 05.00, Sun 16.00-24.00)
An odd mix of bric-a-brac greets you as you approach Ryan's: wooden bow saws, a hammock, a barber's chair, advertising for Bewley's coffee and tea, cricket pads in the window. It's spacious, on two levels and with wooden planked floors. Popular with the young (and young at heart) at night, with live Irish music (Thursday-Saturday) to accompany Guinness and Kilkenny alongside traditional Danish beers.

Finland

Telephone Code: 00 358

Many of the country's major attractions are in the capital, but there is also plenty to see outside, including thousands of lakes and vast forests, Nuuksio National Park and the old wooden town of Porvoo with its brick-faced granite cathedral; lovers of old railways can reach this fascinating town in a 1950s railcar from Helsinki. Ainola was the home of the composer Sibelius, and at Hvitträsk are the studios of the renowned architects Saarinen, Lindgren and Gesellius. In the far north of the country the sun does not set for more than a month in the summer, while in the polar nights (kaamos) of mid-winter it does not rise for nearly two months. The café culture is fairly recent in Finland, and its rapid growth is a reflection of the increase in the travel of Finns outside their homeland. On the eating front, breads, pickled herrings and smoked fish and meats are often presented together in the national favourite seisova pöytä or 'standing table'.

Helsinki

One of the major tourist attractions of Europe's most northerly capital city is Suonmenlinna, a 250-year-old sea fortress built on islands south of the city and now a UNESCO World Heritage Site. The fortress was thought to be unconquerable when it was built, but fell to invading Russians in 1808. It is home to some 900 people, and also to various museums, a 250-ton WWll submarine and a working dockyard. The city itself boasts many museums (the delightful open air museum at Seurasaari should not be missed), while notable among the ecclesiastical buildings are the Lutheran Cathedral, built to original plans by Carl Engel; the Russian Orthodox Cathedral with its bulb-shaped domes; and Temppeliaukio Church, 'the Church inside the rocks', a circular church carved out of rock and topped with a copper dome. It was built in 1969 to a bold modern design by Timo and Tuomo Suomalainen. The Olympic Stadium, Olmpiastadion, was completed in time for the 1940 Games, but war intervened and it was eventually the site of the 1952 Games. Finlandiatalo, a concert hall by Töölönlahti Bay, is the most dramatic work of the leading architect Alvar Aalto. Rally and racing drivers apart, the country's most famous son is Jean Sibelius (1865-1957), whose symphonic poem *Finlandia* evokes the Finnish countryside and the Finns' love of nature. In Sibelius Park is a monument to the composer made from steel tubes and unveiled in 1967. Finland is the home of the sauna, and no visitor should leave without taking the plunge.

Ateneum

Kaivokatu 2, SF-00100 (National Museum Station Square)
Tel: 9 17 33 62 31
Open: Tue & Fri 10.00-18.00, Wed & Thur 10.00-19.00, Sat & Sun 11.00-17.00
Closed: Mon
This is the National Museum of Finnish Art's café, owned by a bakery which supplies cakes and pastries to some of the big department stores like Stockman; the owner also has a small Danish smorrebord place round the corner. People come here to see the standing exhibition and visiting exhibitions, but they also come here to take lunch, and the café offers a little-known outside catering service whose reputation is passed by word of mouth.

Cafe Carelia

Mannerheimintie 56, SF-00260
Tel: 9 270 90 976
Open: 12.00-01.00 (Sat from 13.00, Sun 13.00-23.00)
Opposite the Opera House, a café-cum-restaurant where the elegant people of Helsinki and visitors to the city come to refresh themselves and to dine, while getting away from the bustle and thrust of the centre of town. The speciality is fresh mussels. Previously it was a pharmacy, and much of the old interior has been retained, the bench seating, the burgundy and white diamond-patterned tile floor, the shelving, and the chemist's drawers, and the mahogany-wood panelling. Illy coffee is served with Illy chocolate in smart Illy cups. The long room that runs along Runeberginkatu (it's a corner site) has the bar and smart black table-clothed tables and chairs; the other, looking on to Mannerheimintie, is for non-smokers.

Café Carusel

Merisatamanranta 10, 00150
Tel: 9 622 4522
Open: 10.00-22.00 (winter till 19.00)
Closed: Jan
In 1995 this café was built here on a quay next to a host of marinas and their yachts and motor cruisers. You can sit in the spacious, high-ceilinged circular interior, with picture windows down to the wooden floor giving a panoramic view, or out on the expansive terrace (300+ seats). A draught beer, espresso or delicious white chocolate cappucino may be taken with or without a pastry or perhaps a club sandwich. There's always something to see: pleasure craft, sightseeing boats, private yachts, huge sea-going ferries - there's constantly something on the move. The café hosts occasional jazz or gospel concerts.

Café Ekberg

Bulevardi 9
Tel: 9 681 18660
Open: 07.30-20.00 (Sat 08.30-17.00, Sun 10.00-17.00)
Named after its founder Frederik Eduard Ekberg in 1852, this elegant café and pastry shop lies half way down a tree-lined street with the odd private gallery, towards the flea market in Hietalandenkatori (and its market hall). Away from the busy shopping centre, this is a peaceful café served by girls smartly dressed in black with their money belts carrying the change. Outside on a raised planked platform or inside in the simply but classically decorated room with floral drapes at the windows more mature residents of Helsinki come and enjoy the splendid buffet breakfast, a sweet or savoury pastry with a coffee or a beer, or a late afternoon salad and glass of white wine. Along from the café is their shop with all sorts of confections, including wonderful chocolates.

Café Engel

Aleksanterink 26, 00170
Tel: 9 652 776
Open: 07.45-24.00 (Sun from 11.00, Fri till 01.00, Sat 09.30-01.00)
'Energy' lamps banish the deep winter gloom at this café in the Senate square opposite the Uspensky Cathedral and the University. Named after the architect who designed the University building, it starts the day with a very good value breakfast menu with lots of options: The House Breakfast, French, English, and Energy. The English offers coffee/tea, scrambled eggs, sausage, bacon, bread, marmalade and orange juice. Classical music plays as people sip and munch and chat, in the front room with the wares on display, in the piano room behind (non-smoking), or in the internal courtyard. Also available are light salad dishes, beers by the bottle and wines by the glass. In the evenings it is a busy socialising spot and wine becomes the more common refreshment. The café's walls are hung with a frequently changing exhibition of paintings. The café is associated with the Arts Cinema next door and you can get tickets here; films in Finland are not dubbed.

Fazer

Kluuvikatu 3, SF-00100
Tel: 9 6159 2930
Open: 07.30-22.00 (Sat from 09.00, Sun 12.00-21.00)
A very stylish café-cum-restaurant-cum-bakery just off the Esplanade. Baking is done on the premises, the rolling, cutting and shaping of the delicacies happening before your very eyes. The range of goodies is mouthwatering, a real feast. To the left is the bar, and beyond it the restaurant, black and chrome with modern lighting.

Café Kafka

Pohjoisesplanadi 2/Svenska Teatern, SF-00130
Tel: 9 17 13 80
Open: 09.30-19.00 (Sat from 10.00)
Closed: Sun
The semi-circular foyer of the Swedish Theatre is occupied by this stylish café with cool black-and-white decor. The theatre stages musicals and comedies and has a small bookshop whose stock includes humorous books in English. In the café you can enjoy a peaceful refreshment and read the paper or a book away from the bustle of the shopping centre, or take your drink to the black folding metal tables and chairs outside in summer. In the same ownership are Bar Café Panorama, Mannerheimintie 22-27, Tel: 9 670065; Kanniston Leipomo, Kankurinkatu 6, Tel: 9 669516; and Sand, Bulevardi 32, Tel: 9 6801365.

Kappeli

Eteläesplanadi 1
Tel: 9 179 242
Open: 09.00-02.00 (Fri & Sat till 03.00)
A very stylish glass-covered pavilion, or rather three joined together, in the middle of the Walk. From a central bar pavilion where they brew their own unfiltered beer, tables and chairs spill out on to the terrace, and restaurant areas at either end offer a buffet at one, table service at the other. How do they cope in winter? They have a basement bar where they can escape for a cosy dark ale or one of their wide range of whiskies (opens at 16.00). But the windows of the pavilion are all double-glazed. Recently refurbished.

Kiasma

Mannerheiminaukio 2 SF-00100
Tel: 9 1733 6504
Open: 10.00-22.00 (Tue 09.00-17.00)
Closed: Mon
staccato modern minimalist decor. in modern art museum. opened 1998. art library across foyer. faces parliament. big mannerheim statue outside. oblong pond too. very good espresso. wine and beer to go with salads. green translucent chairs. children's chairs are angels. window wall.

Ravintola Seahorse

Kapteeninkatu 11, SF- 00140
Tel: 9 628 169
Open: 10.30-24.00 (Sat till 01.00)
Established in 1934, this restaurant/café proudly and rightly claims to offer true Finnish food and culture. The food is top-notch: salmon or wild mushroom soup, herrings in various ways, baked perch, steaks with morel and cranberry garnishes and sauces, anchovy butter, meatballs, pancakes and strawberries, cheese and cloudberry jam, blackcurrant sorbet - all at very reasonable prices, with teas and coffees, draught beer and wines by the glass to accompany. The mural at the end is an artistic impression of two sea horses swimming, and the chairs and a row of bench seating are repro in style. This café stands in a quiet suburb south of the city centre towards Eira, while an offshoot is by water in the northern suburb of Niemenmaki. There are coffees and draught beers and wines by the glass.

Robert's Coffee House

Kanavakatu 5, SF-00160
Tel: 9 1733 4458
Open: 09.00-17.00 (Sat from 10.00)
Closed: Sun, also Sat unless there's an exhibition in the building
Dedicated to coffee and tea, this café is located in the docks along from the market by the quays where all the long-haul ferries come in. It occupies the middle of a long building, with a bar at either end and a granite-tiled terrace with folding metal chairs and tables outside (smoking permitted). Inside are sacks of coffee piled up among the quiet comfortable wicker chairs set at tables. Among other offerings are three types of espresso - you choose the bean and the roast. The Robert in the name is Robert Paulig, a real expert in coffee matters, who founded the coffee house in 1987. The 'roastery' imports a selected variety of the finest green coffee from around the world and roasts the beans in small amounts to customers' tastes and requirements. It also sells coffee utensils and a selection of cakes and cookies.

Tomtebo Café

Tamminiementie 1
Tel: 9 484 511
Open: Jun-Aug 12.00-18.00; Sept, Oct & Jan-May Sat & Sun only 11.00-17.00
Closed: Nov & Dec

The centrepiece of the Folklore Centre of Tomtebo, run by the Seurasaari Foundation, is an open-air museum of some 90 years standing. The café is in the summer house (a traditional wooden construction built in 1893) of Gustaf Nyström, the renowned professor of architecture who designed this villa and, among other things, the National Library building. His family used it until the 1960s and it is now owned by the city of Helsinki. For years the citizens have been coming here for quiet summer walks in the park and to picnic on the nearby island, and in winter at weekends to bring their own food to barbecue at bonfire parties. The café has an exhibition of colourful folk costumes worn by Russian refugees escaping the rigours of the old communist state, and most summer evenings folk dancing is performed on a stage behind the café. You can take refreshment both inside the summer house and at wrought-iron tables and chairs in the grounds.

Snellman's

Kauppatori
No telephone
Open: 06.00-14.00 (Sat till 15.00)
Closed: Sun

In the same eponymous family for over 100 years, this splendid little stall stands opposite the Town Hall right by the quayside where all the ferries and excursion boats come and go. The market sells fruit and veg and fish at one end, arts and crafts at the other. If it's too draughty outside under the Coke umbrellas, it's cosier in the bright orange tent. A constant flow of customers arrives for their well-known hot pork and beef pasties, or a hot apple doughnut to go with a coffee. Nearby is the indoor market (1889), Vanha Kauppahalli, where you can buy bread, cheese, meat, sweets and wine from the government-owned Alko stall.

Strindberg

Pohjoisesplanadi/Norra Esplanaden 33, SF- 00100
Tel: 9 270 60 150
Open: 09.00-01.00 (Sun 10.00-23.00)
Closed: Sun (restaurant only)

Opening on to the Esplanade on the corner of Mikongatu (Mikaelsgatan), and inside into the Galleria Kämp shopping mall, this is a very fashionable café owned by Stockman department store, busy at lunchtime with a queue at the self-service counter, and in the evenings a popular spot for a beer, glass of wine, a cocktail or an after dinner coffee and liqueur (good Illy coffee, and café au lait served French style in bowls).

Café Torpanranta

Munkkiniemen Ranta 2, SF- 00330
Tel: 9 484 250
Open: 10.00-212.00 (winter till 16.00)

A pretty pavilion café on the beach in a northwest suburb and parkland. An elderly couple run the place with the help of a young waitress, and there's a cafeteria counter from which you choose your sandwich or pastry to enjoy with some good coffee or a glass of wine. From the large patio, decorated with flowers, you can step straight on to the beach and watch the colourful summertime activity of washing rugs on the bench tables at the nearby jetty. The rugs are left to dry on racks. This activity is particular to certain parts of Helsinki and is much enjoyed by the whole family.

Café Ursula

Ehrenströmintie3, SF-00140
Tel: 9 652 817
Open: 09.00-24.00 (winter till 21.00)
On the water's edge by the Kaivopuisto Brunnsparken Park, in the Embassy district south of the centre, is a pretty pavilion/conservatory café with a terrace, selling snacks, coffees and beers, and a selection of ice creams. In the park, in the summer you can play chess on a paved board with 30"-high chess pieces, or go bungee-jumping (or just watch), or hire roller blades. Otherwise, there's all the activity on the water: jet-skiers jetting, yachtsmen yachting, travellers going to distant places on giant floating hotels.

Tampere

The major industrial city of Finland, and the largest inland city in Scandinavia, Tampere enjoys a peaceful lakeside setting. Parks and lakes provide plenty of opportunity for a quiet stroll, and among the places on the tourist trial are the art galleries, the Workers' Museum of Amuri, which depicts the homes and lives of working people over the past century, and the Lenin Museum - Lenin lived for a time in Finland after the abortive Russian revolution of 1905.

Bodega Salud

Tuomiokirkonkatu 19
Tel: 3 2235 996
Open: 11.00-24.00 (Sun 13.00-22.00)
A friendly and authentic Spanish café/bar, with a restaurant at the back. *Jamon* (hams) hang over the tapas selection along with strings of garlic and salami sausages. There is a good wine list, and several beers. Filter coffee is served in a small pot, or you can have an excellent Illy espresso. As you enter you pass the tapas display and approach the bar, which is made from timber inset with colourful tiles. Pistachio nuts are offered with your drinks, which you can take to the simple wooden tables and chairs spaciously set out. Live Spanish music is played in the evenings, when a small group circulates among the customers.

Café Europa

Aleksanterinkatu 29
Tel: 3 2235 526
Open: 12.00-02.00 (Fri & Sat till 03.00)
A good choice of taking your ease here: lolling in comfortable armchairs and sofas, or sitting at the bar on high-backed stools, or on upright chairs at highly polished antique tables. The walls are hung with antique pictures and mirrors. A cross between French, Italian and Spanish snacks is served here: goat's cheese salad, kidney beans and chorizo, risotto, carpaccio, insalata di mare, tapas tasters. Various good coffees, a big range of whiskies, ciders, beers and wines by the glass from Spain, Italy, France and one from USA, all with information and tasting notes. On Wednesday, Friday and Saturday there's a disco upstairs, starting at 22.00. Newspapers are available to read while you sip your coffee and munch your snack.

Kahvihuone Mestari Brander

Hallituskatu 13
Tel: 3 2125 357
Open: 09.00-18.00 (Sat till 16.00, Sun 12.00-16.00)
The Brander group is a renowned patissier here in Tampere, and they have several outlets. This double-fronted one is in a broad street just behind the big stores on Hameenkatu, where you can park your car. Upstairs is table service, downstairs self-service. There are half-a-dozen terrace tables or you can sit inside the spacious café.

Kauppahallin Kahvila Linkosuo

Hameenkatu 19
Tel: 3 2131 801
Open: 08.00-17.00 (Fri till 17.30, Sat till 15.00)
Closed: Sun
Located in the turn-of-the-century Market Hall (no smoking) on the main street, this fairly roomy café serves coffee of all kinds including good espresso, cappucino, café au lait, tea and hot chocolate with or without cream. Pretty waitresses in navy and white pinafores serve either at high stools at the bar counter or at redwood and metal chairs at plain tables. The stalls are brightly set out with colourful fresh produce of all kinds and there is a buzz of activity about you.

Leivonpesä

Hameenkatu 6
Tel: 3 258 5580
Open: 07.00-18.30 (Sat till 17.00, Sun 09.00-17.30)
Fresh cakes and bread are available here either inside or out on the broad pavement by the bus stop under a big red awning. Customers take advantage of the early opening time to look in on their way to work, or take a break at lunchtime with a sandwich or salad. The tables outside have comfortable aluminium and basket- weave chairs, which at busy times spread out over the brick paving.

Café Rose Rokokoo

Laukontori 6, 33 200
Tel: 3 212 50 65
Open: 11.00-17.00 (Sat till 15.00)
Closed: Sun
A boutique café in a square with a small market selling fresh garden produce and plants, by the quayside for ferries to the holiday island of Viikinsaari. Owners Anne Mattsson and her husband have lived and travelled extensively in Germany, and brought back with them an eclectic mix of dolls, china, and furniture, which they have used to decorate their café. Choice of coffee and a good selection of cakes.

Siilinkari Café

Hameenkatu 9
Tel: 3 222 0861
Open: 07.00-21.00 (Sat from 08.00, Sun 11.00-20.00)
A large café (the name means 'hedgehog') with pavement tables in a roped-off area, serving coffee, wines and beers for passing trade from breakfast right through to the cocktail hour. It is located on Tampere's main street, so shop and office workers mingle with shoppers for refreshment or a snack, perhaps before a visit to the Adams cinema next door.

Teerenpeli (Panimoravintola=Brewery)

Hameenkatu 25, 33200
(also at Vapaudenkatu 20, 15140 Lahti, west of the city centre)
Tel: 3 2234 100
Open: 12.00-02.00 (Fri & Sat till 03.00)
They brew their own beer (one pale, one porter) and cider (one plain, one with blueberry flavour). And they import their own-label Speyside by the cask (cask strength 56%). The first arrived in June 1999 to supplement their already very long (not to say phenomenal) beer, cider and whisky menu. The interior is very spacious, and outside under green awnings is permanent timbered staging with fenced-off tables and basket-weave chairs. Bar snacks can be enjoyed with half a dozen wines by the glass. They also serve coffee!

Tillikka, Tampereen Teatteri Ravintola

Keskustori 2, Teatteritalo

Tel: 3 2544 700

Open: 11.00-01.00 (Fri & Sat till 02.00, Sun 12.00-24.00)

Young people, arty types, would-be actors (Tampere has ten theatres and an annual International Theatre Festival), aspiring intellectuals, even their mentors. They all gather at this cafeteria, either in the long bar with multiglobe chandeliers and a view of the trees across the river and the main street Hameenkatu, or downstairs in the terrace bar with views of the river and the waterfall. Here, too, is an astonishing range of malts; one wonders who drinks them as everyone seems to be drinking beer or stout (except the diet-conscious girls sticking to iced tap water). Cafeteria for snacks, bars for coffees and drinks.

Turku

A small, vivacious city that was once the national capital (it lost that position in 1812). It offers plenty of history and culture and a lively night life thanks in large measure to its two universities. Places to visit include the 13th-century cathedral, the Sibelius Museum and the open-air Luostarinmäki Handicrafts Museum. The Swedish name for Turku is Åbo.

Café Fontana

Aurakatu 1, FIN-20100

Tel: 2 233 3319

Open: 10.00-18.00 (Sat till 16.00)

Closed: Sun

In a building dating from 1898, on a corner site where there has always been a shop, stands this first-class, traditionally decorated café that bakes its own pastries on the premises. The chairs are all original Jugend from around 1910.

Koulu Panimoravintola (The School)

Eerikinkatu 18, FIN 20100
Tel: 2 274 5757
Open: 11.00-02.00 (Fri & Sat till 03.00)

Just along from the Kauppahalli (indoor market) is this grand establishment where various beers and filtered coffee are all made on the premises. It was originally a girls' school, founded in 1889. A few years ago the building had fallen into disrepair, and the City of Turku and the brewery Turun Panimo Oy got together to completely renovate it. This is the result - a fully operational brewery in the ground floor hall and café-bar areas in what were the classrooms. Upstairs, more classrooms have been made into a restaurant, and in the summer there's a kiosk in the grounds.

Old Bank

Aurakatu 3, FIN-20100
Tel: 2 274 5700
Open: 12.00-01.00 (Wed - Sat till 02.00, Sun from 16.00)

As the name suggests, this was once a bank, established in 1907 and converted into its current incarnation in 1992. During the day senior citizens come to relax and read the newspapers in the anteroom set with armchairs like the library of a gentleman's club. The huge bank vault is now the spirit store. Nine draught beers, 120 bottled beers and a few wines accompany a light snack, and there's a big range of malt whisky, served in chilled shot glasses. A few tables are set outside on the pavement.

Puutorin Vessa

Puutori, 20100
Tel: 2 233 8123
Open: 11.00-24.00

The menu at this tastefully converted bar-café contains a history of the square and its uses over the years, and the jokey bill of fare includes snacks such as bratwurst, or frankfurter in a bun with mayonnaise. On the back is an obituary to the lady who sold toilet paper here for over thirty years until forced to retire, aged over 80, when it was converted in 1997. Two months later she died having nothing to do. Also for sale is various merchandise, a beer mug in the shape of a potty, a candle holder in the shape of the building, books written by one of the owners, and, of course, toilet paper!

Sininen Juna (Blue Train)

Turun Kauppahalli / Saluhallen,
Linnankatu/Eerikinkatu 16, 20100
Open: 08.00-17.00 (Sat till 18.00)
Closed: Sun

Make your way to old indoor market and travel down memory lane on the Blue Train! The seating was rescued from an old railway carriage, indeed the café is laid out as a railway carriage with the buffet at the end - even down to the old carriage windows with reflective panels for glass. Its shape is in keeping with the old market itself, which is long and narrow with only two aisles, each wooden stall with its roller shutter - all original. Filter coffee, cakes, filled rolls, soft drinks, and bakery to take home.

Svarte Rudolf/Rudolfilla

Itäinen Rantakatu, Aurajoki, 20100
Tel: 2 250 4567
Open: 11.00-23.00 (Sun till 21.00)

A bar-restaurant on a boat that's permanently moored opposite the Town Hall on the 'better' side of the River Aura, and a stone's throw from the Theatre. The upper deck is an open terrace café that is very popular in the sunshine of the summer when temperatures can reach 30°C. Come November, when it starts to get cold - the first snows come in December and by January the temperature can fall to -20°C - everyone goes down into the saloon. Snacks include a Greek salad. Music is provided by Golden Oldies from the late 50s and early 60s.

Uusi Apteekki

Kaskenkatu 1, FIN-20700
Tel: 2 250 2595
Open: 10.00-03.00

A 1920s chemist's shop was converted around 1992 and its pharmaceutical shelves stocked with a comprehensive range of Scottish single malt whiskies. This, and the same owners' other outlet *Koulu* (qv) sell, among others, their own local draught beer - Kaskenmaen, a darkish unfiltered ale. 'Ordinary' coffee, i.e. filtered cona coffee, is also on offer, but here they sell no snacks. Situated over the bridge from the centre, this is the wealthy part of town with some grand houses and spacious parkland.

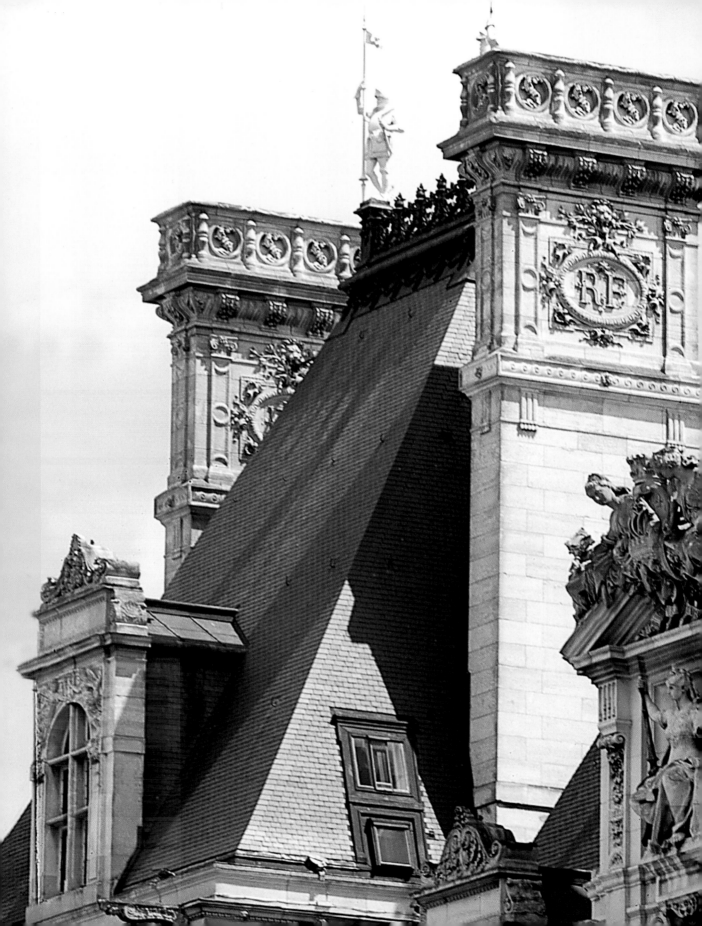

France

Telephone Code: 00 33

The British attraction to France and things French (a few minor differences excepted) is equalled only by the French attraction to Britain and things British. Food and drink are major unifying themes among the diverse population of France, where virtually every town and village has a regular street market as its focal point and social hub. From the major wine-growing areas - Burgundy, Bordeaux, the Loire, Alsace, the Rhone and Champagne - come some of the world's truly great wines and it's a particular delight for the tourist in France to come across village names which are normally seen only on bottle labels. We love their wine (and they love our whisky, getting through more of the hard stuff per head than us!). The café culture is as solidly based as the wine culture, though recently it has been increasingly threatened, certainly in the cities, by the fast food culture. But traditional cafés and bars are still a charming feature of French life, particularly in provincial France, usually giving an accurate snapshot of the daily cycle in each locality. These places range from the tiny zinc-countered bar where the talk these days is likely to be about football to the classic boulevard cafés and *cafés littéraires* of the cities, as well as the stylish themed bars that are bringing a new, international dimension to late-night life.

CAFÉ CRÈME

Paris

The City of Light is an unending joy for the tourist, with so much more to offer than the historic buildings, the museums, the shops, the green spaces, the Seine and the Eiffel Tower. Each of its 20 arrondissements, or districts, has its own town hall, its own market (usually several) and at least some of its old character, though in many areas the streetline, if not the skyline, is being transformed by new developments. Many of the city's old-fashioned cafés have fallen victim to soaring new building schemes or dipping profits, often giving way to fast-food outlets or the themed bars that have their own attractions but are definitely not Parisian. Happily, some of the old zincs can still be found, providing an atmospheric, down-to-earth glimpse of their neighbourhoods and their inhabitants. The Paris Metro is famously quick, quiet and clean, and the buses usually manage to run on time despite the traffic chaos, but the best way by far to discover Paris is on foot, with every turn bringing a new delight, a new dimension, a new insight into this most beguiling of cities.

L'Angevin

168 rue Montmartre, 2nd
Tel: 1 42 36 20 20
Open: 10.00-02.00
Closed: Sun & Mon
An attractive bar in art deco style, where the patron, Jean-Pierre Robineau, and his black-aproned staff have a warm welcome for friends and strangers alike. Jean-Pierre is devoted to wine and cheese, and his wine selection is mostly from western France, the Loire and the South. One of the special wines is an organic Coteaux du Loire made from the chenin grape. They also have a range of Côtes du Rhône from 1988 to 1997. Formerly in rue Richard Lenoir.

"Happiness? A good cigar, a good meal, a good cigar and a good woman – or a bad woman; it depends on how much happiness you can handle."

George Burns

L'Apparement Café

18 rue des Coutures St-Gervais, 3rd
Tel: 1 48 87 12 22
Open: 12.00-02.00 (Sat 16.00-02.00, Sun 12.30-24.00)
A former art gallery whose rooms are named like the rooms in an apartment. The various rooms, each with its own idiosyncratic decor, include the library room with wooden seats and bookcases, from which visitors are welcome to take their pick for a browse with their drink. Board games are also available. 'Le petit salon' is furnished with 1930s armchairs and sofas. A place of real character, great for spending an hour or two with or without a good book. Very close to the Picasso Museum.

Le Baromètre

17 rue Charlot, 3rd
Tel: 1 48 87 04 54
Open: 07.00-21.00
Closed: Sat, Sun, Aug & week Christmas-New Year
A favourite 'local', popular with the wide cross-section of Parisians that inhabit the Marais. It's one of the best *bars à vins* in town, with awards to prove it (including the 1993 *Bouteille d'Or*), and 30 or so well-chosen regional wines available by bottle, carafe or glass. Enjoy your choice with a taste of cheese or charcuterie or one of the two *plats du jour*. Regulars keep their napkins in numbered racks awaiting their next visit.

Bouillon Racine

3 rue Racine, 5th
Tel: 1 44 32 15 60
Open: 12.00-23.30
'La cuisine belge aux couleurs de la bière'. Camille Chartier opened this delightful art nouveau café/restaurant in 1906 and it became one of the most popular workmen's dining halls in Paris, establishing the tradition of taking bouillon (soup) at the counter. Later much favoured by students, it was completely renovated by a young Belgian entrepreneur in 1996, restoring its marvellous bevelled, mirrored panels and intricate woodwork to their original splendour. The tipple is beer (Belgian beers on draught, available by glass or jug), and the cooking is Belgian, with beer an integral part of many dishes.
Nothing changes here, because nothing can - it's a listed historic building.
France Café of the Year 2001

Carette

4 pl du Trocadéro, 16th
Tel: 1 47 27 88 56
Open: 07.30-24.00

A classic *salon de thé* established in 1926 right opposite the enormous Chaillot Palce and the terrace that provides the most impressive view of the Eiffel Tower. It's open all day, every day for coffee, tea, superb pastries and light savoury snacks, with a few *plats du jour* at lunchtime. There's also a busy takeaway trade and a home delivery service.

Au Chai de l'Abbaye

26 rue de Buci, 6th
Tel: 1 43 26 68 26
Open: 08.00-02.00 (Sun 11.00-23.00)

Chai de l'Abbaye is at the heart of the always-lively scene of the street market that runs into Rue de Seine. Bright, friendly and inviting, it attracts both locals and tourists, who come to enjoy the good food, the good wine and the cheerful company.

Café Charbon

109 rue Oberkampf, 11th
Tel: 1 43 57 55 13
Open: 08.00-02.00 (Sat & Sun from 09.00)

An atmospheric café-brasserie in what was originally a dance hall. The turn-of-the-century decor is its chief charm: fading murals above tall mirrors show top-hatted gentlemen being entertained by crinolined can-can girls. Barrels are racked up by a steel pulley system at the bar, providing a large selection of beers. There's also a range of wines, with a dozen available by glass or half bottle. A lively spot - especially when the DJ's doing his stuff - in an up-and-coming part of town.

La Coupole

102 bd du Montparnasse, 14th
Tel: 1 43 20 14 20
Open: 07.30-02.00

The most renowned of the art deco brasseries, and a great favourite with the American set, La Coupole opened its doors in 1927, since when it has remained one of *the* places for people-watching. The columns, painted by different artists, are an eyecatching feature of the decor, whose centrepiece is a revolving modern sculpture. A full brasserie menu is served from 11.30, but before that you can take a coffee at the bar or set yourself up with breakfast on the *terrasse*.

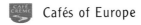

Les Deux Magots

6 pl St-Germain-des-Prés, 6th
Tel: 1 45 48 55 25
Open: 07.30-01.30
Closed: 3-4 days late Jan

This is the one café that almost everyone who ever been in Paris has visited. The two magots are the wise Chinamen whose statues sit in the entrance of what is probably the most famous of all the arty cafés in Paris, founded in 1875 and long associated with the leading lights of 20th-century French and American literature. Artists, too, made it their own, and some say that this is where Picasso created Cubism. The literary connection is still maintained by the owners, but tourists are now a major source of business. Inside are rich red banquettes, brass-edged tables and walls of mirrors; outside is position A for watching Paris pass on the ever-busy boulevard and being entertained by buskers. The waiters wear floor-length aprons and black waistcoats. Hot chocolate is a speciality.

L'Ecluse

15 pl de la Madeleine, 8th
Tel: 1 42 65 34 69
Open: 11.30-01.00

L'Ecluse is a chain of five superior wine bars specialising in the wines of Bordeaux and appealing equally to Parisians and visitors to the city. The Madeleine branch, on the same block as the high-class grocer and traiteur Hédiard, has the look of a private wine-imbibers' club, with seats comfortably clad in velvet, marble panels set into the bar front and the little tables, and wine paraphernalia everywhere. An amusing *carte des vins* lists and describes the extensive range of wines (many of them available by the glass - *verre dégustation* and *verre amateur* - as well as by the bottle) and includes an aide-memoire for tasters. Food is taken seriously, too, and the menu offers a fair selection of hot and cold dishes, plus cheeses and desserts.
Also at: 64 rue François 1er, 8th. Tel: 1 47 20 77 09
15 quai des Grands-Augustins, 6th. Tel: 1 46 33 58 74
13 rue de la Roquette, 11th. Tel: 1 48 05 19 12
1 rue Armaillé, 17th. Tel: 1 47 63 88 29

Bar de l'Entr'acte

7 rue du Montpensier, 1st
Tel: 1 42 97 57 76
Open: 10.00-02.00

Decorated in traditional style, this tiny 300-year-old bar in a side street next to the Palais-Royal remains a popular drinking and snacking place with both actors and spectators at the nearby Comédie Française and Théâtre du Palais-Royal. Diderot was a regular here when it was called something else.

L'Européen

21bis bd Diderot, 12th
Tel: 1 43 43 99 70
Open: 06.00-01.00

'La brasserie très parisienne': their own very fair description of this busy brasserie right opposite the main entrance to Gare de Lyon. The decor features extravagant chrome, Lalique-alike floral lamps and star-cluster chandeliers, and the seats in the front section are on wheels - a comfortable and quite stylish apparent adaptation of executive office chairs. A long bar counter with high stools accommodates travellers in a hurry for the terminus and the terminally thirsty, while the rest of the capacious room is set with tables for dining. Breakfast is served from opening time and the full brasserie menus come on stream at 11.00. An excellent alternative to the catering outlets in the station itself, with a wide choice of dishes (*fruits de mer* and *choucroute* are specialities), reasonable prices and affable, capable service.

Café de Flore

172 bd St-Germain, 6th
Tel: 1 45 48 55 26
Open: 07.00-01.30

The neighbour of *Les Deux Magots* and another of the great *cafés littéraires*, with art deco interior and plenty of seats outside. Service by white-aproned waiters. Pricy, but not to be missed for lapping up the life of the Left Bank. In the 1930s and 1940s Simone de Beauvoir and Jean-Paul Sartre, Camus and Genet were regulars, and Picasso met his mistress Dora Maar here while taking a break from working on his masterpiece *Guernica*.

Bar aux Folies

8 rue de Belleville, 20th
Tel: 1 46 36 65 98
Open: 07.00-23.00

A lively, down-to-earth bar whose name recalls the time when the building was a variety theatre. Much of the interior decor is from that period in the latter part of the 19th century, while other parts are brash 1950s' neon. Belleville is the most cosmopolitan part of Paris, a fact reflected in the cheerful, multi-lingual crowd that fills the place to enjoy a drink and a snack - *jambon au beurre* is the most popular item.

Bar la Fontaine

1 rue de Charonne, 11th
Tel: 1 56 98 03 30
Open: 08.30-02.00 (Sun from 10.00)

Casual, chummy and frequently boisterous, a bar-café that dates from the late 19th century, with a terrace that is always crowded when the weather allows. The atmosphere is cosy, the decor well worn, and there are unusual features, notably a very tight wooden spiral staircase. Salads and gratins and croques.

Le Fouquet's

99 ave des Champs-Elysées, 8th
Tel: 1 47 23 70 60
Open: 09.00-02.00

A notable Parisian landmark, the prestigious Fouquet's (pronounce the 't') is a real institution, the most famous boulevard café-restaurant on the most famous boulevard in the city. Refurbished in the summer of 1999, it continues to attract the rich and famous, the stars and the would-be stars, and the main entrance floor is a rollcall of famous stars, their names engraved in brass plaques.

Harry's Bar

5 rue Daunou, 2nd
Tel: 1 42 61 71 14
Open: 10.00-04.00

Go through the famous swinging wooden doors and discover a piece of America where the spirits of Gershwin and Hemingway and Fitzgerald still linger. Among the 'must' snacks are the hot dogs, smeared with Harry's special blend of Dijon mustard, the club sandwich, home-made chili, savoury tourtes, brownies and fresh grapefruit salad. The barmen are shaker champions and will produce any of 369 cocktails for you, including the Harry's Bar inventions the Bloody Mary and the Sidecar.

Café de l'Industrie

16 rue St-Sabin, 11th
Tel: 1 47 00 13 53
Open: 10.00-02.00
Closed: Sat

Dating from the 1880s, this evocative café comprises three dimly lit rooms whose faded cream walls are a merry jumble of bric-a-brac, including saucy pre-war prints, photographs of the old stars (film), plants, masks, spears, Oriental rugs and crocodile skins. The ambience is happy and relaxed, because the customers, mainly lively youngsters from the Bastille district, make it that way. The rooms open on to a little indoor garden. Drinks, snacks and full meals.

Café de la Mairie

8 pl St-Sulpice, 6th
Tel: 1 43 26 67 82
Open: 07.00-02.00
Closed: Sun (except in June)

A small corner bar with outside tables, a popular haunt of students and writers (Hemingway, Fitzgerald and Samuel Beckett among the past habitués). Good snacks include croque monsieur made with *Poilâne* bread, omelettes and composite salads. The amazing Church of Saint-Sulpice, just along the road, is one of the great buildings of Paris. It took 135 years to build and it was actually never finished, the south tower being crude and obviously incomplete - you couldn't trust builders even in the 17th century! The church and the spectacular fountain in the square are both the work of the architect Visconti.

Café Marly

Cour Napoléon, 93 rue de Rivoli, 1st
Tel: 1 49 26 06 60
Open: 08.00-02.00

One of the most elegant and fashionable cafés in the city, a sumptuous 1994 design by Olivier Gagnère and Yves Taralon in the impressive setting of the grounds of the Louvre, right opposite the Pei glass pyramid. Tables and chairs are arranged outside on the terrace (a long marble-floored forecourt, lined with great stone columns, leading down to the Cour Napoléon itself). Inside, the decor is splendidly extravagant: Venetian chandeliers light black and gold furnishings with grey velvet chairs and sofas, and the magnificent loos are decked out in marble and black china. The chic turns almost to magic at night, when the courtyard is floodlit. Chicest items on the menu are the tartares - steak and salmon. These are fixtures, but the menu changes every two months with the seasons.

Café Martini

11 rue du Pas de la Mule, 4th
Tel: 1 42 77 05 04
Open: 08.30-02.00

A few mule-steps away from Place des Vosges, and a short walk from Bastille, this a dark, low-ceilinged bar-café with heavy beams and crumbly walls. The atmosphere is delightfully laid-back and the little place is often packed. Lunchtime-only fare includes *panini,* salads and a *plat du jour* such as *poulet basquaise. Chocolat à l'ancienne* - very thick and creamy - is a speciality.

Café de la Musique

pl de la Fontaine-aux-Lions, 213 ave Jean-Jaurès, 19th
Tel: 1 48 03 15 91
Open: 08.00-02.00

Grand and elegant, in typical Costes brothers style, the café is at the tip of the Cité de la Musique complex. The atmosphere is warm and inviting thanks to dark-wood panelling, velour-clad tub chairs and discreet lighting, and the live jazz is a major attraction on Wednesdays (not in the summer). Friday is 'World Music Day'. Another Costes signature is the enormous terrace, with seats for 350, that overlooks Parc de la Villette.

Café de la Nouvelle Mairie

19-21 rue des Fossés-St-Jacques, 5th
Tel: 1 44 07 04 41
Open: 08.00-21.00 (Tue & Thur till 24.00)
Closed: Sat,Sun & Aug

Students and locals mingle in a pleasant bar in a leafy side street near the Panthéon and the Sorbonne. French wines by the glass are a major attraction and the bar's 1920s charm remains intact, with leather-clad bench seats, stone walls, tiled floor and a zinc bar. Light snacks and a *plat du jour*, with speciality meats and cheeses from the Aveyron.

Café de la Paix

12 bd des Capucines, 9th
Tel: 1 40 07 30 20
Open: 09.00-00.45

Beneath the Hotel de la Paix (a building listed as a Historic Monument), this is a spacious corner café with a sumptuous Second Empire interior by Charles Garnier, whose masterpiece, the Opéra Garnier, can be seen from the pavement terrace. A classy place, popular with better-off tourists and better-off local workers. Classic menu of fish and meat dishes.

La Palette

43 rue de Seine, 6th
Tel: 1 43 26 68 15
Open: 08.00-02.00
Closed: Sun, 1st 2 wks Aug & 1 week Feb
In a street filled with art galleries and antique shops, this busy, bohemian little place is a popular rendezvous for the shop-owners and for students from the nearby Ecole des Beaux Arts. Palettes and paintings brighten the dark interior, and outside on the flowery terrace is a bronze statue depicting the arts. Food is served at lunchtime only; the *spécialité de la maison* is 'guillotines' - open ham sandwiches made with toasted *Poilâne* bread.

Pause Café

41 rue de Charonnne, 11th
Tel: 1 48 06 80 33
Open: 07.45-02.00 (Sun till 20.30)
A hugely popular and successful café, the friendliest and perhaps the hippest of all the hip places around the Bastille. A changing exhibition of artwork hangs on the walls, and the red and yellow decor is vibrantly cheerful. Drinks are reasonably priced, and the food specialities include dishes cooked à l'ardoise and *tourtes* served with salad. When the sun shines there's fierce competition for a seat on the terrace. Pause Café featured prominently in the film *Chacun Cherche Son Chat* (English title: *While the Cat's Away*).

Bistrot du Peintre

116 ave Ledru-Rollin, 11th
Tel: 1 47 00 34 39
Open: 07.00-02.00 (Sun 10.00-20.00)
An attractive turn-of-the-century café on two floors, with art nouveau decor of tiled floor, frosted glass partitions, long mirrors and a zinc bar. Good food, from sandwiches to full three-course meals, is efficiently served from noon till midnight. Specialities include charcuterie from the Auvergne and *tartine de moelle*.

Le Petit Fer à Cheval

30 rue Vieille-du-Temple, 4th
Tel: 1 42 72 47 47
Open: 09.00-02.00
On a main street of the Marais, one of the oldest and most atmospheric parts of Paris, this pretty and very popular little café has a horseshoe-shaped marble-topped bar (the only original one left in Paris), mirrored walls and a mosaic floor. There is a tiny dining salon behind the bar with old wooden Métro seats and on the bar a tall pewter water-fountain as old as the café, which first opened its doors in 1903; the toilets are in stainless steel, reminding some visitors of Captain Nemo's *Nautilus*, others of Flash Gordon's spaceship. The menu runs from tartines, sandwiches and salads to andouillette, steak tartare, bavette and confit de canard.

Au Petit Suisse

16 rue de Vaugirard, 6th
Tel: 1 43 26 03 81
Open: 07.00-24.00

Across the road from the Luxembourg Gardens and behind the Odéon theatre stands this delightful, idiosyncratic old *café-tabac* with a street-level terrace and steps down to the sunken bar. It has a fascinating history, having been established by Marie de Médicis as a watering-hole for her Swiss guards. Just a few snacks - sandwiches, croque monsieur - and wines to accompany them.

Les Pipos

2 rue Ecole-Polytechnique, 5th
Tel: 1 43 54 11 40
Open: 07.30-23.30 (Sat till 02.00)
Closed: Sun & Aug

A pretty little corner *bar à vins,* friendly and unassuming, with an impressive selection of wines by glass and bottle. Beaujolais wines are the speciality, bought direct from the vineyards by the enthusiastic owner. There's also an extensive range of armagnacs going back more than 30 years. The place attracts a wide cross-section of Parisian society, and tourists also enjoy the buzz. Live accordion and guitar music makes Friday and Saturday nights particularly jolly.

Café de la Place

23 rue d' Odessa, 14th
Tel: 1 42 18 01 55
Open: 07.00-02.00 (Sun 10.00-23.00)

Close to Gare Montparnasse and Edgar Quinet market, this a busy pavement café with 1900-style wooden floors and walls, and a collection of pastis jugs and advertising plaques. The theme is green, for the chairs, for the tables on the *terrasse* and for the sunshades. Good French wines and simple snacks (excellent charcuterie), plus daily specials: *blanquette de veau* is one of the favourites. Breakfast is served until 11.30. A popular meeting place for the young people of the 14th arrondissement.

Le Quasimodo Notre-Dame

11 rue d'Arcole, 4th
Tel: 1 43 54 19 45
Open: 08.00-19.00 (weekends from 09.00)

Just a few steps from the Cathedral, a down-to-earth bar-café serving a day-long selection of sandwiches, crêpes, coffee and drinks (three popular brands of whisky, but no Bell's!). Also a few hot dishes - play your hunch and go for one of the daily specials.

Le Reflet

6 rue Champollion, 5th
Tel: 1 43 29 97 27
Open: 10.00-02.00
Popular with business people during the day, Le Reflet stands in a tiny street running parallel to the Boulevard St-Michel. At night, students from the near-by Sorbonne take over, along with filmgoers and movie buffs (the Médicis Logos cinema is opposite). The decor is black, and the ceiling lighting is made to look like the sort of rig you might find on a film set. Black and white stills from the movies line the walls. At lunchtime, a salad order gets you a free coffee, while the very reasonable price of a hot dish includes a glass of wine. The bar specialises in cider. Live music Monday evening.

Le Sancerre

35 rue des Abbesses, 18th
Tel: 1 42 58 08 20
Open: 07.00-01.30
The wines at this easy-going bar-café are nearly all from the Loire, Rhône and Saône regions, and they accompany some very good snacks. There's also a good selection of beers and whiskies. Daytime jazz turns to raucous rock in the evening, when the young crowd takes over in considerable numbers.

Le Select

99 bd du Montparnasse, 6th
Tel: 1 42 22 65 27
Open: 07.00-03.00 (Sat till 04.00)
The decor, the clientele and the general feel of the place are not very different from the day it opened as an American Bar in 1924. A wide variety of drinks includes great cocktails and more than 60 whiskies, and snacks, light meals and excellent home-made pastries are served throughout the day at this Montparnasse stalwart opposite another (La Coupole). The spacious terrace is very popular in summer.

Parisian pastimes

Surely no two cafés as close to each other have played host to so many creative talents as Paris' Les Deux Magots and Café de Flore. Credited with seeing the flowering of both Existentialism and Surrealism, in the 1930s these two venues were frequented by such luminaries as Simone De Beauvoir and Jean-Paul Sartre, Jean Cocteau, Jean Genêt, Picasso, Max Ernst, Man Ray and Joan Miró.

Raimo

51-61 bd de Reuilly, 12th
Tel: 1 43 43 70 17
Open: 09.00-24.00
Closed: Mon & Feb
The decor is unremarkable, the ices anything but! Raimo is one of the capital's very best ice cream par-lours, in business for 50 years and priding itself on the quality of the fruit and other produce bought from Rungis market. One of the favourites among the many flavours is three chocolate (white, milk and dark). Hot and cold savoury dishes are available at luchtime, but it's the ice creams that bring people out to Raimo, which is located just beyond the handsome lion foun-tain at Place Félix Eboué, Metro Daumesnil.

La Tartine

24 rue de Rivoli, 4th
Tel: 1 42 72 76 85
Open: 09.30-22.00
Closed: Tues & L Wed

Trotsky was once a regular at this lovely old bar à vins, which continues to uphold its original aim of providing good wine and simple snacks at very reasonable prices in what was once a poor part of Paris. It first saw the light of day in the early 1900s, and the owner since 1947, who still watches over the till, seems to be of similar vintage. Today's customers trot along for the tartines made with the wonderful *pain Poilâne* and for something from an impressive range of wines available by glass or bottle (particularly good choice of Beaujolais). Old-fashioned globe lights and pre-war booths add to the character of this hardy perennial.

Terminus Nord

23 rue de Dunkerque, 10th
Tel: 1 42 85 05 15
Open: 08.00-01.00

Railway travellers arriving at Gare du Nord have only to cross the road to be sure of a memorable first taste of Paris. Terminus Nord, with its eyecatching decor, good food, convivial atmosphere and on-the-ball service, also has a large and loyal local following, and is one of the undoubted stars in the Café Flo firmament. It's open for breakfast early in the morning, and the full menu (shellfish a speciality) comes on stream at 11.00. A drink at the bar or in the glassed extension can be had at any time, but it's worth allowing an extra hour or two to sit down to a full meal and start or end a visit to Paris relaxed and content.

Café Zéphyr

12 bd Montmartre, 9th
Tel: 1 47 70 80 14
Open: 08.00-02.00 (Sun till 21.00)

The turn-of-the-century exterior stands out among its flashy modern neighbours and inside, the decor is equally distinctive, with a certain North African inspiration. The food owes most to the Auvergne, majoring on sizeable salads and hearty French country dishes, and the waiters serve cappuccinos with the tallest froth in town.

Aix-en-Provence

The ancient capital of Provence, founded by the Romans around 122BC and now a thriving centre of culture and learning. Many of the boulevards, squares and buildings retain the character of Aix's heyday in the 17th and 18th centuries, and the leafy Cours Mirabeau, with its shops and cafés, is a favourite place for a stroll. Cézanne spent most of his life in and around Aix and his studio is open to the public.

Bistro Romain

13 Cours Mirabeau
Tel: 4 42 91 31 17
Open: 11.30-01.30

On the ground floor of a grand house at the fountain end of Cours Mirabeau, the large Bistro Romain chain opened this outlet in 1998. They completely renovated the place, keeping all the best original features and restoring the impressive ceiling paintings. Beyond the mirrored reception area and Belle Epoque bar are the *salon de thé* and dining room, while outside are lots of tables under an awning, secluded by greenery from the bustle of the pavement. It has proved to be an immediate success, offering anything from an aperitif to a three-course meal.

A la Cour de Rohan

10 rue Vauvenargues (pl de l'Hotel de Ville)
Tel: 4 42 96 18 15
Open: 11.00-19.00 (Thur, Fri & Sat and every day May-Sep till 23.30)

Stables in the 17th century, nougat factory in the 19th, now an excellent brasserie/café in front of the Mairie (Town Hall) in Place de l'Hotel de Ville. It has a pretty internal courtyard reached through the restaurant, with comfortable basket chairs shaded by large parasols. The walls of the yard are either painted or hung with trellised plants; a continuous fine spray keeps the plants green and gives the air the sort of freshness you notice near waterfalls. The restaurant area, back through the french windows, is spacious, with a high ceiling and exposed beams. Through a broad stone arch is the café area in the same style, bringing you out through the open front to terrace tables under mature plane trees and large green canvas parasols. Excellent traditional cuisine includes specialities from Provence.

La Café du Cours (1807)

45-47 cours Mirabeau
Tel: 4 42 26 10 06
Open: 24hrs

Once a convent and then a school for the daughters of the rich; the Revolution ended that line of business, and the premises were sold off in bits. No. 45 became a blacksmith's (*maréchal à cheval*) and then in 1807 a café with a hairdresser's upstairs. Meanwhile No. 47 housed the local newspaper offices and later the ticket office for the bus service. The present owning family are only the third since it opened in 1807 and proudly boast they've kept the same telephone number since 1900, and indeed the same chairs (in style at least). The hairdresser has gone and upstairs is now a capacious restaurant with a kitchen above. Speciality dishes include pig's trotters, kidneys, wild rabbit, composite salads and crêpes.

Les Deux Garçons

cours Mirabeau
Tel: 4 42 26 00 51
Open: 06.00-02.00

A classic French café, dating from the Consular period of 1792, with a fantastic wrought-iron canopy, light-wood panelling, bronze lamps and chandeliers. The splendid terrace, with wicker chairs and marble-topped tables, is shaded by the canopy and the ancient plane trees of Cours Mirabeau. An antiquated plaque outside the bar still advertises the 'Club de Stella Artois', but these days the choice of beer is a good deal more varied, not to mention an excellent selection of wines, coffees and teas. With no *restauration rapide* on offer, dining here is quite a formal affair, confined to the conventional hours of lunch and dinner.

Café Le Grillon

cours Mirabeau
Tel: 4 42 27 58 81
Open: 06.00-02.00

On a corner site that became a café at the turn of the century, Le Grillon has an old oak bar with a brass counter-top, black-and-white tiles on the floor and a frieze of painted cicadas. On the first floor is an air-conditioned restaurant, elaborately decorated, with cameo paintings of pretty desmoiselles. Apart from the cicadas and the pretty desmoiselles the theme is the writer Fréderic Mistral, who was born in Arles but visited hereabouts: at the top of the stairs there's a water fountain with a plaque above showing his profile. At tables under awnings and parasols you can take a drink, or enjoy the Provençal cuisine, which includes both traditional and modern dishes, with some enticing fish specials.

La Madeleine

4 pl des Precheurs
Tel: 4 42 38 28 02
Open: 06.00-24.00

La Madeleine stands opposite the Palais de Justice in a square where a lively market is held every Tuesday, Thursday and Saturday. Well known for its seafood, particularly shellfish, it attracts not only market people but lawyers and teachers from the University. There's bench seating inside and seats at the bar, and a glassed area with folding doors for *restauration en plein air*. Tables on the broad pavement in the shade of a fine old plane tree provide another al fresco option. Coffees and teas, cocktails and beers, wine, Continental breakfast, salads, sandwiches, exotic ice creams.

Le Verdun

20 pl Verdun
Tel: 4 42 27 03 24
Open: 06.00-02.00

Heading down and southwards from the Place des Precheurs through the market you come to the Place Verdun and in the corner this charming French-style tapas bar. It does a roaring trade in the evenings and on market days, and the younger generation come here for the music – live during term time. Outside in the shade of plane trees are lots of tables, with more under the awning as you enter the ample bar area. They specialise in beer, and there's always a 'beer of the month'. The *plat du jour* really does change daily, and in the evening tapas come free with aperitifs.

Bordeaux

'Take Versailles, add Antwerp, and you have Bordeaux.' Victor Hugo admired the grand buildings and the splendid river of a city which was at one time France's chief port, a centre of trade with northern Europe and the Americas. Its chief fame nowadays is for the production of some of the world's finest wines, and a tour of the vineyards should be high on every visitor's list.

Café Le Bal

Eurl le Bal des Grands Hommes
Tel: 5 56 48 55 24
Open: 08.00-19.30
Closed: Sun

Queen Elizabeth, accompanied by the French Minister for Foreign Affairs, opened the imposing glass building that dominates the square in 1992. It stands on three levels, and the ground floor includes a daytime café selling good pastries and light brasserie-style lunchtime snacks. Many of the ingredients come straight from the market which occupies the floor below and which the café overlooks from a balcony.

Le Café Bordelais

15 allées de Tourny
Tel: 5 56 51 73 16
Open: 11.00-01.00/02.00 (Sat from 12.00)

This *bar à vins*/restaurant is on the north side of the Allées de Tourny and gets the evening sun. It has a terrific wine list – lots available by the glass – that changes every week and is probably the best in town for choice. On a corner site, the terrace is cobbled in hand-thrown yellow and red quarry tiles; it is enclosed in glass under a green awning and was clearly once part of the pavement. Before becoming a restaurant it was a garage, so the interior is spacious, with a mezzanine area of the bar for dining. Food specialities are cassoulet and *fondant au chocolat*. Staff are professional and attentive.

Le Castan

2 quai de la Douane
Tel: 5 56 81 85 02
Open: 09.00-02.00
Closed: Mon

One of the celebrated *grands cafés* of France, this unique establishment is famous for its extraordinary sparkling stone grottoes, which form a natural alcove for a variety of ceramic sea pictures dating back to the days when Bordeaux was the main embarkation point for travellers. These pictures were produced at the Boulenger factory in Choisy-le-Roi. Outside, there is additional seating for those who prefer to bask in the sun while having a drink or a meal. Seafood and oysters are the speciality.

Chez Ducou

14 allées de Tourny
Tel: 5 56 81 61 61
Open: 12.00-02.00

A busy brasserie with a long zinc bar and an assortment of caps, kepis and casquettes surrounding a caricature bust of General de Gaulle. The atmosphere is busy, chatty and amusing, and on the walls are some of the funniest photos you'll ever see. Every evening they have a variety of live music to entertain the varied crowd that assembles in the bar or outside on the terrace.

Le Cintra

4 cours 30 Juillet
Tel: 5 56 44 27 05
Open: 07.30-02.00

Next door to the Grand Théatre you'll find this attractive café decorated in the style of the 1900s: a mahogany-fronted bar with banquettes under a leaded glass backlit ceiling leads on to a small room, and stairs ascend to the restaurant area. The terrace has tables for some 30 people, shaded by the red blind and red and white parasols, an ideal spot for breakfast, a light lunch or aperitif as the sun goes down on cocktail hour. Good variety of salads and plenty of wines by the glass. Next door on the other side is the Hotel des Quatre Sœurs, where Wagner stayed in 1850.

Café de la Comédie

52 cours du Chapeau Rouge
Tel: 5 56 51 27 30
Open: 07.30-02.00 (Sat & Sun from 08.00)

Beyond the wide, open frontage is a red granite bar counter with a mahogany-panelled front and Edwardian decor of upside-down silk lampshades on brass fittings. Red upholstered bar stools and chairs and banquette seating stand on granite floor tiles to match the countertop, and mirrored walls give the place a spacious feel. Beyond the bar is another room leading out on the Rue de la Maison Daurade behind, and with the doors open a cool breeze wafts through the place. The café, which is side on to the Grand Théatre, offers a day-long selection of sandwiches, salads and charcuterie.

Café La Concorde

50 rue du Maréchal Joffre
Tel: 5 56 44 68 97
Open: 08.00-22.00
Closed: Sun

This city-centre brasserie/café has a unique feature in the shape of an orangerie - a *jardin d'hiver* - at the back. There are seats for 180 in its lofty rooms with their handsome plasterwork and mirrored walls, and tables and chairs outside overlooking Place de la République, the Palais de Justice and the Saint André hospital, sheltered by a green awning. This is where the legal boys come - the law school is next to the Palais. On the food front are fixed-price and à la carte menus, plus an hors d'oeuvre buffet, a dish of the day and as many oysters as you want.

Café Gourmand

3 rue Buffon
Tel: 5 56 79 23 85
Open: 11.00-01.00 (Mon from 15.00)
Closed: Sun

Café Gourmand, which opened in the mid-1990s, is owned by Bruno Oliver, the fourth generation of great cooks, who dallied with restaurants in the USA before returning to the town of his grandfather's choice. When he took over here it was a café renowned for its wine and cheese. In the tradition of the name he has expanded the repertoire, having an extensive list of local wines. The food is special and he is very inventive, using the best of seasonal, market-fresh products. A snack can be some *jambon* with your wine, or a salad or *patisserie de la maison* with your afternoon tea or coffee. The family tradition is long and honourable, and the walls of the bar are covered with photographs of earlier generations.

Les Noailles

12 allées de Tourny
Tel: 5 56 81 94 45
Open: 08.30-24.00

In the renowned Allées de Tourny, part of the Triangle of Bordeaux that has contained the fashionable restaurants and bars for some two centuries, this is decorated in the style of 1936. A bar-brasserie serving drinks and *grillades* throughout the day from midday to midnight, it has a wide open frontage and a permanent terrace of tables under a green awning. The waiters are resplendent in their white shirts, black waistcoats and trousers, and long white aprons below the knee in classic style. A good choice of wines as you'd expect, or a simple kir with your friends.

Le Bistrot des Quinconces

4 pl des Quinconces
Tel: 5 56 52 84 56
Open: 07.30-01.00/02.00

This 1930s bistro in art deco style has something good to offer throughout the day: a bite on the hop, a business lunch, teatime refreshment after a hard day's shopping, an aperitif with friends after work, an intimate evening or a celebration party with friends for dinner. The welcome is always warm and the staff are never too busy to help; they don't forget you even if you're in an out-of-the-way corner - and however full it seems they will always find you a space. Some evenings there's a live jazz trio. There's a spacious terrace at the front, well shaded by a huge green blind, and while a lot of the interior is laid out for eating at mealtimes, there's a bar and bar area where you can drop in at any time for a drink.

Café Régent

46 pl Gambetta
Tel: 5 56 44 16 20
Open: 08.00-01.00

This brasserie-style café occupies a commanding corner of a square just outside the old town and its ancient gateway Porte Dijeaux. Used a lot by local people and shoppers, it is very spacious inside and all the windows open up to the array of pavement tables outside. The interior is set out in squares with banquette seating, while outside, the small round tables are set with cane chairs, south-facing to get the sun. The Régent has become something of a Bordeaux institution, very popular and very reliable. Ice creams are a speciality.

Cannes

One of the jewels in the Cote d'Azur, its promenades filled with beautiful people and its harbours with beautiful yachts. The film festival is one of the highlights of the year at this renowned luxury holiday resort, which has a year-round tourist and conference trade.

Bar des Célébrités

58 La Croisette
Tel: 4 93 06 40 06
Open: 11.00-02.00

A very spacious room with a high ceiling, pillars and a grand terrace with two handsome palms and a good view out to sea. This must be the smartest café-bar in Cannes and it's part of the Carlton, the smartest hotel in Cannes. Stately rooms are graced with elaborate plasterwork, and the large terrace, *the* place to be when the sun shines, is set discreetly up a few steps from the road. You don't *have* to be rich, famous or good-looking to come here, though it might help to have at least one of those attributes. Having said which, the staff are polite and friendly to all-comers.

La Maison du Porto

1 square Mérimée
Tel: 4 93 39 20 10
Open: 07.30-01.30

One of three adjacent and very popular pavement cafés facing the Palais des Festivals. There's plenty of button-upholstered bench seating inside, together with little wooden tables inlaid with black and orange marble, standing on red granite tiles. The walls of the three rooms are either mirrored or adorned with murals of life at the café. The smartly dressed waiters wear the café's logo over their breast pockets - something to distinguish them as they almost merge with the staff at the terrace tables of the neighbouring establishments. The scampi provençale are the best in town.

> "Each evening after dinner, with my two dogs, I stroll in Park Avenue to walk my cigar."
>
> **Gay Talese.**

Bar des Négociants

pl de la Gare
Tel: 4 93 39 06 35
Open: 07.00-24.00/01.00

Once part of the hotel that until 50 years ago occupied the whole corner, the bar is in austere late-40s style, with simple chairs and bench seating. It's handily placed almost opposite the railway station, so it's popular with the just-arriveds and about-to-leaves. It specialises in beers from all over Europe; sandwiches, snacks and salads are available, along with main meals on a *menu du jour*.

Le Noailles

4 pl de Gaulle, 6 rue d'Antibes
Tel: 4 93 39 21 42
Open: 07.00-02.00

A cool café specialising in crêpes, with banquette seating inside, a sea-facing terrace on the Place de Gaulle and a couple of pavement tables on the street behind (Rue d'Antibes). Other snacks are available and there's a *formule* menu.

Le Bar du Port

16 quai St Pierre
Tel: 4 92 98 82 40
Open: 07.30-01.30
Closed: Wed

The name and the address suggest a seaside location, but the bar is actually set back in a little square, Place Massuque, and nestles under Rue G Clémenceau passing some 30 feet above. It's a fairly peaceful spot, and virtually traffic-free, as the only vehicular access is to the adjoining apartments. Light snacks are available, but this is largely a coffee and beer café that specialises in ice cream. One room is the bar, the other is set with tables and chairs, but in summer the terrace in front of the green-shuttered windows is the place to be.

Carcassonne

Carcassonne is a truly remarkable city with a history dating back four centuries BC. But it is in its history after the Roman period from 46AD that its extraordinary and troubled life is best recorded, with a succession of invaders and marauders all leaving their mark. The commercial centre, with a burgeoning trade in fabrics, developed at the cost of the ancient Citadel and it was not until the mid 19th century that restoration began. What you see today is a remarkable living and working museum of the history of the Citadel, which is now thankfully in very good condition and provides an eye-opener at every turn.

Le Trouvère

1 pl Marcon-La Cité
Tel: 4 68 25 72 60
Open: 08.00-02.00
Closed: Mar except at weekends, all Jan

This was the first bar in the Citadel, certainly the first in the square, and its present ownership dates back some 50 years. It has a low ceiling with exposed beams, an ample bar, a dining room beyond and a busy kitchen in the corner. More tables in the square jostle with competing restaurants and brasseries but this has its own charm and an *esprit* that draws not just the visitors but the local restaurateurs and waiters after a hard night's work. One of the specialities on the menu is the hearty local dish, cassoulet. The wines here are excellent, rich and robust as you'd expect, in the Langue d'Oc Roussillon Corbières style. Don't miss this place – good vibes, good ambience, good drinking and good eating.

Dijon

Important from early days as a strategic point on the merchant routes, Dijon saw its greatest glory as the capital of the Dukes of Burgundy, between the 11th and 14th centuries. It became a major centre of learning and the arts, and today the historic quarter retains much of its medieval charm.

La Concorde

2 pl Darcy
Tel: 3 80 30 69 43
Open: 07.00-01.00

Regional cuisine served in a brasserie on two levels, with a balcony on the approach to the bar and button-backed bench seating set in squares on the main floor. The place dates from 1860 and has been greatly modernised, but the ornate plaster ceiling and the clock are original. The café has a covered terrace, and a splendid arch commemorates the architect of the Cathedral, built about the same time as Notre Dame in Paris (13th century).

Le Grand Café

5 rue du Chateau
Tel: 3 80 30 51 64
Open: 07.00-24.00

Part of the Hotel de la Poste, and dating from the first years of the 20th century, the café is in colonial style, with elaborate angular ceiling lights in opaque glass. Retained from its Belle Epoque origins are the willowy desmoiselles posing in their wispy dresses painted in panels on the wall. Afternoon teas and a *petit faim* snack menu are served by staff who are smartly dressed and as keen as mustard.

Lille

A city of various allegiances - Flemish, Burgundian, Spanish and, since 1667, French. Its accessibility by Eurostar makes it a very real and very agreeable destination for a day trip from England, as a lovely, lively heart beats at the centre of the industrial mass and there's no shortage of places to eat and shop.

La Chicorée

15 pl Rihour
Tel: 3 20 54 81 52
Open: 10.00-04.30 (Sat till 06.00)

A large and busy corner brasserie/café open from late breakfast right through to early breakfast, with only a 4-hour break at the weekend. Centrally located across the square from the tourist office, it has more than enough space, both inside and out on the very comfortable terrace, for the crowds of shoppers, locals and tourists, as well as the stars of the theatre who sometimes drop in. Local cuisine and beers.

La Cloche

13 pl du Théatre
Tel: 3 20 55 35 34
Open: 08.00-24.00

Bar à vins, brasserie and wine merchant on a corner facing the clock of the Commerce Building, with the Opéra on the right and the old Bourse to the side. La Cloche is thus strategically placed for business people, locals and tourists, who come here for anything from a quick drink (20+ wines available by the glass) to a full meal. Snacks to try with your *dégustation* include *rillettes*, croques, smoked eel and leek pie.

Coq Hardi

44 pl du Général de Gaulle
Tel: 3 20 55 21 08
Open: 10.00-24.00

A traditional café-brasserie in a Listed building in what is known as the Grand Place. There is only table service here as the bar itself, just inside the door, is used as a service area. Breakfast is served from opening time, and at mealtimes the place is very popular for its regional cooking, which can be enjoyed inside under exposed beams or sitting outside under the awning.

Jenlain Café

43 pl Rihour
Tel: 3 20 15 14 55
Open: 09.00-02.00
Closed: Sun

This 1860s building, recently re-opened after major renovation, is privately owned and run, even though it carries the name of a leading brewer. They sell a Jenlain *rousse*, a Sebourg *blonde* and a *fraiche* that is made, unfiltered, specially for the café. The ground floor is simply appointed, with different-coloured chairs and tables, and upstairs there's a restaurant and an evening piano bar. Out in the square is a seating area ringed by panelled fencing and shaded by half a dozen trees. Also in the square are an entrance to the Metro and a little fairground roundabout to amuse the children.

M Méert

27 rue Esquermoise
Tel: 3 20 57 07 44
Open: 09.00-19.00 (Sun 09.00-13.00 & 15.00-19.30)

This renowned establishment, one of the most prestigious in Lille was founded in 1761 by a M Delcourt, a maker of sweets and chocolates, and in 1849 passed into the hands of M Méert, who became official provisioner to the King of the Belgians and who left behind many of his excellent recipes. The front room is an elaborate celebration of the work of the architect Cordonnier, responsible also for the Vieille Bourse, built in 1909 in the style of Louis Seize. A second room was opened in 1930 to allow customers to enjoy the goodies on the spot, which they can do to this day with one of the broad selection of teas and infusions that are also available for takeaway and by mail order.

Café du Palais

4 rue du Palais de Justice
Tel: 3 20 74 53 47
Open: 12.00-14.30 & 19.00-22.30 (Thur, Fri & Sat till 23.30)
Closed: L Sat & all Sun

New owners at this bar in traditional bistro style in the old part of the city in the street opposite the front of the Law Courts. It keeps restaurant hours for its food but stays open after lunch to allow regulars to drop in for a coffee and a chat. Its busiest time is Saturday evening after the big market at the nearby Place du Concert has packed up. An exhibition of paintings changes every two months. The last Thursday of each month sees a special event, perhaps a cabaret evening, a Mexican night or a 1950s night.

Paul

8 rue de Paris
Tel: 3 20 78 20 78
Open: 07.00-19.30

One of several notable premises of the prestigious patissier, glacier, chocolatier and baker Paul, which started business in 1889. This is the grandest, with exposed beams in the café area, where you sit on leather-upholstered chairs at chunky tables enjoying your pastry, listening to gentle classical music and admiring the hand-painted ceramics. Nine-branch brass chandeliers hang from the ceiling and a wide oak staircase sweeps up to the restaurant. Outside are slatted tables and chairs sheltered by red sunshades in an area ringed by dwarf fir trees. The shop, as grand as the rest of the place, deals with a constant flow of customers seeking anything from a loaf of bread to savoury filled baps, elaborate pastries or a box of chocolates.

Taverne de L'Ecu

9 rue Esquermoise/4 rue du Pas
Tel: 3 20 57 55 66
Open: 11.30-02.00 (Sun, Mon & Tue till 24.00)

The tavern that was on this site in the 1860s combined with a German tavern in the street behind it to become a brewery with a winter garden and a first-class restaurant. More recently it was an arts cinema which came and went, and in 1994 it was refurbished and opened as the excellent tavern it is today. Beer is brewed on the premises, as in the old days, in *blanche, blonde* and *ambré* varieties, and the menu includes such classics as *carbonnade flamande, jam-bonette aux herbes* and *travers de porc*. There is also a large selection of pizzas which political correctness demands be called *'pate à pain cuite au four'*. Vive L'Académie Française!

Taverne Le Rihour's

29 pl Rihour
Tel: 3 20 13 70 25
Open: 08.00-21.30 (Sat till 24.00)

Beers in profusion and snacks aplenty keep the customers happy at this spacious bar tucked away in a corner of the Place. The new owner (March 2000) has made some changes: a bigger terrace; a new upstairs room in 'pub anglais' style; a buffet serving salads and crêpes both sweet and savoury.

Les Trois Brasseurs

22 pl de la Gare
Tel: 3 20 06 46 29
Open: 11.00-24.00

A café and fully-functioning brewery situated opposite the railway station for local journeys. Beer is of course the speciality and four types are brewed - *blonde, ambré, scotch* and *blanche de Lille*. Also beers of the moment eg Christmas Ale. The brewing process takes place in full view of the customers and sacks are stacked ready for the next brew. The beer is drawn straight from the vat - high fermentation, pure malt, non-pasteurised. A news sheet explains the methods and the results and also contains a little quiz. Snacks include *croques*, salads, grills, *choucroute* cooked in *blonde* beer and even cheeses flavoured with beer.

Lyons

A big, bustling city, important strategically and commercially since Roman times. The banking, printing and textile trades brought it to prominence, and it also has claims to the title of the gastronomic centre of France. It is bursting with food shops, bistros and restaurants, and Lyonnais chefs, both male and female, have spread their influence far and wide. There's also plenty of choice among the less formal bars and cafés.

Bar Américain

24 rue de la République
Tel: 4 78 42 52 91
Open: 06.30-01.00

The only café in France to have been listed on the Paris Bourse (stock market), with a 170-year history that the charming patronne will happily relate to visitors. Faithful renovations include a wonderful trompe l'oeil ceiling of clouds and angels, and some engraved mirrors with bronze trappings. Some 19th-century paintings have recently been added. Good fresh food is always on offer and there's usually an interesting guest beer on tap.

Café Bellecour

33 pl Bellecour
Tel: 4 78 37 03 63
Open: 07.00-20.00 (Sat 09.00-15.00)
Closed: Sun & Aug

An old-fashioned brasserie with a large summer terrace that makes a perfect spot for a refreshment break for visitors to the largest square in Lyons, famous for its statue of Louis XIV as a Roman emperor. Salads and a *plat du jour* at lunchtime.

Café Chantecler

151 bd de la Croix Rousse
Tel: 4 78 28 13 69
Open: 07.30-01.00 (Sun 08.30-21.00)

Draught bitter is brewed on the premises, so it's not a total surprise that the patron is an Englishman, Raymond Rushforth. The smoked-oak panelling, surrounding veranda and terrace make this a pretty much ideal spot to enjoy a drink and perhaps a *plat du jour*. Live music on Thursdays.

Le Cintra

42 rue de la Bourse
Tel: 4 78 42 54 08
Open: 07.00-05.00
Closed: Sun

Seventy years old and still going strong, Le Cintra is a fun café-restaurant and piano-bar all in wood, with a coffered ceiling, a classic tiled floor and motifs in brass. This has been a popular choice for cocktail drinkers and beer fans (there are nine beers on tap) and diners (last orders 02.00) for all those 70 years.

Grand Café des Négociants

1 pl Francisque Regaud
Tel: 4 78 42 50 05
Open: 07.00-24.00 (Fri & Sat till 01.00)
Closed: 1 May

Already 60 years old when Le Cintra opened, this is a wonderfully traditional *grand café*, from the five-light chandeliers, period hatstands, leather banquettes and tall arched mirrors to the immaculate waiters in their long white aprons (*rondeaux*). People come from near and far to this marvellous place in the Cordeliers district between the Rhône and the Saône to enjoy a wide selection of drinks and their choice from the extensive menus. Large terrace.

Le Régent

9 pl Bellecour
Tel: 4 78 42 25 38
Open: 08.00 01.00 (Sun & Mon from 14.00)
Closed: Sun & Aug

An Italian Regency café on the imposing Place Bellecour, with an interior mezzanine. The menu is based on the local cuisine, with omelettes, crêpes, quenelles and *saucisses briochées*. Good choice of teas and draught beer.

Marseilles

The oldest city and chief port of France, established as a trading post around 600BC under the name of Massalia. Italian and North African influences are strong in the city, which has a colourful, vibrant atmosphere with more than a hint of excitement. The Old Port is particularly well worth a visit, whether to watch the world go by from a stylish café or to settle down to a mighty bouillabaisse.

Les Flots Bleus

82 corniche Kennedy, 7th
Tel: 4 91 52 10 34
Open: 10.00-02.00 (sometimes till 04.00)
A spectacularly romantic location for a totally charming café on the *corniche* (cliff road) overlooking the evil island prison fortress of Chateau d'If, immortalised in Alexandre Dumas' *The Count of Monte Cristo*. No one ever escaped from the Chateau, and no one ever wants to escape from this super café: opened in 1916, it remains a great place to visit at any time, whether it's for a drink, a snack or a full meal. Thursday is couscous day, Friday brings salt cod with aïoli.

Café Parisien

1 pl Sadi-Carnot, 2nd
Tel: 4 91 90 05 77
Open: 04.00-22.00 (Thur & Fri till 24.00)
Closed: Sun pm
Café and cultural centre, with grand marble pillars and turn-of-the-century splendour contrasting with Philippe Starck furniture and eye-catching modern art. On the café side is the usual selection of brasserie cheer, plus the less usual features of 150 *appellation* wines and 43 goat's cheeses. The early opening time makes it a revival point for late-night revellers. Culture comes in the shape of musicians performing, artists exhibiting, lecturers lecturing and even the occasional film or mini-play.

Montpellier

Home of one of the first schools of medicine and a centre of trade for a thousand years, Montpellier is notable for its fine architecture, from handsome town houses put up in the 17th and 18th centuries to adventurous contemporary projects.

Le Manneken Pis

10 rue Alexandre Cabanel
Tel: 4 67 66 15 85
Open: 11.00-02.00 (winter till 01.00)
Closed: Sun

In a small street parallel to the main boulevard (Jeu de Paume) leading to the railway station and the tunnel under Place de la Comédie (spacious underground parking) serious beer drinkers will be well rewarded to discover this 'temple' dedicated to their favourite tipple. There are over one hundred to choose from, with almost two-thirds from Belgium (hence the name). Beer is the motif, with posters, coasters, labels, bottles and even special brand glasses. On the food front: moules frites, daily specials.

Bar du Musée

1/3 rue du Montpellieret
Tel: 4 67 60 45 65
Open: 08.00-01.00
Closed: Sun

A typical French bistro (one of the very few in the city) beside the Musée Fabre (which is also very much worth a visit, closed on Sundays and Mondays) in the 'old city'. It has a village feel about it and French-speakers will enjoy having the patron tell them about its history and that of the museum (created between 1825 and 1837 by François-Xavier Fabre, a student of the painter David). It has what the French call 'l'esprit zinc' (translating as true bistro spirit perhaps?). Solid bistro fare and some good local wines at reasonable prices.

Grand Café Riche

pl de la Comédie
Tel: 4 67 60 75 76
Open: 06.00-02.00

This is the centre of Montpellier where the old city meets the new in a spacious pedestrian zone. The enormous Place, known locally as *L'Oeuf* (the Egg) because of its oval shape, takes its name from the imposing theatre which stands at one 'end'; also in the Place is the 18th-century Etienne Antoine fountain of The Three Graces. Founded over 100 years ago, the Riche has a major asset in its vast terrace, the place for being seen and for watching the world go by. Coffee and croissants are available in the morning; salads, sandwiches (hot and cold) and crêpes (savoury or sweet) throughout the day and evening. The art deco interior has recently been totally renovated. Decent wines by the glass.

Moulins

The principal town in the department of Allier, in the northern Auvergne some 165 miles south of Paris. For centuries it was the seat of the Dukes of Bourbon and its architecture shows influences from the 15th century onwards. It was visited by Joan of Arc, and the Cathedral dates partly from her day (the rest from enlargement in the 19th century, a time of prosperity). It is now a pretty, welcoming town with a population of around 28,000.

Café Américain

21 cours Anatole France
Tel: 4 70 44 01 29
Open: 09.00-24.00 (Sat till 02.00)
Closed: Sat & Sun Oct-Feb

1900 vintage, with a striking facade that's classified as a historic monument. In its early days it gave silent movie shows, with the projector on the first floor and the screen in the courtyard at the front. Those shows stopped long ago, but now the café welcomes jazz and cabaret performers, and a nearby bandstand is sometimes used for the entertainment of customers. Worthies of the community gather by day to discuss the world in general and the exploits of the local hunting fraternity in particular: a poster lists the days of the hunting season, and photographs show some of their more successful bags. This delightfully traditional *bar à vins* has an extensive all-French wine list, a small selection of beers and a broad, day-long choice of snacks both hot and cold, with fresh local produce and some good charcuterie.

Le Grand Café

49 pl d'Allier
Tel: 4 70 44 00 05
Open: 08.00-01.00
Closed: Sun Oct-Feb

Grand is definitely the word for this wonderful *grand café*, built in 1899 in dazzling rococo style by a former waiter, one M Renoux, at a cost of a quarter of a million francs. The richly ornate garlands of leaves upon which the ceiling appears to rest are the work of the Italian artist Golfione, while the ceiling fresco telling the story of Gambrinus is by Sauroy. In the early days of the *grands cafés* the clientele were mostly dignitaries and wealthy merchants who would take simple refreshments and enjoy a game of chess or draughts during the day and early evening; only when the shutters went down would the serious business start, with the champagne flowing and poker played till dawn. After the Second World War the *grands cafés* lost a lot of this clientele, so students began to frequent them, along with their teachers, artists, musicians and, of course, tourists. Today, the gallery is still used for concerts, but now it tends to be jazz and the modern music of the young. Outside, a large green awning shelters the terrace tables, while inside, the front part is for café drinkers and the back has tables set with gingham cloths for lunch and supper.

Nancy

The capital of Lorraine was founded in the 11th century but first hit the headlines when Charles the Bold was killed during a siege in 1477. In the early part of the 20th century it became a driving force in the Art Nouveau movement, and one of its museums has fine examples of period furniture and glass. The town had previously been redeveloped in particularly fine style in the 18th century by the last of the independent Dukes of Lorraine, Stanislas Lezczynski, one-time King of Poland and father-in-law of Louis XV. He is remembered in the very elegant main square, Place Stanislas, the work of the architect Emmanuel Héré, who also designed the Town Hall and surrounding buildings.

Ch'Timi

17 pl St Epure
Tel: 3 83 32 82 76
Open: 10.00-02.00 (Sun till 20.00)

Facing the Basilica of St Epure, this deceptively small bar, formerly a butcher's shop, keeps a most impressive range of beers, easily the best in town for both choice and quality. Sixteen draught beers are stored in the cellar to be pumped at the panelled bar, and the range of bottled beers exceeds 200, with their beer mats pinned to the timbered ceiling. Snacks include *tartines* and *croques*.

Café du Commerce

1 pl Stanislas
Tel: 3 83 35 52 67
Open: 07.00-02.00

Place Stanislas, named in honour of the last Duke of Lorraine, is an extravagantly ornate square with splendid gateways and fountains dedicated to Neptune and Venus. The café comprises two rooms, one in the elaborate style of the building (crystal chandeliers, paintings of cherubs), the other contrastingly austere and modern. It's a popular rendezvous for breakfast and lunch, but really comes into its own in the evening. Beers are something of a speciality, with eight kept on draught and a list of 13 bottled varieties with a full description of each - history, taste, colour, strength and best serving temperature. A further ten bottled beers and some beer cocktails are also described. Five wines by the glass and a good range of snacks.

Excelsior

50 rue Henri Poincaré
Tel: 3 83 35 24 57
Open: 08.00-00.30 (Sun till 23.00)

A wonderfully extravagant Belle Epoque brasserie in the safe hands of the Flo Group. At the turn of the century the Nancy School of Art was founded and all the greatest names in the Art Nouveau movement had their works shown here. One of the salons is named after Louis Majorelle, cabinet-maker and craftsman in ironwork design, who designed the furniture for the Excelsior. Here you can enjoy the most exuberant expression of the art while you take a coffee or an apéritif or something from the extensive range of snacks and light meals - seafood is a speciality. Worthy of particular mention are the lights and the chandeliers (Antonin Daum), the frieze of sunflowers, the glass porch decorated in pine cones and the ferns that adorn the columns, repeated in the etched glass (the work of the painter Grüber) and complemented by the real thing in huge silver planters.
Special Award 2001

Le Grand Café Foy

1 pl Stanislas
Tel: 3 83 32 15 97
Open: 07.00-02.00

Named after an important general in Napoleon's army, Foy was opened at the turn of the century in the elegant Place Stanislas, itself commemorating the former King of Poland, who as the last Duke of Lorraine was a major benefactor of Nancy. The café is much now as it was then; smart, efficient staff serve you in intimate booths, while outside is a cluster of pavement tables sheltered by a blue and white striped awning. On offer are breakfast with Viennese pastries, home-made ice creams and brasserie dishes at mealtimes.

Le Merle Blanc

7 rue Saint-Jean
Tel: 3 83 19 36 36
Open: 07.00-19.00 (non-stop Sat am - Sun eve)

This delightful little café with its stone and wood interior is much as it was when it opened 50 years ago. A cup of tea and a pastry are just right for a short break and a chat, while hungrier souls can choose from the selection of grills and *plats du jour* and enjoy their meal with a glass of wine or a beer. Note that it's open non-stop at the weekend.

Nantes

Once the seat of the Dukes of Brittany, now the capital of the Loire Valley region. Its imposing castle, the Chateau des Ducs, has seen many notable guests, willing or otherwise, down the years, including Bonnie Prince Charlie and Bluebeard the pirate (the latter was burned to death here in 1440). The Edict of Nantes, which marked an end to the Religious Wars, was signed at the castle by Henri IV in 1598. Jules Verne was born in Nantes and a museum in the city is full of Vernabilia.

La Cigale

4 pl Graslin
Tel: 2 51 84 94 94
Open: 07.30-00.30

Built in 1895 opposite the theatre in elaborate art nouveau style, La Cigale rapidly became the chosen rendezvous of the noble families of Nantes and the wealthy middle classes, mixing with the dancers and actors from the theatre. It was classed as a national monument in 1964 but nevertheless fell into decline. In 1982 it was revived with a complete restoration, becoming once again the most famous meeting place in Nantes, which it remains to this day. The theme of La Cigale (the Cicada) is repeated in various styles and techniques and the painted panels, the ornate carvings and the marvellous patterned tiles shine in all their fin-de-siècle glory; the inner room still has its 1895 cut-flock wallpaper and a dazzling ceiling painting. On the terrace, comfortable cane chairs are sheltered by greenery, trelliswork and large white sunshades. A staff of 50 is employed here, and everything on the menu, from patisserie to full meals, is made on the premises from ingredients fresh from the market. The Jacques Demy film *Lola* was shot here in 1961.

Café Molière

pl Graslin
Tel: 2 40 73 20 53
Open: 08.00-23.00 (Sat till 24.00)
Closed: Sun

Closely linked with the theatre next door, Molière first opened its doors (as Café de la Comédie) more than 100 years ago. Molière appears in pictures on the walls, mirrors are decorated in art nouveau style and over the bar is an art nouveau splayed light in pale turquoise. Snacks are always available, along with several draught beers and speciality cocktails; students come here to finish an essay, shoppers to take tea and the passing businessman to grab a bite to eat. Opposite La Cigale, it is especially popular with the younger generation. Recedoration, with more wood for the interior, has made it cosier.

Nice

The English first came here in any number in the 18th century and the Promenade des Anglais (so called because it was actually laid out by English residents) remains a marvellous place for a leisurely stroll. Up from the seafront are museums dedicated to the works of Chagall and Matisse. Plenty of restaurants, cafés and bars, mainly in the Old Town, a colourful flower market and an annual two-week carnival. An ideal base for visiting the 30km stretch of the Riviera from Cannes to the west to the Italian border.

Bar des Fleurs

13 cours Saleya
Tel: 4 93 62 31 33
Open: 05.00-02.00 (Oct-Mar 05.30-20.00)
A *tabac* and PMU (tote) point that's used by both stall-holders and visitors to the flower market. You buy your ciggies, get a drink and place your bet in that order down the lefthand side, or take a table in the very spacious room and study form over a cup of coffee. Croissants and *pains au chocolat* are made on the premises, and ice creams and crêpes are other popular choices. Lit by globe lights, it becomes a brasserie at lunchtime. Wide-screen TV for watching football.

Le Gambetta

pl de la Libération (pl Général de Gaulle)
Tel: 4 93 84 76 07
Open: 07.00-24.00 (Sun till 15.00)
Next to the derelict once-grand station of the *Chemins de Fer de Provence*, this café is also a brasserie (seafood a speciality) and up a couple of steps inside the tables are set for meals. Leaded lights and engraved glass panels are among the eye-catching decorative features.

Le Globe

56 bd Jean Jaurès
Tel: 4 93 62 31 74
Open: 07.00-23.00/24.00
Same name, same role for more than 100 years. During the morning the customers are mainly locals, many from the hotel and restaurant industry, while as the day draws on the tourists begin to make their presence felt. Around the walls are tiled tableaux of local coastal scenes - Cap d'Ail, Cannes, Nice, Antibes, Villefranche and St-Jean.

Le Grand Café de Lyon et du Centre

33 ave J Médecin
Tel: 4 93 88 13 17
Open: 07.00-24.00
A long established pavement café in art deco style, one of a genre that it becoming increasingly rare. It stands on the corner with Rue Clémenceau, about halfway up Nice's main shopping street and opposite the Nice Etoile shopping arcade. Always busy, especially as a welcome pit stop when the shops are open, it offers a day-long choice of snacks, crêpes, croques and speciality ice creams. At lunchtime much of it becomes a brasserie. Four beers on draught plus many more in bottles.

Le Café du Palais

1 pl du Palais
Tel: 4 93 85 77 63
Open: 07.00-02.00 (Oct-Mar till 21.00)
Closed: Sun
Facing the Palais Lascaris (now the Palais de Justice) in an attractive square behind the flower market. A daytime bar, it is decorated in Belle Epoque style, and outside there are seats for 100 set at little round tables. Lunchtime *plat du jour*, otherwise pastries and rolls, coffees and cocktails. New owner for Millennium Year has acquired the next-door premises, thus doubling the size and adding still more outside seating.

Les Ponchettes

3 pl Charles Félix
Tel: 4 93 92 16 13
Open: 07.00-01.00
Place Charles Félix bustles in the morning with the life of the market but at night half of Nice seems to be here to party. You can always get a table inside at Les Ponchettes (named after the arcaded gallery on the seafront), but outside is where everyone wants to be on a fine night. There must be 100 tables here, and at midnight nobody wants to go home, except perhaps the staff. The bar itself is on the corner of Rue de la Poissonnerie, with a back-lit leaded coloured glass ceiling depicting the gallery's arches. Music plays inside, while on the street it's the hubbub of animated conversation. Snacks are served, but people mostly order drinks or ice creams.

Chez René, Bar Socca

2 rue Miralhetti
Tel: 4 93 92 05 73
Open: 08.30-21.00 (Oct-Mar till 22.30)
Closed: Mon

On one side of the street in Old Nice is Bar Socca, with tables outside, on the other the rustic restaurant Chez René. The popular orders here are chips, pizza, and the local specialities *socca,* which is a bit like a poppadom, and *pan bagnat,* a round loaf scooped out and filled with a Niçois mixture of salad, egg, tuna and anchovies. The crowd here is a cheerful mix of locals and tourists who've picked up a thirst and an appetite wandering through the streets of Old Nice.

Le Rossetti

32 rue Centrale (pl Rossetti)
Tel: 4 93 92 17 10
Open: 08.00-00.30 (Sun from 10.00)

A cosy little café facing the baroque Cathedral dedicated to the young martyr St Réparate, patron saint of Nice. In the old part of town, it appeals equally to local Niçois and tourists. A long terrace of green tables and chairs under white sunshades stretches along to the fountain and to the cluster of cafés that fill the square. On Sunday mornings there's a secondhand book market in front of the Cathedral.

Périgueux

A bustling market town with an interesting Old Quarter, the fascinating Romanesque Cathedral of St-Front with its square, pineapple-topped belfry and some notable Roman remains. The prehistoric caves of the Vézère valley are well worth the drive out of town.

Le Café de la Place

7 pl du Marché au Bois
Tel: 5 53 08 21 11
Open: 09.00-02.00

A large brasserie-style café with posters for decor, a substantial zinc-topped bar and a central chandelier of globe lighting supplementing the pinky glass-shaded wall lights. Three fans keep it cool inside, where there are stools at the bar and tables and bentwood chairs lower down. Outside, on a spacious purpose-built platform, are square green tables and cane chairs under a green awning. Snacks include soups, omelettes and salads, and ice creams are a speciality. French wines and a good range of beers.

Reims

Along with Epernay, this is the champagne centre of France. Twenty-six kings of France were crowned here between 1123 and 1825, but for most of them it was not to the popping of champagne corks. Documents show that wine has been produced in the region from ancient times, but it was Dom Pérignon (1638-1715) who first put the bubbles in by using a double fermentation process. The cellars of many of the leading producers are in the Champs de Mars district and most are open to visitors. The process of making champagne is depicted in the south transept of the marvellous Gothic Cathedral of Notre Dame, which also contains some very fine statuary and some dazzling stained glass by Marc Chagall.

Le Black Face

81 pl Drouet d'Erlon
Tel: 3 26 40 19 46
Open: 11.00-02.30 (Sun from 15.00)
The former Jour et Nuit is reincarnated in the style of an Irish pub, with draught Guinness and Irish whiskey.

Brasserie du Boulingrin

48 rue de Mars
Tel: 3 26 40 96 22
Open: 08.00-23.00 (Fri till 24.00, Sat 07.00-24.00)
Closed: Sun
Opposite the historic Boulingrin market halls, this popular corner-site brasserie had double main doors that lead to a curved zinc-topped bar with some simple chairs and marble-topped tables. Further in is the restaurant area with art nouveau decoration on the pillars and a full-length mural depicting a wine harvest scene in the 1920s. Champagne and oysters are the specialities.

Le Cardinal

1 pl des Martyrs de la Résistance
Tel: 3 26 40 33 19
Open: 07.30-21.00 (Sat from 08.30)
Closed: Sun except sometimes in Jul & Aug (open 09.00-19.00)
A well-liked corner rendezvous at the back of the Cathedral, with tables spread across the broad pavement and some more under a glassed-in area before the bar. You can take a snack outside, at the bar or at tables in the two side rooms. Newspapers are available for browsing with your glass of champagne or a cup of excellent coffee. Wine is also for sale to take home. Notably friendly young staff.

Le Carnot

5 rue Carnot
Tel: 3 26 47 69 31
Open: 07.00-20.30
Closed: Sun & Aug
The look of the 1950s lives on at Le Carnot, typified by the plastic laminate finishes and the *bébé foot* (bar football) table that's still serviced by the original supplier. Next to Place Royale and its Préfecture, it specialises in breakfasts and simple lunches; also on offer are *coupes* of champagne and first-class coffee.

Les Colonnes

69 pl Drouet d'Erlon
Tel: 3 26 47 20 41
Open: 08.00-24.00
Les Colonnes is named after the stone pillars that support a stone arch at the grand entrance. Inside, the floor is laid with white tiles, and smart, comfortable seating stretches away from the bar, where young waitresses in white aprons provide pleasant service. The bar is also licensed as a *tabac*.

Les Comices

4 pl du Forum
Tel: 3 26 47 23 97
Open: 08.30-24.00
Closed: Sun
A member of the *Chartre de Qualité*, an organisation whose seven-point charter includes a guarantee of good food, service, price, welcome and help for visitors. Daniel Diot and his family maintain high standards here, with Daniel himself in the kitchen and his wife and two daughters serving a clientele composed mainly of young professionals and middle-aged regulars. Old oak doors on the fridge behind the oak bar complement the wooden tables, which are dressed with place mats if you want to eat. Every day there's a *plat du jour* and Friday night is mussel night - always a very popular occasion. Good wines accompany the good food.

Le Condorcet

6 rue Condorcet
Tel: 3 26 40 37 31
Open: 07.00-21.00 (Fri & Sat till 01.00)
Closed: Sun

This is a popular meeting place for shoppers and shop-workers, a two-storey café with pavement tables in a pedestrian street that gets the morning sunshine. Breakfast and lunchtime snacks (*croques*, baguette sandwiches) keep the wolf from the door, and seven bar-top pumps provide draught beer, with which they offer peanuts.

Le Grand Café

92 pl Drouet d'Erlon
Tel: 3 26 47 61 50
Open: 09.30-01.00

Champagne, available in great variety by glass, half bottle, bottle or magnum, is the popular tipple at this comfortable, elegant café at the station end of Erlon. Specialities on the menu include hot and cold salads, mussels (they get through 9 tonnes a month!) and pasta with great sauces including parma ham and clams. The staff are a major asset - young, cheerful, chatty but also busy and attentive - and the customers always seem to be having a good time. Don't leave without having a good look - and a good laugh - at the amusing black-and-white photographs that line the walls.

Café Leffe

85 pl Drouet d'Erlon
Tel: 3 26 40 16 32
Open: 07.00-03.00

It's very hard to beat a draught Leffe *brune*, whether before, instead of, during or after a meal, especially when it's served perfectly, as at this blue and white-liveried café next to the offices of the newspaper L'Union. The hacks use it throughout the day, along with shoppers and office workers, while in the evening a younger crowd takes over, with music to suit. Lots of outside tables. Ice creams and cocktails

Le Lion de Belfort

37 pl Drouet d'Erlon
Tel: 3 26 47 48 17
Open: 07.00-03.00

Exotic animals provide a decorative theme at this pleasant café-brasserie, including a zebra skin, a bronze lion at the bottom of the stairs, a hippo's head over the entrance to the back room, and elephant's heads carved in wood over the bar shelves. *Croques* are a favourite snack, while beer is the major tipple. An interesting variation on our yard of ale is their metre of beer, a wooden box with ten holes for 25cl glasses of ten different beers. You pay for nine and get the tenth free.

La Lorraine

7 pl Drouet d'Erlon
Tel: 3 26 47 32 73
Open: 09.30-24.00
Closed: Mon Oct-Apr

A modern café in classic bar/restaurant style, with globe lighting and silk lampshades in some snug alcoves. Champagne is what you drink here, and the speciality on the menu is *choucroute au champagne*. Mussels are also popular, and *flammekuche* is one of the dishes that represents the region from which the brasserie takes its name. Tables on the terrace, as at all the many cafés and restaurant in this broad pedestrian boulevard.

Café Martin

30-32 pl Drouet d'Erlon
Tel: 3 26 50 02 02
Open: 07.00-24.00

They do a metre of beer here, as at *Lion de Belfort*, but of course you can also get a single beer, served with little pastries. Inside, it's a choice of a stool at the long mahogany bar or a table against the mirror-panelled wall; outside there are lots of pavement tables and folding chairs under the awning or out in the sunshine. Good service from smartly turned-out waiters. The café, which offers a hearty plat du jour, is also a traiteur, with a full takeaway service.

Café du Palais

14 pl Meyron-Herrick
Tel: 3 26 47 52 54
Open: 08.00-21.00
Closed: Sun

A warm and cheerful welcome starts a visit to this pleasant café in a street named after the American Ambassador to France just before the First World War. A family concern since 1930, it is owned by the Vogt family, who over the years have accumulated the large collection of bric-a-brac on display. Jean-Louis well remembers the year his father sent him to London's Hyde Park Hotel, where on one occasion he waited on Queen Elizabeth. He and his son continue the tradition of bistro cuisine at lunchtime, in the restaurant area beyond the bar. The café is opposite the Palais de Justice and the theatre, and its decor reflects the dramas of both.

Strasbourg

'The City of Roads', the capital of Alsace, is an important port, a seat of learning, home to a prestigious music festival and a major player on the European political stage. The city is set in two concentric circles of canals served with 'bateau mouche'-style tours and floating restaurants. Visit the stunning Cathedral in red Vosges sandstone, wonder at the beautiful interiors in the Palais Rohan, take a trip on the canals or the Rhine, eat choucroute and foie gras. On Bastille day join the rest of the city to watch fantastic public fireworks set to music.

Au Bureau

2 pl Benjamin Zix
Tel: 3 88 75 15 80
Open: 10.00-01.00

Au Bureau stands in a picturesque square overlooking the canal and the island of Petite France, where you can see the black-and-white timber-framed buildings that are typical of the district. Alongside others in the square, it has a large number of terrace tables where you can sit and enjoy a coffee with friends or watch the world pass by amid the chatter of others – for this is a very popular place. Snacks on offer include large pretzels, pizzas and salads with ham and goat's cheese.

Maison Kammerzell

16 pl de la Cathédrale
Tel: 3 88 32 42 14
Open: 12.00-15.00 & 19.00-23.30

Any building in the shadow of the stupendous Cathedral is likely to stay in the shadow, but Maison Kammerzell is a fairly amazing sight in itself, a historic monument and the epitome of Alsatian Renaissance. The outside, with its ornate stonework (the oldest parts date from the 15th century) and elaborate carved wood, is matched by the equally startling vaulted and painted rooms inside, which serve partly as a small hotel and partly as a restaurant. This is Strasbourg, so it must be foie gras and choucroute (the fish version is a speciality) or onion tart with a glass or two of Alsatian wine.

Maitre Kanter

11-13 rue des Grandes Arcades
Tel: 3 88 32 15 93
Open: 07.00-24.00

Brasserie, restaurant and tea room: this is *the* place to go in Place Kléber, and in the square, which gets the sun virtually all day, there are terrace tables for 140. Inside, on the ground floor is the shop, and above it a salon in honey-hued wood with velvety red sofas where full meals (shellfish a speciality) are served from noon till midnight. One of the Maitre Kanter's pastries makes a great start to the day and a return trip for another at teatime is a definite possibility, with perhaps a look in at the shop to buy some of their renowned chocolates. Drinks include a house beer and a good selection of Alsatian wines.

Meisberger

39 rue du Vieux Marché aux Vins
Tel: 3 88 32 13 51
Open: 07.00-19.00
Closed: Sun

A family business of many generations' standing, making fine cakes, brownies, chocolates and ice cream. Authentic artisan products with no artificial colouring or flavouring are made to recipes passed down through the family and using local ingredients. They have won several international awards for their terrific patisserie, and the staff also deserve a prize for their friendly, helpful attitude. Light meals are served at lunchtime, with hot sandwiches and 20 kinds of quiche among the offerings.

A La Ville de Bale

24 rue d'Austerlitz
Tel: 3 88 25 53 82
Open: 07.00-02.00

The beers and the cuisine of Alsace are a speciality at this large café-brasserie on a corner in Place d'Austerlitz just outside the inner canal circle. Open very early until very late, and always ready with a friendly welcome, it has a spacious bar and a comfortable dining area inside, and a large number of tables on the pavements outside. Most of the custom is local, and includes other restaurateurs - a recommendation in itself.

Toulouse

Long honoured for its artistic and cultural heritage, Toulouse has more recently added high-tech industry, notably aeronautics - both Concorde and the Airbus were conceived here. The aviation tradition is actually a long-established one, for it was from here that St-Exupéry and others started their pioneering flights to Africa in the 1920s. Toulouse is an important centre of learning, with a student population second in France only to that of Paris. A great place for walking, with many grand houses, some spectacular churches and perhaps the most beautiful town hall in all of France.

Le Bar Basque

7 pl St Pierre
Tel: 5 61 21 55 64
Open: 07.00-02.00

Rugby fans, British visitors and students from the nearby business schools like to meet at this bar on a corner site in a leafy square down near the river. There's not a lot of Basque about it apart from the name, the colour green and a wooden bench or two, nor is it a *bar à vins* as it claims on the awning: Beer is King of the Drinks here, reflecting the taste of its clientele. Next door is L'Annexe, where they have salsa most nights. A lively duo!

Le Café Bibent

5 pl du Capitole
Tel: 5 61 23 89 03
Open: 07.00-02.00

Something of a treasure, and definitely to be cherished: this is the only remaining really old bar in the grand café style in Toulouse. The original co-ordination of marble for the floors, the table-tops and the bar counter is an all too rare sight, and Bibent also has elaborate plasterwork on the walls and ceiling with mirrors in baroque style and large crystal chandeliers. The walls have representations of devils, with Bacchus as the centrepiece. It first opened at the end of the 18th century and attracts the senior citizens of Toulouse with its speciality teas (34 varieties!). It also offers coffee, chocolate and plenty of stronger brews, plus simple snacks both hot and cold, including some good fish dishes.

Chez Tonton

16 pl St Pierre
Tel: 5 61 21 89 54
Open: 08.00-02.00 (Sat 09.00-04.00)
No credit cards

Also known as 'Pastis O Metre', which represents seventeen glasses in a row. Intrepid drinkers sink all 17, one after the other. After the colour of the pastis, the decor here is all yellow, though you might not be aware of this after passing, or indeed failing, the Metre test. A favourite meeting place for the pétanque experts.

Café Le Florida

12 pl du Capitole
Tel: 5 61 21 49 92
Open: 07.00-02.00 (Sat till dawn!)

A grand café, decorated mainly in pink, in a magnificent arcade facing the Town Hall. The ceiling of the arcade over the pavement tables is painted with tableaux by Raymond Moretti depicting the history of Toulouse. Equally eye-catching inside this turn-of-the-century café is a wonderful mahogany bar with a zinc counter. There are two faces to Le Florida - elegant shoppers and business people pause for refreshment in the daytime, while at night the students come for a longer stay to enjoy the music and to debate the world's problems.

Bistrot Montmartre

7 pl St Georges
Tel: 5 61 29 05 42
Open: 07.30-02.00 (winter till 21.00)
One of several bistros in one of the city's prettiest squares. At mealtimes the tables are reserved for eaters, but you are always welcome at the bar.

Le Père Léon

2 pl Esquirol
Tel: 5 61 23 90 95
Open: 06.30-00.30
Closed: Sun
Tradition rules at the Sablis family's brasserie, with a stern portrait of father Léon hanging on the wall and, high above the bar, shelves of wines untouched for over a hundred years with about two inches of dust on them! It's very much a brasserie-style venue, with globe lighting and cane chairs on two levels inside. There's also a glass-enclosed terrace and more tables on the pavement outside in this main cross street coming from the Pont Neuf, right in the heart of Toulouse.

Au Père Louis

45 rue des Tourneurs
Tel: 5 61 21 33 45
Open: 09.00-22.00
Closed: Sun & 2 weeks Aug
Probably the oldest bar in Toulouse, with a few pavement tables, barrels in the bar to rest your drink on, and old paintings on the walls and ceilings, hard to make out under a patina of nicotine but depicting the bridges of the Garonne and the Canal du Midi and lit by a distinctive central chandelier. Open in the morning for coffee and a glance through the newspapers, at lunchtime they serve *plats du jour*. Thereafter you can get a tartine through the rest of the day. The busy time is aperitifs at 18.00, when it's packed, and as the evening wears on the students arrive, often to perform their own music. They've been producing wine and fortified wine for sale in the bar since time immemorial and among their specialities are *Quinquina* - a liqueur with bitter oranges, *Maury* (port-like) and *Muscat*.

Bar Le Quartier Latin

1 pl Rouaix
Tel: 5 61 52 33 82
Open: 07.00-02.00
The time of day determines the style and mood of this agreeable little bar in a square at the bottom of the Avenue Alsace-Lorraine. A breakfast café on your way to work and a place to take a break from shopping, it becomes a sandwich bar at lunchtime and then as the day wears on it takes on a lighter tone in readiness for the cocktail hour. Between 19.00 and 21.00 on Wednesday to Saturday they offer little tapas with drinks. Then it gets very busy with a happy young crowd and stays that way into the night. One of the walls inside has a very large and striking abstract painting in oils by Nikos.

Café Wallace

15 pl St Georges
Tel: 5 61 21 07 18
Open: 07.30-01.00 or 02.00
Closed: Sun am
The great delight at this simple, spacious bar is to sit out in front or in the square in the shade of plane trees with an aperitif or one of their amazing speciality ice creams. Snacks are also available, and wines by the glass.

Germany

Telephone Code: 00 49

When the Germans let their hair down they do it in style, as any visitor to Munich's October beer festival will testify. There's another annual funfest in Cologne, while other gala occasions are rather more sober affairs, notably the Bayreuth Wagner Festival and the Oberammergau Passion Play. German's well-trodden tourist trails offer scenic attractions that can rival any in Europe, and for many the castles are a highlight: in the Bavarian Alps, including Mad King Ludwig's all-time fairytale Neuschwanstein; at Heidelberg (where the university and the 50,000-gallon great vat are rival highlights); at Schleissheim near Munich; and, above all, along the valley of the Rhine, home of the Lorelei and resting place of the treasure of the Nibelungen. A walk in the Black Forest, a trip on Lake Constance or a spell on the ski slopes will generate the right sort of appetite for more of that beer and some hearty German cooking. And if you overdo things, a brief spell in one of the spa resorts will put things right.

CAFÉ CRÈME

Berlin

The wall that divided the city for almost 30 years exists only in a few places, mainly well protected from souvenir-hunters, and Berlin is revelling in a new era of cultural and economic unity. The look of the place is resolutely modern, with new buildings springing up everywhere, and leading architects are transforming areas such as Potsdamer Platz, where the British, American and Russian sectors used to meet. Berlin's chief hooly is the annual Love Parade, which started small time in the late 1980s and has grown into one of Europe's largest festivals.

The cake shops and konditoreis of Berlin, where quite often a few tables and chairs have been added to form a café, are one extreme contrasting with the grand cafés that form part of Berlin's historic past. Everywhere people enjoy the vast array of cakes, gateaux and pastries that have traditionally been one of the strong points of culinary Germany. Night life is as varied as any visitor could wish, though the Cabaret days of the 20s and 30s have gone, and the licensing laws are notably liberal, particularly to British eyes. The Kreuzberg district still has some of the feel of the radical 1960s, while Oranienburgerstrasse, in the Mitte area, has been transformed from virtual desolation into one of the top spots on the bar, café and arts scene.

Adler

Friedrichstrasse 206
Tel: 30 251 89 65
Open: 09.30-24.00 (Sun from 19.00)
An old-fashioned corner café with small white marble tables and wooden chairs. Light snacks, cakes, beers, wines and coffee are the order of the day, but its other, unique, attraction is a location right next to Checkpoint Charlie and its Museum, which tells the story of the Berlin Wall in vivid detail. Originally a pharmacy, it became a café in the mid-80s and was, of course, the first stop for East Germans coming to the West; now, happily, everyone uses it. Twelve tables and their smart new chairs are set outside in summer.

Café Aedes

Die Hackeschen Höfe, Rosenthalerstrasse 40-41, 10178
Tel: 30 285 82 75
Open: 10.00-02.00 (Fri & Sat till 03.00)
A courtyard and the buildings around it were restored and converted into cafés with apartments above, and a cinema. The whole area has been transformed with such projects, which have really caught the imagination of Berliners. Inside Aedes is a roomy, comfortable bar, while outside there's a huge parasol covering tables and chairs to hold about 40. Good menu and wine list + 75 whiskies.

Astor

Oranienburgerstrasse 84
Tel: 30 283 68 34
Open: 10.00-01.00 (Fri & Sat till 02.00, Sun from 10.00)
A quintessentially English bar/restaurant where fish & chips, jacket potatoes and other favourites are washed down with tea and beer by local Anglophiles and occasional packs of Brits abroad. Despite the extraordinary montage of photos and press cuttings of the Royals and other patriotic memorabilia, evidence of an identity crisis emerges on the menu in the shape of various American specialities such as cheesecake, brownies and pecan or pumpkin pie.

Café Bleibtreu

Bleibtreustrasse 45, 10623
Tel: 30 881 47 56
Open: 09.30-01.00 (Fri & Sat 09.00-02.00)
A highly individualistic café-bar with black-painted tables and chairs at the front and bench seating at the back in red upholstery. There are also some rather more quirky design features, such as an English telephone box, alongside photographs of Hollywood greats from Laurel & Hardy and Chaplin to Bogart and Wayne, Bardot and Hepburn. Soft lighting and candles help to complete the intimate atmosphere in the evenings. Excellent fresh orange juice and a good selection of newspapers are two good reasons to make a stop-off here at breakfast time. Special evening menus.

Dressler

Kurfürstendamm 207-8
Tel: 30 883 35 30
Open: 08.00-01.00

A small company established in 1997 to open cafés in French brasserie style: art nouveau, globe lights and shaded uplighters, black and white decor, ditto staff outfits. The wall-hangings are in Expressionist style. Two thirds of the lofty interior is taken up by the restaurant, while the bar section extends outside to terrace tables. The speciality drink is the romantic 'chandelier', two glasses of pink Moët sitting prettily in a little chandelier, and there are other champagnes, German and French wines, beers, coffees and teas; great patisserie, and hot and cold snacks, salads and full meals served from 11.00. Also at Unter den Linden 39, where owner Herr Waernd is usually to be found.

Café Einstein

Kurfürstenstrasse 58, 10785
Tel: 30 261 50 96
Open: 09.00-02.00

On the ground floor of an elegant villa-like private house built in 1898, this is an opulent Viennese-style coffee house with a lofty main room and various other majestic rooms leading through into the leafy garden. Come here to read the papers over a leisurely breakfast, to sip a cup of superb coffee with a wonderful apple strudel, or to sit down to a full-scale meal (hot food served noon till midnight). A popular choice for well-to-do Berliners'. Service is friendly and helpful, even at the busiest times, and children are welcome as long as they don't disturb the peace.

Filmbuhne am Steinplatz

Hardenbergstrasse 12, 10623
Tel: 30 312 65 89
Open: 09.00-03.00 (Sun till 02.00)

Opposite the HDK concert hall, this intellectuals' meeting place is a large café with a sizeable terrace beyond the tall windows. Breakfast is served from a buffet that includes lots of fresh fruit. Plenty of teas and coffees to choose from. It is incorporated into one of the many independent cinemas which are so popular in Berlin. Films start at 19.30 and 21.30 (+23.30 Fri & Sat).

Hoeck

Wilmerdorfstrasse 149, 10585
Tel: 30 341 81 74
Open: 08.00-24.00
Closed: Sun

Hoeck opened its doors in 1862, and its most famous owner was a gold medallist in the 1932 Los Angeles Olympics; around the walls are bottles with his name on: Host Hoeck. The house speciality is the Berlin Kindl original Weiss Schankbier, served in a broad tumbler, an ideal accompaniment to the robust German fare on the menu, including the famous *Schweinehackse* (knuckle of pork). A listed building, and the oldest of its kind in Charlottenberg.

Kempinski

Kurfürstendamm 27, 10719
Tel: 30 884 34734
Open: 06.30-01.00

The ground-floor café of the Hotel Bristol is a favourite place of refreshment for the Berlin smart set, the terrace for drinks and snacks, inside for meals. Soups, salads, terrific fruity ice creams. Wine by the glass is served in a 20cl glass pot.

Leydicke

Mansteinstrasse 4
Tel: 30 216 29 73
Open: 16.00-24.00
Closed: Sun

Fruit wines are the speciality of this grand old family enterprise, where the introduction of electricity is one of the few changes to have come about since the doors first opened in 1877. Gooseberry, raspberry and plum are just three of the many varieties on offer, served in generous tumblers to be enjoyed in the most traditional of surroundings. Four candelabras provide the illumination and some yellowed newspaper obituaries framed in a glass cabinet stand as a tribute to members of the founding family. Wine buffs of all ages come here, but it is mainly the older generation who like to sit quietly with a good drink and a newspaper.

> "In a hectic world, cigars give people a chance for a pause. It's a ritual."
> **Michael Douglas.**

Café Leysieffer

Kurfürstendamm 218
Tel: 30 885 74 80
Open: 09.00-02.00 (Sat & Sun till 22.00)

Established in 1909 and with outlets throughout Germany, this could just be the best sweetie shop in the whole wide world. Try a cake, torte or chocolate confection on the terrace outside the shop, or in the café/bar in the gallery upstairs, with a glass of champagne or house wine or a liqueur while they wrap the gift you have chosen from the brochure. A splendid place for a little spot of self-indulgence, and an excellent source of an extra-special gift (Christmas hampers a speciality). The building used to be the Chinese Embassy.

Pranzo e Cena

Goltzstrasse 32, 10781
Tel: 30 216 3514
Open: 09.00-01.00

Opened in July 1999 by two enterprising second-generation Turkish waiters who have thereby realised their dream. The food and wine are Italian, with some real bargains among the bottles: Barbera 1997, Salice Salentino Reserve. This has not in the past been a good site, but the owners know what they are doing and deserve to succeed. Note that they're now open for breakfast.

Rampenlicht am Sudstern

Korterstrasse 33
Tel: 30 692 1301
Open: 09.00-01.00 (Sun from 10.00)

Tucked away in the residential area of Kreuzberg and close to the Volkspark Hasenheide Gardens, this double-fronted café is a versatile place that serves breakfasts, light lunches and evening meals in bistro style as well as being an all-day café. It is particularly busy in the evening and the bench tables on the terrace are much in demand when the weather is kind. Plenty of choice among the wines and beers: try the Czech beer Budvar.

Rost

Knesebeckstrasse 29, 10623
Tel: 30 881 95 01
Open: 09.00-24.00/01.00

A busy arts café, modern and sparsely decorated, in a residential area just south of the overland metro line by Savignyplatz. Seating comprises stools at the slate-topped bar, benches and chairs around the walls, and outside chairs at a small line of terrace tables. There's a stage for poetry, jazz and many other events.

Sale e Tabacchi

Kochstrasse 18
Tel: 30 252 11 55
Open: 09.00-01.00 (Sat & Sun from 10.00)

The full-height glass front of this modern Italian café creates a naturally bright and airy interior, and the comfortable wooden seats are a further invitation. Just a block away from Checkpoint Charlie, it offers a good opportunity to combine a visit to the CPC Museum with some excellent real Italian coffee and authentic Italian food.

Wintergarten im Literaturhaus

Fasanenstrasse 23, 10719
Tel: 30 882 54 14
Open: 09.30-01.00

A large, comfortable café/bar that never fails to impress. With its conservatory and garden terrace in Berlin's central library, it is a social and cultural centre as well as a treasury of books. There is a full programme of recitals, readings and performances to dazzle the most seasoned of café intellectuals, but customers are equally at home just reading one of the many newspapers provided. The clientele are mostly young, mostly wine-drinkers. Breakfast is available until 14.00, bistro-style cooking from 11.30.

Cologne

In the centre of Europe, Cologne has a history dating back to Roman times. The city's crowning glory is its cathedral dedicated to St Peter, which stands in imposing contrast to the modern blocks around it. Work on the cathedral spanned 600 years, ending in the second half of the 19th century, and at the time of their building the twin towers on the west facade were the tallest structures in the world. Cologne is a centre for art, culture and music, as well as hosting some 30 trade fairs each year. Germany's fourth most populous city is largely Catholic, and the annual carnival, leading up to Holy Week, is an enormously popular event. The season begins as early as November, and at the height of the festivities the bars never close.

Bootshaus Rodenkirchen

Rodenkirchener Yachthafen, Am Leinpfad 50996
Tel: 221 39 51 84
Open: 14.00-22.00 (Sat & Sun from 11.00)
Closed: Tue
Owned by Helmut Ammel and Sabine Weiss, this permanently moored café-bar-restaurant was established over 30 years ago, and offers the pleasure, winter or summer, of sitting and watching the busy traffic on the Rhine over a beer, glass of wine or a coffee. Snacks are available, but the kitchen doesn't cater for full meals until after 17.30.

Engelbät

Engelbertstrasse 7, 50674
Tel: 221 24 69 14
Open: 11.00-01.00
Creperie und Kneipe (Crepes and Snacks)
Engelbät offers a huge range of crepes, sweet and savoury, and the excellent Illy coffee, also wines by the glass from Germany, Italy, France, Spain and Argentina, and a range of salads. An upright piano stands in the corner of this dimly lit young café that's very popular with young people including many students; enamelled adverts decorate the walls, well-used sturdy bar stools attend the bar and the tall tables, and in the window wooden tables are set on the quarry-tiled floor. A music centre with a library of tapes and CDs stands next to the pre-war till.

Café Fleur

Lindenstrasse 10, 50674
Tel: 221 24 48 97
Open: 09.00-01.00 (Fri & Sat till 02.00)
A pretty corner café offering a range of coffees and teas (in the summer also iced specials), attracting customers in their 20s and 30s who come to read the papers or chat in the afternoons over a cup or glass. There are four white three red and a rosé in 10cl or 20cl glasses and lots of spirits and cocktails. Snacks are served at meal times, and a salad is available throughout the afternoon.

Guildenhaus

Grosse Budengasse 10, 50667
Tel: 221 257 5966
Open: 08.00-03.00
Tucked away in a side street around the corner from the Cathedral, the Opera and the Old Market, the building dates back to the 13th century, and since 1990 has been offering solid refreshment from breakfast time to midnight and liquid sustenance until well into the small hours. It's very popular with locals, and on May Day musicians meet here for a big party, when they play and sing and dance. Several beers are available from the hop-hung bar, and the recommended draught is the local Kölsch served in 20cl slips. A good little snack is the Mett, a crusty roll with steak tartare and onion.

Haus Schwan

Dürenerstrasse 235, 50931
Tel: 221 40 33 68
Open: 11.00-01.00
In a well-known street leading west out of town, this café-bar is a favourite among the gregarious townsfolk. At Carnival time (in February) each district has its own float, and Haus Schwan is the focus for this district. Marionettes hang above the bar, along with badges representing the various districts. The food is good at good prices, and can be enjoyed at the bleached tables set on the scrubbed oak floors to the left of the bar. Excellent local brews can be supped with a chat with the jovial staff at the bar.

Café Orlando

Engelbertstrasse 9
Tel: 221 237 523
Open: 09.00-01.00
A dear little café in the student district very near the university, and renowned for its home cooking. Coffee is served with a delicious little biscuit, and the prices are all very reasonable. They do eight fruit juices, eight milk shakes, chili con carne, omelettes etc, and have a very reasonable wine list: whites include pinot grigio, verdicchio, and a German white; reds a German, Côtes du Rhône, and a Dao.

Peters Brauhaus

Mübalengasse 1, 50667
Tel: 221 257 39 50
Open: 11.00-24.00

In the Altstadt, and not far from the Philharmonie and the Rathaus, this building was a bar for successive brewers for many years, and in 1994 Peters Brauhaus took it over as their first outlet to sell direct to the public. From 1847 they had been a brewer supplying only to the trade. A second outlet was opened in Düsseldorf in 1996. The brewery is about 15 kilometres from here. Herr Lenz says the busiest time is in the winter, especially in the four or five weeks leading up to Christmas, when he wishes it was twice the size! He also serves food here, mainly traditional Cologne fare - snacks like cheese, or boiled salt beef with bread, or more substantial (*very* substantial) dishes such as sausages with fried potatoes, pork with mashed potatoes, knuckle of pork, black pudding etc. Businessmen come during the day and mingle with the tourists and shoppers, while at night opera-goers mix with locals and visitors here for a good night out.

Pomp

Lindenstrasse 38, 50674
Tel: 221 21 11 12

Open: 09.00-02.00 (Fri & Sat till 03.00, Sun from 10.00)
Established by an Iraqi owner in 1997, this has a Mediterranean flavour. In the entrance is an internet station where you can log in to pick up your e-mails. The pavement tables are shaded by leafy trees, and the tables inside are packed with young café-goers, dipping into the newspapers or enjoying the cheerful ambience and the company of friends. A well-known and well-loved meeting place.

Café Reichard

Unter Feltenhennen 11
Tel: 221 2 57 85 42
Open: 08.00-20.00

Established in 1855, this is a seriously smart bar, tea room, restaurant and shop - one of the very best in Cologne and part of a group of four. From the large terrace (which in summer is set with tables and chairs), or from the conservatory, you can see the front of the impressive cathedral (Dom) in the centre of the Altstadt. The shop sells pralines, sweets and cakes as colourful and as enticing as anywhere in the world. In the mornings there's a breakfast buffet as good or better than in a top-class hotel, with hot and cold food, and of course, a selection of their pastries. The restaurant has an extensive cold buffet, with strudels among the specialities. Another real treat is the coffee, and yet another the ice cream. There's a choice of five Italian wines by the glass and two draught beers.

Vintage

Pfeilstrasse 31-35, 50672
Tel: 221 92 07 10
Open: 10.00-24.00 (kitchen: 12.00-15.00 & 18.00-23.00) (Fri till 24.00, Sat 12.00-24.00)
Closed: Sun

Owned by Claudia and Michael Stern, with Jürgen Hammer as sommelier, this is probably the best wine bar/café in Cologne. The wine list is extensive, imaginative and very reasonably priced by UK standards; it's available for retail off-sale, and if you drink it on the premises there's a modest corkage. They also stock some excellent produce from Italy, including charcuterie and olive oil, and the espresso coffee is first-rate. The design of the place is modern, and as you enter through the shop with its enticing wares, attentive staff welcome you and show you to comfortable, light wooden tables and chairs. There is also a private courtyard terrace for warm days where many a merry evening can been enjoyed.

Waschsalon

Ehrenstrasse 77, 50672
Tel: 221 13 33 78
Open: 09.00-01.00 (Fri & Sat till 03.00)

Opened in 1998, this was at first a launderette where you could have a coffee while using the machines. But that didn't wash with the customers, so they used the machines in the decor - carcasses in the bar front, drums for light shades, bases of stools at the bar etc, and now they come! Big and open, with bench seating under huge umbrellas in the pedestrianised street, the café offers breakfast in the mornings, from the simple to the truly filling, and at weekends a buffet brunch. Four wines are offered by the 15cl glass including one red; good espresso; other snacks include pizzas, salads, chicken wings and fries.

Wippenbekk Café (Restaurant and Hotel)

Karlstrasse 7-9, D-50996
Tel: 221 93 53 150
Open: 11.00-01.00 (Sat & Sun from 10.00)

In the pretty suburb of Rodenkirchen, with a conservatory open to the bar, and stepped-down terraces open to the elements, Wippenbekk offers the perfect view of the Rhine and its constant traffic. It serves Segafredo coffee and several wines by the 10cl glass, and you can prolong your stay with a snack such as soup or a ciabatta sandwich, or a meal from the à la carte menu, or the 2- or 3-course fixed price menu during the day. A haunt for tourists and city dwellers who come for the view. The open-plan island bar is manned by friendly staff.

Dortmund

Once a Hanseatic League city famous for its steel and brewing industries. Now a service industry city for the Westphalia Ruhr area, it continues its brewing tradition and also supports a thriving café society. It has many notable architectural sights, both ancient (four beautifully restored medieval churches) and modern, including one of Europe's largest exhibition halls.

Capriccio

Kleppingstrasse 4, 44135
Tel: 231 58 600 47
Open: 11.00-24.00 (summer till 03.00)

Established in July 1994, this is *the* Italian café of Dortmund, specialising in very good Italian ice cream and coffee. It is a well-known local meeting place, and in the summer it has tables spread out over the broad boulevard. Lots of young people and some of the Italian expatriates use it. One white wine, two reds, prosecco and champagne. The favourite snack is croque monsieur.

Cotton's

Markt 5, 44137
Tel: 231 58 600 49
Open: 10.00-01.00

Music, coffee, beers, light snacks - breakfast, baguettes, soups, salads, tapas etc, this is in the Alter Markt (old market place), a busy modern café with people of all ages but predominantly in their 20s and 30s, meeting here for a drink and a chat. It's set on two floors with an all-glass frontage so you can watch the pedestrian traffic in the square. Wine (three white, three, two rosé) available in 20cl glasses. Split level, with the bar at the back.

Hövels Haus-Brauerei

Hoher Wall 5-7, 44137
Tel: 231 14 10 44
Open: 10.00-01.00

This was established in the early 1980s as a breakaway from the main brewery behind it when a big outside brewer took it over. Hövels brew on the premises, 20 hectolitres at a time, and two to three times a week in the winter, daily in summer. Their beer is also made under licence by the big brewer for sales elsewhere. A pleasant bar area is attached to a much larger restaurant, where substantial meals are sold, and from where you can see the Brewmaster, and his 'Stub'.

Rathaus à la Carte

Freidensplatz
Tel: 231 586 12 11
Open: 10.30-21.30
Closed: Sun

Dortmund was largely destroyed in World War ll, with one tower and its piece of wall remaining of the original walled town. Its new Town Hall (Rathaus) is here in Freedom Square. In common with most German towns, there's a café in the Town Hall where the City Fathers entertain, and where local food and drink specialities are sold. It's now leased to Andreas and Eberhard Gerbig, who propose the specialities of Westphalia, including potato soup (*kartoffelsuppe*), *Westfälischer bauernsalat*, and *kasslersteak mett* (raw minced beef and onions) *bratkartoffen*. Other more international fare such as pasta and filled baguettes are also available, and there's always a dish of the day - and, of course, some local beers. On the 2nd and 4th Fridays of the month from May to September live jazz concerts start at 19.00.

Zum Alten Markt

Markt 3, 44137
Tel: 231 57 22 17
Open: 11.00-01.00

Established in 1983, the old and the new blend here to make a busy bar with people popping in for a beer and a roll, or a simple sausage dish at lunchtime, or a sparkling wine and a glance at the TV. The bar has a surrounding gallery and a huge false fireplace surmounted by a boar's head, and customers can stand at the bar or the tall counters set around the ground floor. The tables upstairs are for more formal meals. The new counters contrast in age with the pillars and beams that support the gallery. A large chandelier hangs in the middle, and a medley of 60s' German songs plays quietly in the background. This is where the older locals meet, while the youngsters gather next door (at Cotton's).

Dresden

Spread on either side of the River Elbe, Dresden was the seat of the Duchy of Saxony, kings of Poland. It was heavily bombed in 1945 but many of its grand buildings have been restored, notably the Zwinger, a magnificent baroque edifice built by Augustus the Strong. The bridge that bears his name has been an inspiration for many artists, including Canaletto. Nearby is Meissen, famed for its china and ceramics (see PFUND).

Barococo

Altmarkt 10, 01067
Tel: 351 8 62 30 40
Open: 08.00-01.00

The Old Market was originally much smaller than it is today. It was largely rebuilt in the 1950s after everything but the Kreuzkirche was destroyed in the war. The imposing houses on the east and west sides were rebuilt in the Dresden baroque style, while here on the south side the market bar is part of the commercial and office development of the square. The Altmarkt hosts lively markets through the year, the most famous being the Striezelmarkt at Christmas time. Barococo is the market bar and has cane terrace tables and chairs stretching into the square under large cream parasols. The café on the ground floor leads to the all-day restaurant upstairs and to the cellar, which is often used for functions.

Blumenau

Louisenstrasse 67, 01099
Tel: 351 8 02 65 02
Open: 10.00-03.00

Here's just the business for the young and students of the city: located in the new town along from Jazz Café, it's busy with chattering people, trying to talk over the beat music. Lots of coffees and beers, a good wine selection by the glass on the blackboard behind the bar. Up to the right and towards the back is the restaurant area, which is used as a café overflow when they're busy.

Brazil

Kleine Brüdergasse 1, 01067
Tel: 351 8 62 12 00
Open: 10.00-24.00

Impressive corner site on two floors joined by a sweeping stair and mezzanine, with a semicircular bar from which the tables radiate. The wine list includes 22 white, four rosé and 19 red from the New World - South Africa, Mexico, South America - and the local Saxon Radebeuler. All the food is in Portuguese, with German subtitles. There's a daily card, lots of cakes, and plenty of ways to spoil a good cup of coffee (by adding liquor). The glass sides of the building allow an unimpaired view of the Zwinger Garden and the promenading people.

El Español

An der Dreikönigkirsche 7, 01097
Tel: 351 8 04 86 70
Open: 10.30-01.00 (Thur, Fri & Sat till 02.00)

In the smart part of town in the shadow of the famous Three Kings church is this busy tapas bar in a building dating from the 1730s. It was supposed be assimilated into the surrounding landscape, which it would do if it were not for the impressive clock tower and steeple. El Español is more a café/restaurant than the Basque original, however, but popular for all that. The rooms are small and intimate, there's a small area of bar you can sit at, and the place buzzes with happy chatter. Decent wines by the glass and good coffee.

Kempinski Hotel: Allegro Bar/Vestibule

Taschenbergpalais, Taschenberg 3, 01067
Tel: 351 49 12 712
Open: 19.00-02.00/09.00-24.00

The place to stay in Dresden, if you have the money. This restored palace is something to be seen. Central to all the monumental buildings in the Altstadt, the castle (whose restoration is scheduled to be complete in 2005/6); the cholera fountain (commemorating the fact that the cholera plague didn't hit Dresden); the Zwinger, built by August the Strong and originally the open-air ballroom of the royal family (Wettin); the former Catholic Hofkirche (court chapel, with statues of 78 saints); the Semper Opera.... it's all here. Within the palace are a café, a bar, an inner courtyard with tables and chairs under umbrellas, a restaurant, and much more.

Lloyd's Kaffeehus

Martin Luther strasse 17, 01099
Tel: 351 8 03 57 90
Open: 09.00-24.00

Facing the Martin Luther church in the square, host to classical concerts as well as religious services, this corner café advertises 'coffee & books', 'cigars & wine'. Splendid! Elegant round and oval tables with bentwood chairs, and a bookcase with some heavy tomes give the first impression inside. Then you see that to the right is the bar and beyond that a further room with some inviting armchairs. For breakfast the choice runs from two croissants with jam and honey 6DM to the full works or something from the à la carte menu; for the rest of the day the options include soups, salads, omelettes, pasta and steaks. A reasonable list of wines is available, served in large Paris goblets: we're in the suburbs of the 'new' town.

Löwe

Hauptstrasse 48, 01097
Tel: 351 8 04 11 38
Open: 10.00-24.00

Around the corner from the Königstrasse, in the High Street, is the smart café Löwe. The interior is quite intimate, with small triangular leather upholstered seats set at tables in the bar area, but the popular conservatory attached is more communal, and this spills out on to the pavement under umbrellas. There's a good selection of teas, coffees and wines by the glass, served by smartly dressed waitresses. The mature shrubbery surrounding the conservatory softens the angular architecture in this newly built part of town.

PFUND Gebrüder, Dresdner Molkerei

Bautznerstrasse 79, 01099
Tel: 351 80 80 80
Open: 09.00-20.00 (Sat & Sun 10.00-16.00)

Probably the most extraordinary dairy you'll ever see, with floor, ceiling and walls in the ground-floor rooms covered in Meissen tiles! There's a display of cheese for sale to take away, or to sample with fresh bread and a glass of wine or milk. Upstairs, in elegant rooms extending over neighbouring shops, is the café/restaurant. The dairy was founded by the Pfund brothers in 1880.

Café Schinkelwache

Sophienstrasse am Theaterplatz, 01067
Tel: 351 4 90 39 09
Open: 10.00-24.00

Next door to the tourist board is this traditional café serving lots of cakes to lots of tourists. Inside are conventional tables and waitress service, while outside are comfortable terrace tables and chairs under broad parasols. And what a view: the Zwinger, the Castle, the Semper Opera House, the Cathedral. Espresso coffee and plenty of wines by the glass.

Café Strauss

Königstrasse 1, 91097
Tel: 351 8 04 52 42
Open: 11.00-23.00 (Fri & Sat 10.00-24.00)

Perhaps they're used to severe weather, or is it that 'outdoors' is for a mere few weeks of the year? In any event, in this upmarket residential area just across the River Elbe from the Opera and the ancient royal residences of the rulers of Saxony, this part of a side street has been glazed over (double-glazed to reduce neighbour-rage) making it a permanent pavement space to sit 'outdoors'. The two or three shops face the Café and a tavern. Strauss sells Illy, and you really can taste the difference. Port wine is alive and well in Dresden, here served in 5cl measures from six houses, eleven different ports in all. Wine, plenty available by the glass, comes from Germany, Chile, France, Italy and Australia. Breakfast, served from 10.00, could be a quick roll or croissant with butter and jam or the full Strauss including coffee and a prosecco. Later there's pasta or a baguette or toast - an open sandwich Norwegian style.

Düsseldorf

A confident, prosperous city on the banks of the Rhine, a major centre for heavy industry, finance and fashion; the fashion houses are found mainly along the famous Königsallee. Its café life is particularly lively in the Aldstadt, the charming old part of town with its narrow streets and little squares.

Bagel

Alte Stadt 12-14
Tel: 211 863 92 22
Open: 10.00-02.00 (Fri & Sat till 03.00)

In what was once part of a monastery, hence the spectacularly plastered ceiling, it first became a café in the 1980s after spells as a grocer's and an undertaker's. It then became popular as Bagel, was closed, re-opened under other names and finally, under Stephan, took its first name and now has a fight on his hands to use that name, the previous owner having registered it as his own. Tucked away in the north of the Altstadt, it serves - of course - filled bagels, along with salads and other snacks to enjoy with a good espresso or a glass of wine. Inside, the place is simple and minimalist in contrast to the ceiling, and outside are trestle tables and bench seating.

Balthasar

Bolkersstrasse 63, 40213
Tel: 211 32 27 70
Open: 09.00-01.00 (Fri & Sat till 02.00, Sun from 10.00)

On the edge of the Alt Stadt, on two floors, a busy bar and meeting place for 20 to 30-year-olds, offering decent espresso and house wines by glass or bottle and a separate list of bottles. On the food side are soups, salads and lots of pasta, and a variety of choices for breakfast. The long bar at the back looks out on to the tables for two or four and, through the tall glass windows, to the street. Favoured by young pleasure seekers include some visitors to Düsseldorf.

Café Bernstein

Oststrasse 158
Tel: 211 35 65 20
Open: 09.00-01.00 (Fri & Sat till 03.00)

A twice-lifesize Mogul in plaster of Paris stands against one wall watching the scene and on either side there is bench seating. Opposite is the simple granite bar, and granite-topped tables have bentwood chairs at which the 20-30something customers sit laughing and joking over their refreshments in the evenings. Mornings are more peaceful, times to reflect over breakfast with coffee and the papers. The simple daily menu offers the likes of mushroom soup, rocket salad and pasta, perhaps a steak if you're seriously hungry. A simple wine list accompanies: five white, two reds and a rosé by the glass, or to celebrate, Pommery, Veuve or Dom Perignon by the bottle.

Et Kadüffke

Flingerstrasse 1
Tel: 211 13 32 69
Open: 11.00-24.00
Closed: Sun

Hans and Willi (Busch) were sitting in their air-raid shelter during World War ll, as they often did while the bombs were dropping, "Hans, if it goes on like this they're going to KILL us", said Willi. "Not while we've got liquor to 'pitsch' (drink)", he replied. "But it's all finished", he moaned. "That's impossible", Hans said, "after all, you make it!". " How can I? the Nazis won't let me have any more alcohol. But if we do survive I'll make a liquor to die for". Sure enough, after ten years experimenting with fruit and herbs, he came up with *killepitsch*, which remains a popular alternative to a glass of wine in the crowded bar. Peter Busch and his aged mother carry on a family tradition that dates from 1858, when the first Peter Busch established his *likör-fabrik*. This the favourite spot for the older Altstädters to come for refreshment, and besides the thronging bar and balcony drinks can be ordered through an open window on the pavement, where there are trestled tables for resting glasses. And if beer is their tipple, the Zum Uerige brewery is just across the road.
Special Award 2001

g@rden

Rathausufer 8, 40213
Tel: 211 86 61 60
Open: 11.00-01.00

On the banks of the Rhine, with loads of aluminium chairs and tables outside, stands this internet café (www.garden.de), which at night becomes a discothèque. Very spacious, and split level, it was established in 1997; the decor includes indoor palms and lots of orange, extending to the staff's tennis shirts and the logo on their long black aprons. Refreshments include soups, salads, pasta and burgers, and more filling choices like chicken, duck and beef, often with an Eastern flavour. Cocktails are popular, but also offered are wines by the glass, coffee and the dark Düsseldorf beer. It's very popular with 20-30 year-olds, and on busy warm summer evenings they open another bar outside.

Goldenen Ring

Burgplatz 21-22, 40213
Tel: 211 13 31 61
Open: 10.00-01.00

Facing the square on the right bank of the Rhine in the old part of the city is a single house brewery, with a history going back to 1873. The food is traditional and very reasonable, and the beer excellent. Also offered are house red, white and rosé wines. A robust building dominating one end of the square, inside is spacious with scrubbed solid tables in ash, while outside is a large area shaded by pollarded plane trees, whose leafy branches shade comfortable terrace tables and chairs for hot summer days, while other tables stand out in the open for those wishing to take the sun.

Café Knülle

Oberbilker Allee 24, 40215
Tel: 211 31 84 43
Open: 10.00-01.00 (Fri & Sat till 03.00)

Owned by Gilbert and Jürgen Knülle, this is a comfortable students' bar selling good coffee (often bowls of it), beer and a selection of wines by the glass. Double fronted, with tall windows, this is a café for the young intellectuals, who come here for a quiet read or earnest discussions, or a game of chess until the daylight fails. At night the dimmed chandelier and the candle-lit wooden tables lend an intimacy to the large open room, and on the walls above the panelling is exhibited a collection of works by a single artist. The bar is a popular rendezvous in the early evening before going on to more energetic entertainment, but many of the regulars linger on here. Snacks include salads, baguettes, soup and chili con carne - all familiar student fare.

Café Madrid & Café Cico

Bolkerstrasse 23-25, 40213
Tel: 211 13 33 24
Open: 09.00-02.00

In a Spanish enclave right in the heart of the Alt Stadt stand these popular neighbours with oak bars, tables and cabinets. Some good house wines are available by the glass, along with a list of bottles from around Spain, to accompany a large range of tapas and snacks, including slices from the whole jamón (pata negra) that is held in a clamp on the bar. Full meals are also available, and Düsseldorfer beer too. Breakfast is served from opening time, offering anything from a Colombian espresso with a brioche to the full cooked Ibiza. Ice cream is another favourite, along with iced coffee and banana split. Air is circulated by old aircraft propellers worked by an elaborate belt system. Good *cave à cigares* from Havana.

Muggel

Dominikanerstrasse 4, 40545
Tel: 211 55 41 82
Open: 09.00-01.00 (Fri & Sat till 02.00)

Pony-tailed Alex Exposito is the owner of this very popular café/restaurant, which offers a feel of Italy here in this leafy, well-heeled suburb of Düsseldorf on the left bank. Refreshment has three phases, with the breakfast-lunch menu from opening time until 15.00, tapas in the afternoon until 18.00 and thereafter the evening menu. Smart local people of all ages come to be served by elegant young girls in black tops and long white aprons. The hot spot in the winter is in the window on the slatted seat over the radiator, otherwise there are bar stools and scrubbed-top tables, with restaurant seating up a short flight at the back. Look out for the modern art on the plain plastered walls here. Good coffee, excellent list of wines by glass or bottle.

Otto Bittner

Karlplatz 20-21 (+6 others)
Tel: 211 3 10 9840
Open: 09.30-18.30

A big cake and sweetie shop, with a line-up running from gingerbread men to pralines. The other half is a café selling coffee, tea, hot chocolate, sparkling and still wines, beers and spirits. The square is in the middle of Düsseldorf's main shopping district, and in its centre is a food market selling fruit, vegetables, fish, meat and flowers. The restaurateurs shop in the market early in the morning, as well as the local residents, but Otto Bittner, established in 1905, serves the shoppers in the Königsallee. An institution, it produces 20,000 kilos of champagne truffles alone each year, and the busy staff make up parcels and hampers which are sent all over the world. Mrs Kreutz runs the shop, and her two sons, Ingo and Guido, are the managers, one in production, the other in administration.

Paulaner Botschaft

Hüttenstrasse 30, 40215
Tel: 211 37 60 97
Open: 11.00-24.00

Owned by the Lohmann and Mitarbeitar families, this is a Bavarian-style hostelry with an enormous bar in the round made of good oak. Here the standard measure is 30cl rather than the more usual 20cl, and the beer is the light Munich beer rather than the darker Düsseldorfer. There are six beers on draught, but beware of the Salvator Starkbier - its abv is a staggering (literally!) 7%. They also sell rib-sticking food - knuckle of pork boiled or grilled, with sauerkraut and mashed potatoes, or you can have a selection of sausages with the same, all day round, for about £6. There are also more simple snacks - omelettes, salads, soups - and a selection of puddings. Five wines by the 20cl glass.

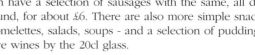

Essen

Once the centre of the coal and steel industry and home of the Krupp family, recently visited by Queen Elizabeth and Prince Philip. Evidence of its industrial past has been well disguised - the Baldeney Lake, once a scar of open-cast mining, is now filled with water from the Ruhr and surrounded by trees; it has been turned into one of the largest inland leisure resorts, hosting Germany's biggest inland sailing regatta.

Café Extrablatt

Kennedy Platz 5, 45127
Tel: 201 23 68 55
Open: 08.00-24.00 (Fri & Sat till 02.00)
A popular and successful café on two levels, which spreads into the enormous square (Essen's town centre is almost entirely post-war). A central bar commands a view of all its clientele, and hip hop music plays while young people sip their beer and wine and snack on wraps and bruschetta and pasta. There's also a long breakfast menu that includes an eat-as-much-as-you-like buffet. Lots of fruit for juicing, for breakfast and for cocktails. An older crowd fills the place at the weekend.

Café Rendezvous

Weberplatz 2
Tel: 201 20 06 74
Open: 11.00-01.00
A Greek-owned café serving Essen's expat Greek community, a role reflected in the food and drink on offer. It has a pleasant interior with an aspect through picture windows on to the square, where apartment blocks and a community centre are its neighbours. Lots of blue and white outside, for tables, chairs and awning, but it is only the appearance that is French.

Tapas

Theaterpassage 3, 45127
Tel: 201 23 74 16
Open: 09.00-01.00 (Fri & Sat till 02.00, Sun from 10.30)
A huge café-restaurant with a grand piano, leafy palms, an indoor fountain, and a big terrace partly under permanent canvas, partly shaded by pollarded plane trees in Hirschlandplatz behind. Tapas head the menu, but more substantial meals are also available. Weekends see live music entertainment on the terrace. The venue for the well-heeled, where stylish older ladies feel they can come unaccompanied.

Temple Bar

Saltzmarkt 1
Tel: 201 24 37 184
Open: 10.00-01.00 (winter from 12.00, Fri & Sat till 04.00)
Opened in 1990, and under the present German ownership for the last three years, it still gets Irish customers who remember it from the beginning, but now there's also plenty of local custom. Two of the three partners work in Joseph Music, and many of their international clientele are regulars at Temple Bar. Breakfast is served in the morning, and other snacks include baguettes, salads and pasta. It is renowned, of course, for its Guinness.

Frankfurt

Frankfurt boasts the largest airport in Europe after London Heathrow, a sign of its prosperity and its importance as a centre of banking and finance. There are concerts in the Alte Oper, shows at the International Theatre, a throbbing nightclub scene and plenty of cafés in the thriving shopping centres and the suburb of Sachsenhausen across the Main. And Goethe was born here in 1749.

Café au Lait/Bistro Maria

Am Weingarten 12, Bockenheim
Tel: 69 70 10 39
Open: 09.00-01.00 (Sun 10.00-18.00)

Out to the north-west of town, among the residential streets, is a narrow 'high street' called Leipzigerstrasse, at the top of which is Café au Lait, aka Bistro Maria. There's just enough room outside for a narrow line of pavement tables, while up some steps inside there's the bar and a good view through the windows. The place is renowned for its excellent variety of breakfasts, from the simple French at 3.20DM to the 'extrem' for two at 55DM. Apart from that, there is a daily card of hot and cold dishes, and a reasonable range of wines by the glass.

Café Bar 13

Am Wilhelmsplatz 13, Offenbach
Tel: 82 35 62 68
Open: 09.00-01.00 (Sat till 02.00)

Refreshments and meals are offered here from breakfast time to the cocktail hour; soups, salads, pasta, fish, vegetarian dishes and all sorts cooked in the wok. Specialities here include their breakfasts (5.50-14.50DM), starring the Sunday buffet served from 09.30 to 15.00; and their cocktail list, which is as cheap as you'll find in Frankfurt.

Chez Daniel

Brückenstrasse 35, Sachsenhausen
Tel: 69 61 82 47
Open: 10.00-01.00 (Sat & Sun from 17.00)

Located just south of the river from the old city centre, Chez Daniel is roomy, friendly and unashamedly French - the name is emblazoned across a tricolore. It is firmly established in the gastronomic centre of Frankfurt, with tables spilling out on to the pavement under aquamarine awnings. The menu is typified by snails in a calvados cream sauce, and bouillabaisse with all the trimmings, while simpler snacks take the form of filled baguettes. With an emphasis on the Alsace, the wines by the glass include riesling and pinot blanc; also edelzwicker (tokay by the bottle) and the German white sylvaner. Annual events here include an Alsace week and a French Bistro week.

Café Extrablatt

Bockenheimer Landstrasse 141, Bockenheim
Tel: 79 40 39 99
Open: 10.00-24.00

North-west of the city centre, in a district of reasonably-priced accommodation favoured by students and young single people, this new Extrablatt Café is in the modern idiom of a coffee house, and serves an extensive range of breakfasts, notably a buffet that extends to midday on weekdays and until 14.00 on Sundays. Other snacks include American/Italian dishes like pizzas, pasta and salads. The standard Extrablatt range of two red and two white wines by the glass, choice of beers, very good coffee and hot chocolate.

Holbein's

Holbeinstrasse 1, Sachsenhausen
Tel: 69 66 05 66 66
Open: 10.00-24.00
Closed: Mon

This very grand café-restaurant is the result of a collaboration between the gourmet Gregor Meyer and the well-known Frankfurt designers' guild. It stands in a mature garden, with imposing gates and glass walls extending up through three storeys; wide steps lead up to terrace tables with basket-weave chairs under parasols. Renowned for its seafood, this is the in place to eat in Frankfurt, to meet your friends for a prosecco in the heart of the gastronomic district, Sachsenhausen. If money's no object, stay on for Holbein's Menu Surprise at 69DM.

Café Karin

Grosse Hirschgraben 28
Tel: 69 29 52 17
Open: 09.00-01.00 (Fri & Sat till 02.00, Sun 10.00-19.00)

In the heart of the city, this is a busy café in classical style, with globe and chandelier lighting, comfortable round wooden tables, newspapers, and lots of people coming to meet friends to chat over a drink or a snack. Karin offers a range of breakfasts and a lunchtime menu, with dishes served by friendly, professional staff. A macaroon accompanies espresso served in the familiar gold-rimmed, green Apilco china; they even serve Ovaltine! The evenings attract thirsty locals with a decent variety of wines by the glass and good draught beer.

Café Liliput

Neue Kräme 29/Sandhof Passage
Tel: 69 28 57 27
Open: 09.00-22.00

Tucked away in a shopping arcade just off the Römerberg in the city centre, this is a typical little up-town café, small and cosy within, but also with a garden with flowers and shrubs. Drinks range from tea, coffee and hot chocolate to kir royal; for the hungry, three or four different cakes, a choice of soups and a variety of French and German breakfasts.

Living XXL

Kaiserstrasse 29
Tel: 69 24 29 37 10
Open: 11.30-01.00 (Fri till 03.00, Sat 16.00-03.00, Sun 19.00-02.00)

The middle of town is where Living is: facing the Theatre, by the Eurobank, Living XXL caters for those here for business or for culture. Look up through the glass roof and the Europe Tower looms above. This is skyscraper terrain. Fortunately, although it reaches out from the basement on two levels leading to the bar and terrace, its aspect is open space. The long bar facing you as you enter serves good espresso, several wines by the glass and draught beers. Downstairs is the restaurant, and a dance floor for evenings. Food is good and imaginative, from a rocket salad with tomato, mozzarella and pesto sauce to a large steak, salad and handcut chips. Sunday nights for the gay crowd, and their friends.

Opéra

Opernplatz 1/Alte Oper
Tel: 69 13 40 215
Open: 10.30-24.00 (restaurant 12.00-01.00)

The Frankfurt Opera house is an imposing building standing alone in a huge pedestrian piazza. To the right is a cluster of smart red parasols and traditional pavement tables that would look equally at home outside a Parisian café. Beyond them is the entrance to the Café Rosso, which with its highly ornate ceiling, smart bar, elegant tables and loose-covered chairs looks out through the tall windows. It feels immediately chic with the ruched curtains and patterned tile floor, elegant globe chandeliers and gilded ornamental plasterwork. Yet it is inexpensive, and the friendly professional service makes you feel comfortable at once. There's a simple menu including tomato soup, salad, Oriental chicken, rumpsteak, salmon (9-19.50DM). Espresso is 3.50DM, and wine by the glass is 8-14.50DM/20cl. The torte is luxuriant with fruit, nuts, cream and chocolate. Upstairs is Opéra, a larger and even more elegant room with even more to offer.

Cafébar Relativ

Friedberger Landstrasse 88, Nordend
Tel: 69 43 05 83 35
Open: 16.00-01.00 (Sat & Sun from 09.00, Sun till 24.00)

At weekends the Greek brothers Aristotle and Kosta offer a quick start breakfast of croissant with jam and coffee; or the substantial breakfast feast for two comprising a selection of salamis, cheeses, two eggs, fresh bread rolls and a glass of prosecco each. As the day wears on, Aristotle offers sweet and savoury crepes - spinach, garlic, tomato and sheep's cheese, tuna, onion and egg, while Kosta may serve you a glass of beer or chardonnay to wash it down. There's a daily evening menu offering chicken dishes, smoked salmon and a variety of pasta, with tiramisu to finish.

Schiffer Café

Schifferstrasse 36, Sachsenhausen
Tel: 69 61 99 32 21
Open: 08.00-20.00 (Sat till 19.00, Sun 09.00-19.00)

In the residential area, south of the River Main, stands this 'L'-shaped corner café-cum-larder. Behind the bar are shelves with some of those things that get forgotten on the shopping list, the biscuits, coffee and tea and drinking chocolate, jam and preserves, demerara sugar. A tiny amaretto biscuit accompanies the espresso, the coffee being from the excellent firm of Wacker. Wine by the 20cl glass. A good range of breakfasts is offered, and assorted blends of tea. A tall ceiling and a floor tiled in pale beige, create a good of feeling of space, and there's a rack of papers to read.

Schirn Café

Römerberg 6a
Tel: 69 29 17 32
Open: 11.00-01.00 (Sun till 24.00, Mon from 19.00)

Classical in the sense of high intellect, and artistic learning, this is in the centrally located Veranstalungs Gallery. A horseshoe central bar serves glass-topped coffee tables at the entrance to the right, and to the left, tall tables (pedestal swagged) and a grand piano stands; all is columns and curves, and beyond the bar are restaurant tables. Modern is the one word to sum up.

> "I smoke in moderation. Only one cigar at a time."
>
> **Mark Twain.**

Hamburg

Germany's first seaport, and one of the busiest in the world, Hamburg has known almost constant prosperity since it joined the Hanseatic League in 1358. The harbour area is well worth exploring, along with the city's innumerable galleries, and Hamburg is notably well endowed with lakes and parks. There's a strong tradition of theatre, opera and ballet, and a varied café-bar and nightlife scene.

Bobby Reich

Fernsicht 2
Tel: 40 487 824
Open: 10.00-24.00

There are two main lakes in the centre of the city, and Bobby Reich stands at the northern end of Aussalter, the larger. It's a great place to be in summer, when tables are set out across a raft terrace. The decor consists of variations on a musical theme with marine bits and pieces thrown in.

Die Brücke

Innocentiastrasse 82
Tel: 40 422 55 25
Open: 11.00-02.00 (Sun 19.00-24.00)

A bar-restaurant with a different appeal for every part of the day. Coffee and little snacks are served throughout the day, joined at noon for lunch with a largely business clientele. It's back to snacks until the early evening, when the dinner menu comes into operation (last orders 23.00). From mid-evening, a mainly young set takes over till the wee hours, transforming the atmosphere into that of a loud and trendy bar.

Eisenstein

Fridensallee 5
Tel: 40 390 46 06
Open: 11.00-01.30

In business for 12 very successful years, this trendy café-bar in a converted factory is set back from the road in a side street to the west of the Altstadt. Spacious and open-plan with a sweeping bar, it is part of modern shopping mall development – among the other shops is an excellent wine merchant. Pizza and pasta are the specialities, and Sunday brunch is served from 10.00 to 15.00. Plenty of outside seats.

Brasserie Gröninger

Ost-West-Strasse 47
Tel: 40 331 381
Open: 11.00-24.00 (Sat 17.00-02.00)
Closed: Sun

The cellar of the town brewery (which is still visible through glass panels) is the setting for this vast and atmospheric brasserie and the old brass brew-pots that were once part of the daily operations upstairs are now on display in the bar. The beer is available in anything from a small glass to a barrel holding 20 litres which is brought to your table on a stand for you and your party to help yourselves. Hearty German dishes provide the blotting paper.

Open

Eppendorferlandstrasse 31
Tel: 40 480 36 07
Open: 10.00-22.00 (Sat & Sun till 20.00)

A firm favourite with the locals, Open is a modern bar with marble bar-top and tables. Modern music (often Latin American) plays in the background and service is unrushed and unpretentious. The menu changes every fortnight.

Hanover

The capital of Lower Saxony is a city of immense appeal, a focal point for the arts as well as an important centre for conferences and trade fairs - it has just hosted World Exposition 2000, the first EXPO has come to Germany. The ties with Britain are strong, stemming from the Act of Settlement of 1701, which resulted in Georg Ludwig of Hanover becoming George 1 of England. Notable sights include the Royal Gardens of Herrenhausen, among the most spectacular in Europe.

Broker's Café

Nikolaistrasse 3
Tel: 511 169 61 55
Open: 09.00-01.00

In a central location, this is Hanover's first stock exchange café, where you can listen to broking gossip, while overhead the monitors flicker with news of the world's share movements. Specialist literature for the budding careerist is available for background information from New York through Frankfurt to Tokyo. At the bar you should find a remedy for share fever in a coffee, a glass of wine and a snack.

Café Casa Nova

Am Markt 12, 30159
Tel: 511 32 17 97
Open: 09.00-22.00 (Sun till 21.00)

Breakfast is an important meal in Germany, some say the most important, certainly in the cafés. Here there are several options, including goods from their own bakery. This modern café looks out on an ancient view of the now Lutheran 14th-century Church of Sts Jacob and George in the market square, centre of the old town. Another speciality is the selection of ice creams. Also on offer are soups and pasta, with which you can have a glass of wine.

Espada

Theaterstrasse 14
Tel: 511 32 23 89
Open: 09.00-02.00 (Fri & Sat till 03.00) kitchen open till 20.00 (Fri & Sat till 18.00)

The green marble-topped tables and their stools, both inside and out, and their terrace tables, invite you to enjoy the various offerings that start with a long breakfast list. Located near the Opera house, in the city centre, it's an ideal spot to come at coffee time for one of their home-made cakes. The interior is lit with art nouveau style lighting; there's a modern art picture on one wall, a torso sculpture on another. The copper-fronted, marble-topped bar displays the café's wares, and a spiral stair leads to the upper floor. An excellent daily-changing lunchtime menu offers spaghetti, tagliatelle, gnocchi and goulash, salads and crostini; specialities of the house include fillet steak, and tuna with a crust of almonds and breadcrumbs with the special Espada sauce. The wine list offers two white and two red by the 20cl glass (8-9.50DM), three more of each by the bottle and lots of champagne. A range of whiskies complements the selection of Cuban cigars. Good espresso. Newspapers. 'See and be seen' runs the nightcrowd motto.

Expo-Café

Ständehausstrasse 6
Tel: 511 882 000
Open: 09.00-24.00 (Sun from 10.00)

In 1870, Swiss-born Johann George Robby, impressed with the Great Exhibition in Paris with its cast-iron pavilions, came to Hanover and built one here on the junction with Georgstrasse. It was managed by a man called Wilhelm Kröpcke, who became so well known that the original café (now long gone) and the junction are now named after him. On the site now is Expo Café, so named as 2000 is the first year the World Exposition comes to Germany, and to Hanover in particular. A range of coffees from Java, Colombia, Ethiopia and Guatemala is available, also hot chocolate and a wide range of teas. Wines from around the world are available by the glass and some very special ones by the bottle (Luce 1993/4 Frescobaldi-Mondavi 180DM). Snacks and meals include a breakfast bar, a lunchtime salad buffet and an eat-as-much-as-you-like evening buffet.

Café Extrablatt

Grupenstrasse 2
Tel: 511 363 12 74
Open: 08.00-01.00 (Fri & Sat till 02.00, Sun from 10.00)
A quick coffee after a stroll through the shops per-haps? There's a pleasant atmosphere at this ideally placed café in the pedestrian area, where the break-fast menu is available throughout the day (7.90-16.90DM). Seating is on two floors, with more tables and chairs on the terrace outside. Other hot and cold snacks are always available, with extra choices from 10.00 till 14.00 on Sundays. A couple of white and red house wines are offered by the glass.

Fresko

Moltkeplatz 11, List 30163
Tel: 511 66 49 75
Open: 09.00-01.00 (Fri & Sat till 02.00)
On the square named after the Count, German Chief of Staff until 1916 (or his uncle before him, Chief of Staff for the Prussians), this spacious, high-ceilinged café is reminiscent of a Tuscan villa, with marbled walls, trompe l'oeil arches and a marble floor. There's a breakfast card (from mini to American) and a daily-changing lunch card, both of which are published for the whole week in advance. There's a range of coffees and cocoa drinks to go with them. The lunch menu includes a grilled fish platter with salad consisting of fillets of salmon, red snapper, 'exotic' fish and American catfish for 21DM. For snacks there are sand-wiches and crepes. A wide range of wines is available by the 10cl or 20cl glass. A private fenced-in terrace outside is inviting, and there are newspapers on sticks.

La Gauloise

Limburgstrasse 8
Tel: 511 363 13 72
Open: 08.00-22.00 (Sat till 18.00)
Closed: Sun
In what is one of the first and best street cafés in Hanover, Franz Rheinlander has been practising his French flair for over 20 years. A short pause between stressful shopping excursions can be rewarded with one of his cafés-au-lait and his très tasty baguettes. Breakfast is served between until 10.30 and there's a take-away service.

Georxx

Georgplatz 3, 30159
Tel: 511 30 61 47
Open: 09.30-01.00 (kitchen 12.00-23.00)
If you find yourself sauntering through the city centre, or your shopping's finished and packed away, make your way to Georxx opposite the Opera. In a long, tall, elegant room, the ceiling supported on pillars, and light streaming in through the windows, breakfast with the papers is served until 15.00, and later, nachos and pasta. In this civilised, metropolitan atmosphere, a milky coffee's a popular choice, while at night pros-ecco's the thing, or a glass from their international wine list - a Fetzer from California perhaps. Outside, on the broad pavement of the square, comfortably spaced tables invite you to take the sun.

Holländische Kakaostube

Ständerhausstrasse 2-3
Tel: 511 30 41 00
Open: 09.00-19.30 (Sat 08.30-17.00)
Closed: Sun
In 1895 Van Houten proudly opened the first cocoa-tasting house in Ständerhausstrasse, and his successor Friedrich Bartels inaugurated the Holländische Kakao-Stube in 1921. Eighty years on it's as popular as ever, and the clatter of cups, saucers and plates can be heard from the kitchen as the waitresses in blue aprons carry fully laden trays to the tables. Grandparents with their grandchildren, elegant matrons and younger folk come here to this most tra-ditional of cafés, a large, lofty room with simple chan-delier lighting and blue-and-white tiles depicting windmills, sailing ships and lighthouses. There's a wide range of teas: Darjeeling, Ceylon, Assam, green, mint and camomile; coffee and, naturally, hot choco-late (kakao) with or without alcohol. Then there's the pleasant problem of choosing what to eat - a cake, perhaps, or something savoury like an onion or leek tart or a bowl of nourishing oxtail soup. But the Kakaostube is much more than just a place of refresh-ment, it's a step back into the gentler, more civilised days before the war. The wines by the glass include pinot grigio, edelzwicker (pinot blanc/gewürtz), ries-ling, spätburgunder and a rosé. Breakfasts cater for all appetites, and other choices include salads, herren-toast, pasta and kartoffelgratin; the speciality ice creams and milk shakes should not be missed.
Germany Café of the Year 2001

Café International

Ottenstrasse 1, Linden
Tel: 511 210 79 42
Open: 17.00-01.00 (Sun from 10.00)
Closed: Mon

A colourful scene of culinary art is what you get at Café International, tucked away in the suburb of Linden. The menu is testament to its international claim - its house speciality is Kazakhstan cuisine. Particularly pleasing is that these people have initiated the backing of a child culture programme, and to underscore that they stage culture events on Thursdays. On a corner site, the interior is decorated with lots of plants, and outside there's a fenced-off area for terrace tables.

Café K

Egestorffstrasse 18, Linden
Tel: 511 21 34 49 6
Open: 10.00-01.00

This long narrow café in the centre of Linden suburb is especially popular at the weekends and on Sundays you should plan on a long wait to get one of the sought-after tables, unless you get there early. The breakfasts are positively sumptuous. Proprietor, Ralf Schnorr, offers an espresso for 2.60DM (a home-made praline is given away with each hot drink), and wonderful cakes, which are his passion (try the raspberry cheesecake). There are tables under parasols and under the tree on the pavement opposite the entrance. Inside, the new interior designed by Sarah Atashfashan, is a well-lit terracotta with quarry tiles to match. Three white and three red wines are served by the 20cl glass, as well as prosecco. A well-priced daily lunch menu (available from noon) changes every week.

Café Konrad

Knochenhauerstrasse 34, 30159
Tel: 511 32 36 66
Open: 10.00-24.00 (Fri Sat till 01.00)

Part of the gay scene in the old part of town, but Café Konrad attracts a mixed crowd who fill the place, chatting and laughing and joking. In a narrow pedestrian shopping street, it's always busy, so getting a seat is a matter of luck. The café opens on to the street, and the customers spill out among the blue plastic garden chairs and tables. Breakfasts are a feature, the various combinations named after stars of stage and screen, Edith Piaf, Bette Midler, Gina Lollabrigida, Barbara Rütting, and strangely (for two) the Weather Girls. Also popular are the large white bowls of frothing coffee. Wines by the glass, and snacks include filled baguettes, salads and pasta. There's also a special dish of the week.

Kramer's 12

Kramerstrasse 12
Tel: 511 300 80 88
Open: 10.00-24.00

Daily from opening time there's a super breakfast menu, with a brunch at weekends. During a stroll around the city centre, drop in for a snack - soups, salads, baked potatoes with fillings such as North Sea crab, and other things. Summertime encourages them to offer great cocktails (try frozen daiquiri) and ice creams.

Café Lohengrin

Sedanstrasse 35, List 30161
Tel: 511 33 28 35
Open: 09.00-00.30 (Fri & Sat till 01.00, Sun 10.00-23.30)

Smart suburban café run by energetic ladies, and their girls: there are rose marble table-tops and window sills, and lots of plants, magazines (for women) and newspapers (for men). Off the shopping street bordering the residential streets around, it captures breakfasters and a lunchtime trade who can look forward to soups, salads and dishes of the day, and a long wine list - 11 white, six red and a rosé served in 10cl, 20cl or half-litre measures. For fair-weather days there's a fenced-in terrace bordered by flowering plants.

Naoum's

Hildesheimerstrasse 81, Südstadt 30169
Tel: 511 980 54 28
Open: 09.00-01.00 (Fri & Sat till 02.00, Sat & Sun from 11.00)

Hildesheimer street is a long, wide and busy road running south out of the city centre, a desert for café lovers. Until you reach Naoum's. This new establishment fills that void. Italian-designed, with attractive use of leather and marble, mirrors and curves, it has a sense of spaciousness enhanced by doors that open on to the pavement, where tables and chairs are set. Snacks include pizzas, sandwiches and pasta. A speciality for the evenings is a range of cocktails mixed by manager Georgios.

Das Neue Kaffeehaus

Schillerstrasse 34
Tel: 511 32 33 62
Open: 09.00-23.00 (kitchen 11.00-21.00)
Closed: Sun

This inner-city traditional café offers various cakes, cream tarts and other bakery from 09.00, as well as a huge breakfast bar. The big choice of salads, and the deliciously filled baguettes are an ideal reason for a pause in shopping. Now and then there's live music, and there's a take-away service. Best to book on Saturdays.

Café Tabac

Ferdinand-Wallbrecht strasse 44, List 30163
Tel: 511 66 94 59
Open: 09.00-01.30 (Fri & Sat till 02.30, Sun from 09.30)
A long breakfast menu and a short lunch menu, on Sundays a buffet till 15.00. Lunch includes gnocchi/pasta in tomato sauce and filled baked potatoes. Purple is the thread linking the conservatory (or wintergarten) to the bar into the café room, and outside in the leafy avenue there are terrace tables. Five wines from France, four from Italy, rosé from Germany and an Austrian are offered by 10cl glass.

Teestübchen

Ballhofstrasse 10, 30159
Tel: 511 363 16 82
Open: 10.00-01.00 (Fri & Sat till 02.00)
Established in 1970, and still in the same family, there is a comfortable Victorian feel to the building, but on a busy weekend the staff have a struggle to keep up with demand - even Madame helps out. The coffee is good, but the real speciality is the tea list. The tall lidded cup of hot water is delivered, within a strainer containing the tea of your choice (no bags here), the reversed lid becomes a saucer for it when the brew has reached the required strength. Big fluffy homemade slices of cake accompany, or a glass of wine or prosecco. Takeaway available. On Saturdays, live jazz is played between 11.00 and 15.00.

Victors

Lister Meile 10/Friesenstrasse 14, Oststadt
Tel: 511 38 76 00
Open: 09.00-02.00 (Thur till 03.00, Fri & Sat till 05.00)
Victors is a real all-rounder - during the day a café-cum-restaurant, in the evening a bar, and at night a pulsing club. This is a spacious corner site with its own extensive pavement area, light wood and royal blue livery, sandy beige walls and glass shade uplighters. The daily menu, published for the week, includes (in season) the delight of comparing the white asparagus and the green. The wine list offers two whites, two reds and a rosé.

Wiener Café

Ernst August Platz 4
Tel: 511 368 3120
Open: 06.30-21.00
A classic Vienna-style café on several levels round a corner site, offering a range of rich cakes and pastries to eat in or take away. For the former, there's also a range of baguettes and other snacks, and a fine list of wines by the glass from five German regions, Austria, Italy and France. Smartly aproned ladies serve at inside tables with two tablecloths, or out on the terrace looking across the square towards the main line station. Most of the customers are in their 50s or older. They feel comfortable and relaxed here: it's not the sort of place to attract rowdy youths!

Magdeburg

On the River Elbe, the ancient capital of Saxony Anhalt has some fine historic buildings. The Cathedral of St Maurice and St Catherine, begun in the 13th century, is the first major example of Gothic architecture in Germany, while the Central Post Office is an example of late Dutch Gothic. A fountain commemorates one of Magdeburg's most famous sons, the natural scientist Otto von Guerice. The city has strong links with Protestantism and Martin Luther.

Alex

Ulrichplatz 1, Altstadt 39104
Tel: 391 5 43 32 16
Open: 08.00-01.00 (Sat till 03.00, Sun from 09.00)
This new café-bar is set on two floors with a full glass frontage at the fountain in a large square in the old city centre. The fountain is a splendid affair, and can be refreshingly enjoyed at close quarters from the terrace tables (seating 400 in summer!). The terrace is the best place to be, especially on warm weekends, but otherwise the upper floor has the best view. In the mornings they offer a breakfast buffet, including everything from a fruit yoghurt to the full works with meat, cheese, eggs and cereals. During the day it has a bistro character and is frequented by the older crowd. In the evenings, however, the young take over and make it their own.

Altstadtcafé

Erzbergerstrasse 11, Altstadt
Tel: 391 5 31 33 16
Open: 11.30-22.00 (Sat & Sun from 13.00)
A relatively new café, unfortunately overlooking the ugly city treasury building. But its saving grace is the little beer garden hidden away at the back, where guests can escape the view and the traffic noise. Coffee very reasonably priced at 2DM, and cakes from 3DM.

Babylon

Ulrichplatz 10, Altstadt 39104
Tel: 391 5 31 32 36
Open: 11.00-24.00 (Sat till 02.00)
Situated next door to Palazzo in Otto von Guericke strasse, Babylon offers Magdeburg its first taste of Iraqi food; indeed, it is probably unique in the whole of Sachsen Anhalt (the region of which Magdeburg is the capital). The really fresh, appetising Arab cuisine includes home-made falafel and houmous, but also some of the ancient Mesopotamian recipes using potato, rice and cracked wheat, as in tabbouleh. And the prices are good, starters 5-12DM, main dishes (which are substantial) 8.50-16DM.

Le Cochon

Hegelstrasse 39, Altstadt 39104
Tel: 391 5 41 98 57
Open: 09.00-24.00
Since opening in 1995, Le Cochon has been consistently the best and most popular French restaurant in Magdeburg, and now an à la carte breakfast menu adds to the attraction. It's a modern building set in a broad cobbled street of elegant houses, but behind the ordinary facade Le Cochon has the friendliness and charm of a well-loved home. The style is reminiscent of a Parisian bistro, yet more intimate, more polished, with candle-lit, lacquered tables comfortably spaced. Outside on the open-air terrace there are comfortable basket-weave chairs and tables under scarlet awnings. Good coffee, excellent wine list.

Deep

Breiter weg 231, Altstadt
Tel: 171 3 84 68 47
Open: 20.00-01.00 (Fri & Sat till 02.00)
A few steps lead down to the entrance to Deep, a night-time lounge-café-bar created by Guido Maiwald. The busiest nights are Tuesday and Friday, when local DJs spin their vinyl magic, tripping from Pop to House music and back. On the walls is an ever-changing display of works by local artists. The speciality is the cocktail list, at astonishingly low prices.

Café am Dom

Breiter weg 213, Altstadt
Tel: 391 5 43 28 50
Open: 09.00-20.00 (Sat & Sun from 11.00)

This slightly pompously named 'Café at the Cathedral' has been around since 1985. As you enter you pass a piece of bronze artwork by Heinrich Apel labelled 'The Sins of Mankind', the main sin likely to be committed here is to break your diet and try the delicious hot apple strudel - their popular speciality. Other items on the extensive menu run from a bowl of soup to a grand dish of pork steak with mushrooms. Occupying a corner site, the café has a permanently extended glazed terrace that looks towards the Cathedral of St Maurice and St Catherine, which was begun in the 13th century.

Café Extrablatt

Maxim Gorki strasse 24b, Stadtfeld
Tel: 391 7 33 82 42
Open: 09.00-21.00 (Sun 10.00-20.00)

Very different from the trendy hip hop image further west, this café is located in the desirable residential suburb of Stadtfeld. The formal tables with lacy cloths greet you as you enter the corner of the building, while towards the bar is a reading table laden with magazines and newspapers from all over Germany, all neatly laid out. These are the ideal accompaniment to breakfast, served à la carte. The range of publications reflects the proximity of the local Education Institute and the High School. The customers are smartly casual, the music subdued and the waitress mature. Cakes, ices, good lunch card and evening menu.

Flair

Breiter weg 21, Altstadt 39104
Tel: 391 5 61 89 55
Open: 08.30-01.00 (Sat till 02.00, Sun 10.00-24.00)

Spawned by the same owners as *Le Frog* (qv), with a customer base that changes with the time of day: up to and around lunch time the older crowd come in for their coffee and cakes, while the evenings attract the pleasure seekers intent on beer and wine, which, in summer, can be enjoyed on the terrace seated in basket-work armchairs. Ices and cakes; speciality: a combination of both. Tasty regional cooking and a breakfast buffet.

Le Frog

Heinrich Heine platz 1, Stadtpark 39114
Tel: 391 5 31 35 56
Open: 11.00-24.00 (Sun from 10.00)

Le Frog, which opened in 1999 replacing some unsightly kiosks, stands in the park on the Island of Rotehorn in the middle of the River Elbe, among mature chestnut trees on the shore of the Adolf Mittag lake. It enjoys splendid views through its floor-to-ceiling glass on three sides, the fourth being the bar with the kitchen behind. The ambience and the offerings change with the seasons. In winter the customers snuggle up inside by the fire, while on busy summer days everyone moves outside, through the fully opening glass doors, and service is complemented by an extra bar among the slatted bench seating - orange is the theme colour. First eats are breakfasts; at lunchtime the menu starts with excellent soup, and other choices among the many dishes both traditional and imaginatively modern include a cheese platter of which they are justly proud. Several wines are offered by 20cl elegant glasses, including a Californian cabernet sauvignon. Good espresso and a large range of teas. Once a month there's a 'Big Frog Night' with live music, and on Sundays a band plays in a nearby pavilion.

George

Breiter weg 214, Altstadt 39104
Tel: 391 5 31 47 30
Open: 08.30-01.00

Very new, George is in the Bundesbank building, opposite the imposing Cathedral, which is currently undergoing restoration and cleaning. The decor is light wood, aluminium and blue, and the food offerings are pan-European, emphasis being on the Mediterranean, with wines also from southern Europe: Côtes du Rhône 20cl in a large balloon 7.50DM. Mornings offer a big breakfast buffet, lunchtimes a hot buffet - pasta, excellent paella, bouillabaisse - and at weekends the brunch is very popular. The espresso is also good, and the staff are friendly and eager to please.

"Happiness? A good cigar, a good meal, a good cigar and a good woman – or a bad woman; it depends on how much happiness you can handle."

George Burns

Café in der Goethestrasse

Goethestrasse 5, Stadtfeld
Tel: 391 5 32 90 07
Open: 12.00-22.00 (Sun 14.00-19.00)
Closed: Sat

A quiet, sedate little local café in a treelined avenue, offering newspapers on sticks to be pored over with a glass of wine or an espresso at lacquered tables, each set with a doily and small bunch of honeysuckle. Classical music plays gently, and candles are lit at your table as mein host Klaus Jürgen Mansfeld or Ulrika Knape serves. The customers here are all locals, but the occasional stranger is always greeted with courtesy and charm. Snacks include cakes, toast, salads and some simple dishes, all of which can be enjoyed inside or on the tiny terrace in the front among the trees.

Hemmingway

Breiter weg 227, Altstadt
Tel: 391 5 31 34 42
Open: from 17.00-late

What's this, the Buena Vista Social Club in Magdeburg? It could be, as far as living life to the full is concerned. In the Hemmingway you can at least get a mojito or a margarita and dance the night away. From street level the reveller takes the long stairs down into the bar to be engulfed by Salsa rhythm. The place is full to bursting at the weekends, with many coming to watch the dancing. The bar offers a large range of cocktails, and, until 02.00, a selection of Cuban, Spanish and Creole dishes.

Kokospalme

Uniplatz/Gareisstrasse 15, Altstadt
Tel: 391 5 61 05 74
Open: 10.00-18.00 (Thur & Fri till 24.00, Sat 15.00-24.00, Sun from 14.00-18.00)

For ten years now many Magdeburgers have frequented the Kokospalme café, following it to this busy square when it relocated in 1993. While the traffic whirrs around the square, the café-goer can be found relaxing here in his velvet upholstered chair, enjoying a traditional *baumkuche* (a spit-baked cake looking like a tree trunk) and supping a cup of coffee or a glass of ale. Fresh cakes daily, lots of coffee options and cooling ices.

Mausefalle

Breiter weg 224, Altstadt
Tel: 391 5 43 01 35
Open: 08.30-03.00

Mausefalle, meaning mousetrap but also a play on the proprietor's name, now opens up on weekdays for breakfast (08.30-12.00): the 'super breakfast' includes rolls, salami, cheese, jam, coffee, orange juice (or sekt), and boiled or scrambled egg, and costs just 9.50DM. Before midday the sun shines on the street terrace, and in the evenings the clientele, from the young crowd to the suits and ties, meet at the long bar counter. Detlef Maus, celebrated for his skill in cocktail making, now leaves it to the young barmaids. Every Saturday, there's a different special cocktail for only 5DM, and a disco to lift the party mood.

Palazzo

Ulrichplatz 10, Aldstadt
Tel: 391 5 31 32 33
Open: 09.00-24.00 (Fri & Sat till 02.00)

In an unprepossessing postwar government building, Abdul Mijthab has, at great expense, created a splendid art nouveau-style café. From the first, Palazzo has been on everybody's lips, and not just figuratively, because the elaborately decorated ice cream sundaes are truly special. At 10DM they offer great value for money, and the Palazzo bowl of ice cream for eight (50DM) has to be seen to be believed. Since ice cream is not everyone's cup of tea in the morning, Abdul also offers a wide choice of breakfasts. Draught beers, limited wine list. Next door to *Babylon* (qv).

Café Pfeiffer

Ulrichplatz 1
Tel: 391 5 62 03 55
Open: 09.00-19.00 (Sun 14.00-18.00)

The time-honoured, traditional combination of Café and Patisserie (Konditorei) is alive, well and in very safe hands in Café Pfeiffer. But this is also an ice cream specialist and in your comfortable basket chair you can enjoy the magic they do when they mix ice cream with drinks. Next door to *Alex* (qv).

"I only smoke cigars with people I trust."
Saddam Hussein.

Rathaus Café

Alten Markt, Altstadt
Tel: 391 5 61 19 37
Open: 10.00-22.00 (Sun till 20.00)

There's been a Rathaus Kaffee here for generations, and the tradition happily lives on in this building, a reconstruction of one destroyed in the war. Outside, the market stalls offer clothes, flowers, fruit, vegetables and meat. In Rathaus you can eat in the traditional way: tomato, broccoli, mushroom or goulash soup, salads, eggs and ham, pasta (here nudeln), a cheese and cold meat platter, fish, pork and beef steaks - hearty, rib-sticking stuff. German wines by the glass 6.50DM, espresso 3.50DM, plain coffee 2.80DM. The customers are almost all local, and of all ages.

Café Yellow

Immermannstrasse 35, Stadtfeld
Tel: 391 5 39 19 64
Open: 11.00-20.00 (Sat till 22.00)

A brightly decorated café in the quiet, tree-lined suburban street across the railway lines and the ring road from the old city centre. A very agreeable half-hour can be spent sitting on the terrace enjoying an ice cream and a cake.

Munich

The capital of Bavaria, its links are more with the Mediterranean way of life than with northern Europe, a fact reflected in its markets, its cuisine and the outlook of its people. Located on the River Isar, it is no distance from Strasbourg in France, Salzburg in Austria, Bolzano in Italy and Zurich in Switzerland. Nearby are great lakes and the Alps. All these influences are evident in the townspeople's attitude to life and in their café society.

Arzmiller Konditorei-Café

Salvatorstrasse 2, 8000-2
Tal 11, Böhmler-Passage
Tel: 89 29 42 73
Open: 08.00-18.30 (Sat 09.00-18.00)
Closed: Sun

These two patisserie outlets are difficult to find, tucked away as they are, the first in the inner courtyard of the Theatinerhof (theatre house), and the other through the shopping arcade Böhmler. They both use the very good Alfredo coffee, which can be enriched with one of their wide range of pastries and cakes. There's a large offering of alcoholic drinks, which can be enjoyed away from the hubbub of traffic in these secluded pedestrian areas.

Café am Beethoven platz

Goethestrasse 51, 80336
Tel: 89 54 40 43 48
Open: 09.00-01.00

Established in 1899, this is a Konzertcafé, and one that sells good beer, good wine (14 wines available by the glass), tasty pastries and other meals too, salads and dishes of the day, and a good espresso. It has had a chequered history - at one time it was an American nightclub - but for the last 20 years it's been a concert café. A bust of Beethoven stands in the middle of the café, and there's a grand piano just inside the door. Live music most nights, usually starting around 19.30.

Kaffee Dukatz

Literaturhaus, Salvatorplatz 1, 80333
Tel: 89 29 19 60-0
Open: 10.00-01.00

A very large and busy café-bar-restaurant in the Literaturhaus, with a balcony built above and behind the bar under the long, high-vaulted ceiling. The style is very French - behind the bar are bottles of pastis, calvados, cognac and armagnac, and also on display is the standard document summarising the French regulations regarding the sale of liquor to minors. People come here to read, chat, meet, have lunch... mid-afternoon the place is buzzing, with all the staff busy. Opened in the spring of 1997, this is the 'in' place for the 30- and 40-year-olds. Newspapers on sticks. Meals are served 12.00 to 14.30 and 18.30 to 23.00.

Faun

Hans Sachs strasse 17
Tel: 89 263 798
Open: 10.00-01.00 (Fri & Sat till 02.00)

On the apex of a fork in the road with Jahnstrasse, this busy, busy bar, formerly a discothèque, was established in 1994 and is a great favourite with the 20s and 30s. The bar and tables are in light oak, the ceiling high, with art nouveau decor in aquamarine. There's plenty of seating at tables or on bar stools, and the slatted chairs and tables outside are always popular. Breakfast is served from 10.00 to 16.00, and at weekends until 21.00! The main menu offers a good selection of dishes, including some game (rabbit, duck, venison), and two lunchtime specials widen the choice. Beers start at 2.80DM for half a litre, wines at 7.50DM for a 20cl glass; there's a range of teas, and good espresso is 3.50DM. Many regulars drink the Munich Weissbier - it's bottled and comes up cloudy. Lots of newspapers and magazines on sticks if you're alone, but on Friday nights everyone talks to everyone.

Café Freiheit

Leonrodstrasse 20
Tel: 89 134 686
Open: 09.00-01.00

Going northwest from the centre of town towards the Schloss Nymhenburg, in the Neuhausen district, is this comfortable café run by affable young girls and with a clientele of both local residents and students. The all-Italian wine list comprises 12 white wines, 14 reds and a rosé, and there are special promotions each month, perhaps Grattamacco, Castegnetto Carducci among the whites, and Chianti Castelnuovo Bernardegna for a red. The breakfast menu is served until 16.00 and dinner from 18.00. They do a fixed-price menu for 36DM for three courses. Bossanova music plays in the background. Outside tables in the summer.

Glockenspiel Café

Marienplatz 28
Tel: 89 264 256
Open: 10.00-01.00
Closed: Sun in Jul & Aug

The entrance is in Rosenstrasse through an arcade, almost next door to the Metropolitan, and on the fifth floor, but at the back of the building, it is a terrace bar (with a canopy for winter). Slatted bench seating and wicker chairs were designed to give it a Mediterranean feel, assisted by Spanish music playing. Espresso 3.50DM, latte machiato 5.60DM. Lots of beers and wines - and of course, cocktails - are available with light snacks. The restaurant at the front of the building faces the Glockenspiel.

Iwan

Josephspitalstrasse 15
Tel: 89 554 933
Open: 12.00-02.00 (Sun from 17.00)

On the ring road, but happily in a courtyard away from the traffic, and with terrace tables around a wide dish fountain, Iwan is located behind the Swedish Embassy, and in the same building. It is essentially a wine bar - but there are no German bottles except their sekt. There's wine from France, Portugal, Italy and Spain; snacks are available, there's a salad bar and pasta dishes are served at lunchtime. Jazz/swing music plays. The tables, bar and bar front feature lots of steely grey granite, and in the day the light streams through the virtually all-glass outside wall, while at night the red lighting over the bar creates an intimate atmosphere. Lots of bar stools, little snacks served free 21.50-23.50, balcony restaurant over the ground-floor bar.

Café Luitpold

Briennerstrasse 11
Tel: 89 292 865
Open: 09.00-18.00 (Sat 08.00-19.00)

Originally opened in 1888, this was Munich's answer to the famous cafés in Paris, Vienna and Berlin, and bears the name of the then Prince Regent of Bavaria. A venue favoured from the beginning by aristocracy and literary figures, and later by musicians and artists, the café of those early years was destroyed by fire at the end of the Second World War. The rebuilding, later to incorporate the petites boutiques of well-known high street names in the 1989 refurbishment, was initiated by the Buchner family, who became owners in 1960. Paul, a confectioner, ran the café for some 26 years, and in 1989 handed over its management to Gerhard Brenner, master confectioner. Paul's daughter Tina carries on the tradition, being part of the administration since 1994. It is a very large café with a patisserie in the middle, and tables extend into an inner courtyard where businessmen, shoppers and tourists flock in for lunch.

Metropolitan Café

Marienplatz 22
Tel: 89 230 970
Open: 09.00-01.00 (Sun from 10.00)

Taking up the top two floors of the Metropolitan building, and reached by a fast glass lift, the café overlooks the Marienplatz, the scene of many a dramatic event in Munich's history. Uppermost is the café-bar and cocktails, below, the restaurant. In the square there are also bench café tables. Directly in front is the exotic clock where, when it strikes 11 o'clock (and also 5 o'clock on summer afternoons), two groups of figures perform, one above the other. The first re-enacts the tournament held at the wedding of Renata of Lorraine to Duke Wilhelm V, while the second commemorates the coopers' dance celebrating the exorcism of the Plague of 1517. The very elegant, airy, modern bar-café has royal blue suede chairs and beech-topped tables on stainless steel frames, recessed low-voltage ceiling lighting, and tall windows to the floor to make the most of the view. Among the items on offer are coffee, six types of tea, and a choice of eight breakfasts. The light lunch menu reflects the very international feel here in Munich.

Luigi Tambosi am Hofgarten

Odeonsplatz 18, 80539
Tel: 89 29 83 22
Open: 09.00-01.00

This was once called Annast but changed hands in July 1997. German owned, it is named after a well-known Italian who opened the first café here in Munich some 200 years ago (and now long gone). Next door is the spectacular Hofgarten and Palace. Across the road Versace and other top designers have their shops. Food is available, and the style is very Mediterranean, with the emphasis on French and Italian cuisine. Tables are set in the Hofgarten, and there's a terrace at the front, while inside, the velvet-clad chairs sit at little marble tables and a sweeping gallery served by a spiral staircase looks down on the pleasant scene. A small upright piano stands in one corner, *Bolero* builds to its climax in the background. Pepe, the Italian barman, says the new style is very popular.

Münchner Kartoffelhaus

Hochbrückenstrasse 3
Tel: 89 296 331
Open: 11.30-01.00
Closed: Sun

In 1995 Ralph Beister opened this bar-cum-restaurant, where the potato is King - boiled, sauteéd, mashed and especially baked. There's even potato pasta and, of course, potato schnapps! A charming, tall German, with excellent English, he says there are lots of baked potato restaurants in the north of the city, but his was the first; it's in the centre, and it has style. A good selection of beers is served at the oak bar, which gets very busy as the evening wears on. Hot food is served non-stop from opening time through to 23.30. Baked potatoes cost from 10DM with soured cream, to 20.50DM served with pork and mushrooms. There are also dishes like veal or smoked salmon, but you can gamble all your chips that potatoes will creep in somewhere.

Café Reitschule

Königstrasse 34
Tel: 89 333 402
Open: 09.00-01.00

To the north and east of the city centre, the university riding school is beside the Englischer Garten (actually designed by an American with British sympathies by the name of Benjamin Thompson). It has a very big café, bar, restaurant and terrace overlooking the stables, and inside there's a window through which you can watch the indoor school. The long bar is towards the middle, with dining at one end (about 30 covers) and the café at the other (60 covers); the terrace is at the back. Some typical dishes on the menu: spinach soup, cold meats and salads, spaghetti, lamb provençale. Two-course set lunch, weekend brunch. Newspapers are provided.

Café Roma

Maximilianstrasse 31, 80539
Tel: 89 22 74 35
Open: 08.00-03.00

A spacious café with lots of tables outside under large awnings, with space heaters for warmth. This is the beginning of fashion street - all the top names have premises - and the Munich Kempinski is also here, so the faces are here, too. A common scene in the morning is peaceful newspaper reading. As the day wears on the lunchers arrive, and later on the fun starts, with wine lovers, indeed lovers, coming to sip and laugh with their friends. No visit to such a city by the jet-set would be complete without a stylish Italian watering hole, and Roma fits the bill perfectly.

Schlosscafé im Palmenhaus

Schloss Nymphenburg Eingang 43
Tel: 89 175 309
Open: 09.00-18.00 (summer till 18.30)

A very elegant café occupying the long side of the lofty glass palm house in the grounds of the magnificent castle. Take a stroll through the well-groomed symmetrical gardens, with their moat and lakes, before passing through the tall hedge into an enclosed garden with the Palmenhaus and its terrace. The café is a very popular venue, especially at the weekend; on Sundays between 10.00 and 14.00 they play live music, with performers such as the Trio Westend, Roy's Good Time Band, Günter Mayer's Band, and The Souvenirs playing 'Jazz for Breakfast'. The leaseholder is Johann Schmidbauer, who also runs the Botanischengarten Café in Menzingerstrasse.

Schumann's American Bar

Maximilianstrasse 36, 80539
Tel: 89 229 268
Open: 17.00-03.00 (Sun from 18.00)
Closed: Sat

Charles Schumann established this American-style cocktail bar in January 1982. A prolific author on American cocktails, and of stories around them (*Tropical Bar Book*; *Artistry of Mixing Drinks*; *Whisk(e)y Lexicon*), he has decorated the bar in black, with mirrors: the bar, the stools and the tables are all black, and the cupboards and wood panelling are stained dark brown going to black at the frames. The lighting is carefully directed to light surfaces, while maintaining the intimate club-like atmosphere, underscored by gentle jazz piano music. Early evening visitors are besuited businessmen and some elegant couples. There's an impressive list of single malts, and several champagnes, and a coffee costs 4.50DM. Eurosport TV plays silently above the bar.

Café Venezia

Lenbachplatz 8
Tel: 89 545 949
Open: 08.00-24.00

This Mövenpick restaurant offers the same menu in rooms with different decorative themes, all within the same building: the Venetian room has elaborate decor in the Italian Renaissance style. Breakfasts are served from 08.00 till noon, lunch from 11.00, and there's something to eat at any time of day. Mövenpick restaurants, all very popular, can be found all around the country.

Woerner's Café am Dom

Marienplatz 1
Tel: 89 222 7666
Open: 08.00-19.30 (Sat till 18.00, Sun 10.00-18.00)

A smart first-floor café with cream-painted tables and chairs with floral upholstery in dark green, blue and terracotta colours. They sell excellent pastries - a selection from their shop downstairs - and splendid chocolates and pralines. Cut glass chandeliers and smart modern brass wall lights give the room a bright feel and atmosphere. All ages come here, some while on business, some taking a break from shopping, others just to meet up in the centre of town.

Münster

Little changed down the years and largely unaffected by the last war, Munster is a deeply religious city - its name means monastery - and a city of learning with the country's third largest university. It is also known for the breeding of horses. Just a few minutes' walk from the centre is the lovely Aasee Park and its boating lake. One of the treasures in the cathedral is an astronomical clock dating from 1540.

Alex Brasserie

Salzstrasse 35, 48143
Tel: 251 4 01 56
Open: 09.00-01.00 (Fri & Sat till 03.00)

On the perimeter of the old town, by the leafy promenade that runs along what was the moat boundary, Alex is Parisian in style. A long sweeping bar has a buffet for breakfast and lunch, including a tempting display of cakes and pastries; there are filled baguettes, salads and pasta, with pork and beef steaks for the bigger appetite, and a range of teas, coffees and wines to accompany. Families come in the daytime, couples and singles too, and on fine evenings the customers spill outside on to the terrace tables.

Café Extrablatt

Königstrasse 31
Tel: 251 4 33 06
Open: 08.30-01.00 (Sun from 10.00, Sat 09.00-02.00)

This expanding café concept is increasingly popular across all age groups. Here, as in all the outlets, they offer breakfasts daily, light ones on Saturdays, and brunch on Sundays. During the rest of the day there is a standard card of drinks and snacks: coffee, beers in the larger 30cl glass, two red and two white wines by the glass, soups, 'pick and dip'. The doors fold back on one side, allowing the café to spill out on to the street; the floor-to-ceiling windows on the other give a feeling of light and space. The combination of bentwood chairs here and cane there, bench seating against the walls, and stools at the bar give the relatively small site a number of dimensions as well as choice.

G.A.S.O.L.I.N.

Aegidiistrasse 45, 48143
Tel: 251 5 10 58 97
Open: 11.00-03.00

A pavilion in the round with decking outside for trestles and benches, offering light breakfasts, sandwiches, soups, nachos and olives, espresso coffee, and a horseshoe bar serving several beers and house wines. A firm favourite with the students, who park their bikes in the stands outside. This was originally a petrol station - hence the look and the name.

Grotemeyer

Salzstrasse 24, 48143
Tel: 251 4 24 77
Open: 09.00-19.00 (Sat till 18.00, Sun from 10.00)

The classic Viennese Konditorei, with coffee and cakes the treat. Established in 1850, it faces one of the most noble residences in town - the Erbdrostenhof, built in 1753-57 by Johann Conrad Schlaun in the Baroque style, and the setting for the Baroque Festival in June (the building was destroyed in the war and rebuilt to the original plans; it is now the home of the State Curator). On entering the café past the pavement tables, visitors first see the shop that elegantly displays its wares in glass cabinets set in pink marble on a marble floor. Beyond is a large room with a high ceiling and chandelier lighting, where the mature burghers of Münster come for traditional refreshment.

Marktcafé

Domplatz 6-7
Tel: 251 5 75 85
Open: 08.00-01.00 (Sun & Mon from 10.00)
Opposite the Cathedral, across the expanse of the cobbled square where the market is held every date except Sunday and Monday, the centre of activity is this fine café with its wide frontage. Its spacious room, which was once part of the Central Post Office next door, is served by bars at both ends; the flow of young people is constant, the babble of conversation continuous. Inside are plain laminated tables, and out at the front under awnings, and at the back in the garden terrace under umbrellas are aluminium and basket-weave chairs with their tables. After breakfast, the menu extends to soups, salads and filled baguettes, with a dish of the day, and in season a range of mushroom dishes (*pfifferlinge*).

Moccad'or Caffé-Bar-Bistro

Lütke Gasse 21, Rothenburg im Deilmannhof 48143
Tel: 251 4 49 91
Open: 08.00-01.00
A great café, but you should book if you want a table in the evenings - or else take pot luck at the bar. It stands in a passage off a main shopping street in the old town centre, and the surprise is how spacious it is, the bar with a long table for communal enjoyment leading to café tables looking on to the courtyard through wide arched windows, and steps up to more. Below this area is a wine bar, open only in the evenings. The bistro is renowned for its Italian food and confectionery, with pizzas looming large on the menu card, along with bruschetta, carpaccio and salads. A large blackboard, headed 'Schön sie zu sehen' ('great to see you'), lists the dishes of the day. Two red and two white house wines; the draught beers are DAB and Schlösser Alt - the darker one.

Das Piano

Fraüenstrasse 44-46
Tel: 251 4 32 46
Open: 17.00-03.00 (Fri, Sat & Sun from 18.00, Sun till 01.00)
Opposite Collegium Marianum, part of Münster University, Das Piano claims to be the students' and indeed the city's jazz local. They play the Rolling Stones as well. Tucked away in this otherwise quiet street, its old interior has a warm feel, with the bar as you enter, and at the back past the upright piano, split into two levels, something of the look and feel of Amsterdam's brown cafés and bars in the Jordaan district. Good beer and good company.

Stuttgart

A major player on the European industrial scene, with Bosch, Kodak, BMW, Porsche and Daimler-Benz all in residence. The city lies in a deep valley of the River Neckar, and on the higher slopes vines are grown, producing Stuttgart's red wine Trollinger. Germany's first two skyscrapers, known fondly as Romeo and Juliet, were built here. Suttgart has one of the country's finest art galleries (Staatsgalerie), with works from the 14th century onwards and the largest Picasso collection in Europe.

Bar e Tabacchi

Nadlerstrasse 5, 70173
Tel: 711 2 36 49 58
Open: 09.00-01.00 (Fri & Sat till 02.00)
In a street that opens out into a piazza, Bar e Tabacchi is a pavilion with a terrace of parasol-shaded chairs and tables occupied by chic shoppers and workers from the smart end of King's Road, where all the top fashion houses are found. The snacks they serve include baguettes and large pretzels, washed down with good espresso or a variety of other coffee preparations, while their speciality is ice cream. Also selling beer, wine by the glass and spirits, it's a very popular, busy refreshment stop, and, as the name suggests, carries a range of tobacco products.

Bistro Brenner

Brennerstrasse 5, Bohnenviertel
Tel: 711 23 27 08
Open: 08.30-23.20 (Sat till 16.00)
Closed: Sun
A smart café located across the ring road from the city centre in the so-called 'poor' district, once the Jewish quarter, and now occupied by wine merchants and the denizens of the red light district. The café has a small bar area, dining room, and a few pavement tables outside and across the street. It offers some good wines by the glass, Italian-style *vorspeisen* (antipasti) and a daily menu. Very good espresso.

"I owe everything to cigars."

Jimmy Savile.

131

Deli

Geissestrasse 7, 70173
Open: 09.00-01.00 (Fri & Sat till 02.00)
In a charming little pedestrianised square at the south-ern end of the centre is a cluster of restaurants and this café. In the middle of the square is a pretty fountain with a bronze figure struggling with a pig, the whole enclosed in a fine iron 'bird-cage' set on a stone dish. The café is in the ground floor of a stone building occupying one end of the square, with an arcaded facade. Here, terrace tables stretch into the square with their broad white canvas parasols. A 25cl glass of wine or an espresso can be sipped with a deli-style snack while scanning the papers, watching fellow cus-tomers, or gazing at the activity at the other places across the square. At weekends the tempo speeds up with local disc jockeys spinning their turntables for the young crowd to boogie to.

Bistro Einstein

Wilhelmsplatz 5, 70182
Tel: 711 2 34 97 97
Open: 12.00-01.00 (Fri & Sat till 02.00)
The chic split-level interior, with soft furnishings and fine iron and basket-weave chairs, belies the fact that this is the 'poor' district (according to the tourist board); once the Jewish area, it is now the red light district - even at lunchtime it is difficult to walk these side streets without being propositioned. However, with a large terrace and comfortable slatted armchairs shaded by the awning and umbrellas or by the leafy horse chestnut trees, a glass of wine, a baguette or crepe can be enjoyed in peace. The bar has a small piano, and live music is played at the weekend between September and May.

Empore

Markthalle Dorotheer strasse 4, 70173
Tel: 711 24 59 79
Open: 09.00-22.00 (Sat 08.00-16.00)
The city-centre art nouveau market hall, built by Martin Esaesser in 1914, is as colourful as you'd ever find, selling anything from fruit and veg, meat, fish and cheeses, to hardware and flowers. The open-plan café/restaurant overlooking the hall has smartly dressed waiters serving at cloth-covered tables, and at the bar. There is a good wine list and plenty of invit-ing dishes using the freshest of produce. The excellent espresso is 3.80DM, and wine by the glass from 8DM per 20cl glass. It's a joy to come here just for the bus-tle and colour, but all the better for its refreshment offerings. Dieter Looss keeps an attentive eye on everything.

Weinhaus Stetter

Rosenstrasse 32, Bohnenviertel 70182
Tel: 711 24 01 63
Open: 15.00-23.00 (shop 10.00-12.30)
Owned by Roman Stetter, this is a wine merchant's-cum-café. Wine is offered in 250ml glass mugs with blue glass handles. Mid-afternoon, ladies and gentle-men of retirement age come in, often to start with a cup of coffee or tea, and to move on to wine, some-times with a snack. In the morning it is open to the public for off-sales from its extensive wine list; over 90 of the hundreds of wines are later available in the café. Local residents make up the bulk of the evening crowd, as, although English is spoken, this is not on the tourist route. Snacks include potato salad, cheeses and sausages, plus soup and some hot dishes.

Café Culture

Café Inspiration

"I heard the laughter of her heart in ev'ry street café."

One way or another, there's something about cafés which provides a rich vein of inspiration. Their special combination of intimacy and anonymity creates the perfect setting for that poignant moment. Whether it's a wistful, romantic recollection – typified above by Oscar Hammerstein's lyric from that classic 1941 musical *Lady Be Good* – or a moment of revelation, we've all got our café memories.

Artists, writers, composers – from solitary scribblings on napkins to heated debates involving one and all – the list of leading lights that have found inspiration in the cafés of Europe seems endless.

The allure of the favourite café will surely endure. Where better to savour the bitter-sweet memories of a lost love, or take time out to gather one's thoughts, or meet friends and share new ideas? Where better to watch the wonderful swirl of daily life go waltzing by and dream one's dreams?

A coffee, a cognac, a cigar and a world of possibilities await.

To paraphrase that great 18th century poet, critic and bon-viveur, Samuel Johnson, *"When a man is tired of cafés, he is tired of life; for there is in cafés all that life can afford."*

Particular Pleasures
Cigars & Cognac

"If I cannot smoke cigars in Heaven, I shall not go."
Mark Twain

It's not difficult to imagine two of history's great lovers of life, Mark Twain and Samuel Johnson, savouring a cigar and a cognac in their favourite café. Such sparkling personalities would no doubt have been very particular about their pleasures, insisting on enjoying the best cigars and cognac in the convivial atmosphere of the best cafés.

The combination of cigars and cognac has long been a traditional favourite – and with good reason. Cognac's solid cores of vanilla flavours – derived from long years of oak-barrel ageing – and its crisp, clean taste are ideal for keeping the palate alive to the smoothness of a fine cigar.

"Claret is the liquor for boys; port for men; but he who aspires to be a hero must drink brandy."
Samuel Johnson

In fact, cigars and cognac are so well suited that they have even been combined in the much sought-after El Sublimado – a rare cigar from the Dominican Republic which is lightly flavoured with 50-year-old cognac.

But before setting off for your chosen café to delve into the epicurean delights of a cigar and a cognac, you might find the following helpful and enlightening.

The Perfect Location

A casual glance that leads to romance . . . an out-of-the-way rendezvous for clandestine lovers . . . a place to dream of the future and remember the past . . . there's something about cafés that appeals to the imagination like no other venue. Which is surely why they appear so regularly in another enduring pastime of the modern age – the cinema.
Like the diner in America, the café in Europe features in film after film. Here are just a few of our favourites from the '40s, '50s and '60s.

Summertime *(Directed by David Lean, 1955.)*
Katherine Hepburn's sensitive portrayal of the American school teacher – holidaying in Venice and looking for love – evokes a world of fragile hope. Sitting at her café table amidst the cosmopolitan Venetians and tourist groups of St Mark's Square, she cannot help but fall for the city's charm and its promise of romance.

Hunt

Huntley Archive

Brief Encounter
(Directed by David Lean, 1946.)
Another café setting for director David Lean, but this time with an altogether more tragic tone. From the bright sun of Venice to the darker interior of London – setting for the achingly poignant Thursday meetings of two married strangers who fall hopelessly in love.

Darling *(Directed by John Schlesinger, 1965.)*
Staying in London but moving to the city's heyday as the capital of the swinging sixties, this amoral tale of free love brought Julie Christie a Best Actress Academy Award for her portrayal of the vivacious fashion model dedicated to fame and money. Perfectly personifying this unique era, this is film as both drama and historical record – complete with hip and happening café life.

Kobal Collection

The Sun Also Rises
(Directed by Henry King, 1957.)

Taken from the Ernest Hemingway story, this tale of post first world war expatriates – roaming Europe in search of satisfaction and meaning – epitomises the 1920's 'lost generation'. The backdrop of cafés evokes the hedonistic spirit that unites this group of perpetual wanderers.

Huntley Archive

Huntley Archive

The Third Man
(Directed by Carol Reed, 1949.)

Another film about searching, with Joseph Cotton's naïve pulp-fiction writer beginning his quest for the truth about his mysterious friend Harry Lime (Orson Welles), at the infamous Café Mozart in Vienna. Ernst Deutsch's unnerving 'Baron' Kurtz – complete with affected lapdog – tries to muddy the water in this classic evocation of another post-war landscape riven with uncertainty.

Casablanca *(Directed by Michael Curtz, 1942.)*

Not strictly set within Europe, but how could we omit arguably the most famous film café of them all – Rick's Café?

"Play it once, Sam. For old times' sake."
"I don't know what you mean, Miss Elsa."
"Play it, Sam. Play As Time Goes By."
"Oh, I can't remember it, Miss Elsa. I'm a little rusty on it."
"I'll hum it for you. Da-dy-da-dy-da-dum, da-dy-da-dee-da-dum. Sing it, Sam."
"You must remember this,
A kiss is still a kiss,
A sigh is just a sigh.
The fundamental things apply
As time goes by.
And when two lovers woo,
They still say, "I love you"
On that you can rely
No matter what the future brings . . ."
"Sam, I thought I told you never to play . . ."

Now that's one café that will never be forgotten.

Kobal Collection

Smoke Signals

There are literally hundreds of different cigars to choose from. Variations in size, shape, country of origin, manufacturing technique, strength and taste present the newcomer with a bewildering array of options. Indeed, many cigar lovers choose different cigars for different times of the day, situations and moods. But don't be put off – for the smoker who wants to explore the pleasures of cigars, a lifelong journey of revelations awaits.

Having chosen your cigar, a certain amount of ritual is considered de rigueur before you begin smoking. If your cigar has a closed end, it has to be opened to allow the smoke through. So, unless you find yourself in a spaghetti western where the fashion is to bite the end off and spit it out with manful disdain, you'll need a sharp pocket knife or cutter. Generally, aim to cut off about a sixteenth of an inch (1.6mm) to get a good burn and even draw. Don't pierce the closed end with a match (or anything else) as it can cause the smoke and oils of the tobacco down onto the tongue – which is not pleasant.

Time to light up – but beware, don't use sulphur or wax matches, or a petrol lighter, as they can impair the cigar's flavour. Go for a wooden match, spill or a gas lighter. Whatever method you choose, never let the flame actually touch the cigar. Holding the cigar just above the flame tip, rotate it gently so that the entire end (or 'foot') is evenly lit. The trick is to get a wide flame, so go for two or three matches at once if it's a particularly thick cigar.

Enjoy! Take good, even draws to fill your mouth with the cigar smoke. Let the flavours roll around your palate for a moment, then exhale. Cigar smoke is not intended to be inhaled. And don't worry if it goes out – re-lighting a cigar is perfectly acceptable, if not left for too long. Finally, don't grind your finished cigar in an ashtray. This actually releases more odours into the air and is unnecessary – a cigar will extinguish on its own in only a few moments.

Learning Your Labels

Choosing a cognac – the best known type of brandy in the world and a benchmark by which most other brandies are judged – is all about understanding labels. Knowing how to recognise a cognac's pedigree and age from the bottle's label will help you appreciate the remarkable range of subtle differences between different types.

Cognac takes its name from the French town north of Bordeaux. Surrounded by the Charente and Charente-Maritime regions, only brandies from this area can be called a cognac. Further, French law limits the use of the cognac name to only those brandies from this area which are made from the wine of a specified grape variety, distilled twice in special pot stills (known as alembics) and aged for a prescribed period in Limousin oak.

Learning Your Labels

The Charente and Charente-Maritime regions are subdivided into seven growing zones. These, in descending order of quality, are Grande Champagne, Petite Champagne, Borderies, Fins Bois, Bons Bois, Bois Ordinaries and Bois Communs. So, the finest of the fine are cognacs are from Grande Champagne exclusively and tend to be labelled 'Grande Fine Champagne'. A 'Fine Champagne' label denotes a cognac which contains a blend of brandies from the Grande Champagne and Petite Champagne zones.

Most cognacs are a blend of brandies from different vintages and different growing zones. Even those from single vineyards or distilleries tend to be a combination of brandies from different casks. The production of local vineyards is sold to the cognac distillers (or 'houses'), each of which then stores and ages cognacs from different suppliers for its master blenders to combine.

All cognacs start out in new oak to mellow the fiery spirit and give them colour. After a few years, those batches which have been chosen for long-term ageing are transferred to used (or 'seasoned') casks that impart less of the oak flavour notes while the cognac matures.

The designated age of a cognac refers only to the time spent in wood, as distilled spirits cease to age once they are bottled. The older the cognac, the smoother, more complex and more refined it becomes. It is rare, however, for a cognac to remain in wooden casks for longer than 40 or 50 years. Most cognacs spend from one or one and a half to five years in wood, with the final spirit being a blend not just of brandies from different districts, but also of brandies aged for different periods.

Because there are no overt age statements on bottles of cognac, the industry uses some generally accepted terms to indicate the minimum age of each cognac:

V.S./V.S.P./Three Star: A minimum of two years for the youngest cognac in the blend, although the average is four to five years. V.S. stands for 'Very Superior' and V.S.P. for 'Very Superior Pale'.

V.S.O.P.: A minimum of four years, with the average being between 10 and 15 years. V.S.O.P. stands for 'Very Superior Old Pale'.

Napoleon: A minimum of five years, though again usually longer.

X.O./Luxury: A minimum of six years, with the average running to 20 years or older. X.O. stands for 'Extra Old'.

Hungary

Telephone Code: 00 36

The leader of the downfall of Communism in Eastern Europe, Hungary has always had strong ties with the West, and today those ties are as strong as ever; at the same time she has kept her own folk traditions alive in music, song and dance. Outside the capital, Hungary's main tourist spots are Lake Balaton, Europe's largest lake, with its popular holiday resorts, and the Danube Bend, where the past comes alive in such places as Szentendre, a magnet for artists down the years, and Esztergom, founded by the Magyars, dominated by a huge basilica and once the home of the kings of Hungary.

CAFÉ CRÈME

Budapest

A lively, convivial city lying along the two banks of the Danube. Buda and Pest are linked by several bridges over the river, the first and best known being the Chain Bridge guarded by imposing stone lions. The city boasts some very grand architecture, including the magnificent Parliament Building, modelled on London's House of Commons, castles, museums and the old-fashioned, often very grand public baths for which the city is famous. Many of its restaurants are traditional in style, while the cafés range from simple to sumptuous. The patron saint of Hungary is Stephen, in whose honour the 19th-century basilica was built; his mummified right hand is one of its more unusual 'treasures'.

Café Angelika

1 Batthyany Ter 7
Tel: 1 212 3784
Open: 10.00-20.00

A refined, atmospheric café housed in the former crypt of St Anne's Church in Old Budapest, right by the Danube. In summer, a terrace gives views of Parliament across the river, while in winter patrons sit inside in cosy niches lit through dark stained glass and enjoy a variety of coffees and home-made cakes. A nice old-fashioned place and a favourite rendezvous among demure middle class ladies, who come here for a good gossip.

Coquan's Kávé

Ráday utca 15
Tel: 1 215 2444
Open: 09.00-17.00 (Sun from 11.00)

A small, friendly, American-style gourmet coffee bar that brings the art of coffee-making to a very high level. The high ceiling, ochre walls and wooden floor, legacies of its days as a grand shop, provide a naturally light environment, enhanced by halogen spots over the bar. Coffee cocktails provide an added kick. Other Coquan's are at Nrador utca 5 (Tel: 1 266 9936) and Steny utca market (Tel: 1 345 4275).

Incognito

VI Liszt Ferenc tér 3
Tel: 1 267 9428
Open: 10.00-24.00 (Sat & Sun from 12.00)
Still the trendiest café in Budapest, with battered old furniture and the sleeves of rare jazz LPs that cover the walls just visible in the dim light. A young crowd flocks here to sip their coffees and beers and spirits and cocktails, and listen to jazzy beats, having probably started the evening at one of the other bars on not-as-quiet-as-it-was Liszt Ferenc square.

Café Mozart

VII Erzsébet körút 36
Tel: 1 267 8586
Open: 09.00-23.00 (Sat till 24.00)
The decor may be on the naff side, but there is a surprisingly wide selection of coffees and pastries to be enjoyed at this Mozart-themed place. The jazzed-up garden furniture is topped only by the waitresses in tight-laced baroque costume and the mirthmaking murals depicting scenes from the life of the great composer.

Café New York (New York Kavehaz)

Erzebet Korut 9-11
Tel: 1 322 3849
Open: 09.00-24.00
The edifice is a melancholy reminder of past glories when this was the meeting place of the literati of Pest at the turn of the century. Now primitive scaffolding supports a frontage which was rammed in 1956 by a Russian tank. Inside, however, is in sumptuous contrast: a glorious riot of art nouveau decor - twisted columns, wrought iron and gilding - seduces visitors into abandoning thoughts of tea and sandwiches and ordering cocktails, caviar, a mountainous concoction of cream and chocolate, and fabulous coffee.

Ruszwurm

1 Szentharomsag Utca 3
Tel: 1 375 5284
Open: 10.00-20.00
Closed: Wed
Tourists visiting Castle Hill squeeze into this tiny salon, a baroque original high above the city, nestling among the old cobbled streets. Its linzertorte was already renowned in Hapsburg Vienna by the turn of the century. Today its two small rooms still evoke the era, with pastel-coloured walls, a chandelier, antique-filled glass cabinets and a ceramic stove. An elegant spot for sipping iced coffees and ice creams in summer and a range of coffees, teas and hot chocolate in winter.

Ireland

Telephone Code: 00 353

A land of legends whose inhabitants have cultivated the art of living, often through troubled times, putting the emphasis on kindness and hospitality, allied to a determined individualism, a great sense of humour and a wonderful way with words. They also love to down a pint or two of stout, and there's very often live music in the pubs. *The* Irish drink is Guinness, and the brewery, founded by Arthur Guinness in 1759, covers 60 acres and is the largest in Europe. He was wise enough to take a 9,000 year lease on the premises, so there's quite a lot of drinking-up time left. There's a good choice of bars and cafés in Dublin and the major towns, and most of them serve Irish coffee - a potent and very agreeable blend of hot coffee, Irish whiskey and cream. The little fishing port of Kinsale has put itself on the map as one of the gourmet centres of the Republic and its annual four-day Gourmet Festival attracts international interest.

Dublin

A modern city with a young, vigorous population. It's a great place for strolling, either along the shopping streets or lovely parks, and you're never very far from a convivial pub. Dublin's contribution to the arts has been mainly in the field of literature and among the writers who were born or lived here are no fewer than three Nobel Prize winners - WB Yeats (1923), George Bernard Shaw (1925) and Samuel Beckett (1969). The Dublin Writers Museum is a shrine to their achievements and their works are frequently performed at the renowned Abbey Theatre. Handel's Messiah had its first performance in Dublin, in 1742. Places for special visits include the Castle (originally a Viking fortress), Trinity College, where the priceless treasure the Book of Kells is housed, St Patrick's Cathedral, resting place of the writer Jonathan Swift, who was Dean here from 1713 to 1745, the Guinness Brewery and Irish Whiskey Corner. There's a wide variety of restaurants in Dublin and the cafés are a gentler alternative to the city's 800 pubs.

The Bridge Café Bar (Bewley)

10 Westmoreland Street
Tel: 1 670 8133
Open: 10.00-23.00 (Fri & Sat till 01.30, Sun from 12.00)
A broad zinc bar top, tiled panels on the dark, polished wood counter, and behind the bar a large tiled panel of a peacock. The ceiling has three circular panels with relatively modern scenes and the fourth is a verrière of leaded coloured glass. The whole ensemble is a modern interpretation of art nouveau, put in place a few years back as the café-bar of the renowned Bewley chain: the cafeteria, open from 07.30 till 18.00, is next door, and the complex also includes a 70-bed hotel in Fleet Street. The excellent snacks include speciality sandwiches, plain or toasted. Other Bewleys are in Grafton Street and South Great George Street.

Brogan's

75 Dame Street
Tel: 1 679 9570
Open: 10.30-23.00
Guinness, Guinness, Guinness. Brogan's is a virtual museum to all things Guinness. Advertisements, toby jugs, mugs, glasses and a host of other artefacts bearing the Guinness name fill the place - and you can also get a very good glass of the real thing.

The Bruxelles

7 Harry Street
Tel: 1 679 9636
Open: 10.30-01.30 (Sat till 01.00)

In a prime site just off Grafton Street, this always busy place features an extraordinary example of early art nouveau ceramics by JB Rooke as well as etched mirrors and elegant cabinet work. Open for drinks 15 hours a day, it also offers traditional Irish food and a new dinner menu with the likes of chicken wings and burgers. Regular live jazz sessions.

Fitzers

51a Dawson Street
Tel: 1 677 1155
Open: 12.00-23.30

A bright, airy and very popular café-bar just round the corner from the pedestrianised shopping area on fashionable Grafton Street. Eyecatching canopies on an impressive glass frontage are matched by equally striking interior decor that is softened in the evening by lamplight and candle-light. All types of beers and wines are on offer, alongside a varied modern menu that includes dishes from Japan, Italy and California. Outside tables in summer. One of four Fitzers Cafés in Dublin: the others are in Temple Bar Square (1 679 0440), in the National Gallery Merrion Square (1 661 4496) and in the Royal Dublin Society building in Merrion Road (1 667 1301).

Café Java

5 South Anne Street
Tel: 1 670 7239
Open: 07.45-18.00 (Sat from 09.00, Sun from 11.00)

A stylish modern café on two levels; the floor is of light wood, the white walls are decorated with Polynesian murals and the skylight at the back creates a bright, airy atmosphere in which to enjoy good coffee with a sandwich or one of their excellent salads. It's very popular during the day and you might even have a short wait for a table (outside in summer).

La Med

22 East Essex Street
Tel: 1 670 7358
Open: 11.00-23.00 (Fri & Sat till 24.00, Sun till 17.00)
Closed: Mon

Café, restaurant and jazz bar with the look and the feel of Paris and the Mediterranean. The owners are French, too, and that's reflected in the coffee, the wine and the food. La Med opens on to East Essex Street in the heart of Temple Bar, Dublin's Left Bank, but runs through to the quays overlooking the Liffey.

Kaffé Moka

Lower Rathmines Road
No telephone
Open: 08.00-04.00 (Sun from 10.00)

A small café that's popular with students and young professionals, approximately 25 minutes' walk from the city centre and served by a number of bus routes. It has a good selection of coffees and teas, and friendly, mostly young staff. The late opening hours make it a frequent stopping place for revellers on the way home from city-centre night clubs, and it's a popular spot for breakfast.

Kaffé Moka

39 South William Street
Tel: 1 679 8475
Open: 07.30-04.00

A super coffee house on three floors - popular, friendly and a great place to linger with a newspaper or a book from the upstairs library, or to enjoy a game of chess, draughts or even snakes & ladders. You can choose your coffee from the house blend, Java, Columbia, Kenya or Costa Rica and they'll make up a bag of beans (whole or ground) for you to take away. They also have an impressive range of teas and infusions, and they make first-rate sandwiches. Regular events include poetry nights, tarot readings and live music.
Special Award 2001

The Old Stand

37 Exchequer Street
Tel: 1 677 7220
Open: 11.00-23.00

This comfortable, traditional pub in the heart of town close to the tourist office is a great favourite of the local business community and of the sporting fraternity, especially fans of rugby and horseracing. Centuries old (its licence was *renewed* in the reign of Charles ll in 1659!) it serves coffee in the old-fashioned way, in a pot on a tray, or you can choose from a wide range of beers and stouts. Very good straightforward food (steaks a speciality) is served from 12.30 till 21.15 (till 20.15 on Saturday). The tourists are particularly keen on the Old Stand's Irish stew. Sister establishment, in Duke Street, is Davy Byrnes, immortalised in James Joyce's *Ulysses*.

The Oliver St John Gogarty

58-59 Fleet Street
Tel: 1 671 1822/1595/1683
Open: 10.00-23.00 (Left Bank bar till 01.30)
Established in 1850 and later renamed in memory of the distinguished surgeon, poet and politician, this bar-restaurant, loved equally by locals and tourists, also operates as a hotel, with 30 bedrooms and 6 penthouse rooms. Live Irish music is performed every afternoon and evening in the low-beamed main bar, and the Left Bank bar stays open late every night with a DJ till 01.30. Traditional Irish cuisine is served in the 95-cover restaurant. In the early part of the day it's a pleasure to sit quietly with a drink and a newspaper, but before long the crowds begin to gather and everyone joins in the fun.

The Palace

21 Fleet Street
Tel: 1 677 9290
Open: 10.30-23.00 (closed on Sunday between 14.00 & 16.00)
Established in 1828 and associated down the years with Irish writers including James Joyce, Brendan Behan and Patrick Kavanagh, the Palace retains its period decor and frontage in pristine condition; the only real change in the last 100 years has been the introduction of electricity. Very friendly staff, who know all the local gossip and the history of this 'Left Bank' area of Dublin, will serve you a filter coffee or something stronger, which you can take to the comfortable parlour at the far end.

The Temple Bar

47-48 Temple Bar
Tel: 1 672 5286
Open: 10.30-23.00 (Thur & Sun till 24.00, Fri & Sat till 00.30)
The Temple Bar first opened its doors in 1840 and was popular as a bar long before this part of Dublin was designated a cultural development area. It is now just as popular as a café, with seats for 200 and walls cluttered with prints, pictures and photographs which testify to its long standing. The place is always busy, really buzzing in the evenings and at weekends. Live Irish music on Sundays. Just sandwiches for snacks.

Thing Mote

15 Suffolk Street
Tel: 1 677 8030
Open: 10.30-23.00
The name means Assembly Mount in a corruption of the language of the Norsemen who left their stamp on Dublin a thousand years ago. Mainly a bar, Thing Mote is very popular with the students from Trinity College next door, and the warmest and friendliest of Irish welcomes greets every visitor. Light eats include sandwiches, rolls and home-made soup. Look for the elaborate gilt chandelier hanging from the ceiling two-storeys high at the back.

Thomas Read

4 Parliament Street
Tel: 1 671 7283
Open: 10.30-23.00 (Thur, Fri & Sat till 01.30)
A people-watching corner site with tall windows, awnings, double doors, a lofty ceiling supported by two columns, globe lights, round tables and bentwood chairs - this could almost be a Paris pavement café. It's always busy, especially at weekends, with customers of all age joining in the fun. Excellent coffee, light snacks and a wide range of beers. Opposite the entrance to Dublin Castle.

Trastevere

Unit 1, Temple Bar Square
Tel: 1 670 8343
Open: 12.00-23.00 (Fri & Sat till 23.30)
A taste of Italy in Dublin. Trastevere (the name means 'across the Tiber' and is a lively district of Rome), occupying a corner site in the handsomely rebuilt square, is chic and modern, and tall windows let you watch life pass by while enjoying a drink or a snack. That life might easily include street theatre or a music procession, for this part of the city is a designated cultural area. Italian dishes share the menu with the occasional home-grown favourite such as potato and curly kale.

Cork

The Republic's second largest city, a major commercial centre on the River Lee and a fascinating city with a history reaching back to the 7th century. The old quays and warehouses are reminders of its mercantile past, and the prosperity of the 18th and 19th centuries may also be seen in the fine houses and the splendid church architecture. Ring the bells at St Anne's Shandon, kiss the stone at Blarney Castle. Henry Ford was born nearby, and in 1917 the Ford company set up its first overseas factory here.

Bia Beo
MacCurtain Street
Tel: 21 506 422
Open: 09.00-18.00
Closed: Sun

A wine bar-café whose walls display a regularly-changing collection of work by local artists. The name means 'good food' and the day starts with a cup of tea or coffee and one of the irresistible home-baked French pastries or a formidable full Irish breakfast. Light lunches (perhaps a ciabatta sandwich or an omelette with a glass of wine) and a full dinner menu. Newspapers are provided for lone visitors.

Bodega
46-49 Cornmarket Street
Tel: 21 272 878
Open: 12.00-23.00 (summer till 23.30)

A big, open café-bar on the site of St Peter's Market, with beams and transoms on its lofty ceiling, tall mirrors behind the slate-topped bar and tables scattered randomly around the room. They serve a varied selection of wines and beers as well as good espresso coffee food throughout the day. Every Sunday there's a jazz session. On the same premises, the newly-opened 100-cover Coal Quay café is open from 17.30 till late. The same owners have another new venture, The Roundy, a traditional pub venue in Castle Street.

Clancy's
15-16 Princes Street
Tel: 21 4276 097
Open: 10.30-22.30 (Thur till 01.00, Fri till 02.00 Sat till 03.00)

One of Cork's oldest café/bistro-bars, with premises stretching from Princes Street through to Marlboro Street. There are two bars for taking drinks, a spacious area with coffee tables and bench seating, and a downstairs carvery (self-service cafeteria) open at lunchtime. A late breakfast starts the day, and in the evening the food is provided by the first-floor bistro. Fish, steaks, traditional Irish dishes.
Ireland Café of the Year 2001

Farmgate
Old English Market, Princes Street
Tel: 21 278 134
Open: 08.30-17.30
Closed: Sun

This old market has been completely restored and just inside the main entrance (Grand Parade) on the first floor is a café in a gallery from which you can look down on the busy goings-on. Coffee and a pastry provide a good break from shopping, or better still walk through to the waitress-served restaurant to enjoy a light lunch and a glass of wine. The menu, which changes every day, combines traditional Irish cuisine with modern Mediterranean, and with the market on hand, the produce could not be fresher.

Gloria Jean's
Patrick Street
Tel: 21 270 555
Open: 08.30-18.00 (Sun from 12.30)

On two floors overlooking the city's main shopping street, this is part of an American chain of specialist coffee houses and offers an impressive range of coffees in many different preparations to savour with a pastry or an open sandwich. There's also a shop on the premises where you can buy your beans, whole or ground, to take home.

The Goat Broke Loose

Grand Parade
Tel: 21 279 186
Open: 10.30-23.00 (Thur, Fri & Sat till 00.30)
Once a pub but recently extended at the back to make
a café, it takes its name from the song about Paddy
McGinty's goat (the words are written up on a wall).
You enter from the river end of the broad parade, and
beyond the bar are a comfortably furnished reading
room and a raised area with conservatory-style benches and chairs. They make a good cup of coffee here,
and at lunchtime there's a selection of snacks. Night
time is party time. A second bar has recently been
added.

Maguire's Warehouse

Paul Street/Patrick Street
Tel: 21 277 825
Open: 10.30-23.00 (Fri & Sat till later)
A spacious former warehouse with exposed brick
walls, a lofty beamed ceiling and a tall, elaborate,
glass-fronted cabinet running the length of the wall
behind the counter in the spacious bar area. At
lunchtime a daily menu offers four or five Irish dishes. Very busy in the evening, with late-night partying
at the weekend.

Italy

Telephone Code: 00 39

The grandeur that was Rome' lives on not only in the capital city but throughout this country of diverse charms, from its beautiful language (spoken at its purest in Tuscany) to the splendour of the great cities, the glorious lakes and mountains, the ravishing, romantic coastline and the unrivalled feeling of history. The Italians are rightly proud of their monumental past but also have a great interest in making the most of the present. Living life to the full is the watchword, as shown in the interest in good food and good wine, the colourful carnivals and festivals, the evening stroll with family and friends. Cafés fit into the Italian way of life throughout Italy, but are treated differently in city and country. In the busy city life the café provides a haven for the harassed business person, shopper or weary tourist, while in the country or smaller towns, the café is the focal point of the area, often doubling as a post office and sometimes a general store. Italy produces some superb wines, while for something somewhat stronger grappa is the answer. And should you overdo things, Fernet Branca will cure almost anything.

Rome

The River Tiber snakes through this endlessly fascinating city, where 2,700 years of history come alive in the glorious ruins. The most famous of these include the Colosseum, built in 80AD to hold 50,000 bloodthirsty spectators, the Forums, the Emperor Hadrian's Pantheon and the Baths of Caracalla, the hugely atmospheric setting for operas and concerts. Among the more recent attractions are the amazingly ornate Fontana di Trevi (have your loose change ready) and the Spanish Steps, one of the most popular and best-loved meeting places in the whole city. The fountain and the steps both date from the 18th century. Outside the walls of Rome, the Catacombs contain the first examples of Christian art, while within its confines lies Vatican City, the smallest state in the world (107 acres) with the largest Cathedral in the world and some of its greatest art treasures including Michelangelo's *Pietà* and his breathtaking ceiling in the Sistine Chapel.

The Rome of today is much more than a giant museum: it's a vibrant, exciting and go-ahead city, spruced up for the new millennium, a great place for shopping and eating, and enjoying a varied and convivial night life, with plenty of music, dancing and clubbing. The cafés of Rome are vibrant with the chatter of the customers, the hiss of the espresso machine and the general background noise of a city that seems constantly in a state of excitement and expectation.

Babington's

Piazza di Spagna 23
Tel: 06 6786027
Open: 09.00-20.15
Closed: Tue

A century of history here. Two Victorian spinsters Anna Maria Babington from Derbyshire and Isabel Cargill from New Zealand set up shop in this prime location by the Spanish Steps, bringing a touch of English class Fortnum & Mason-style to the citizens of Rome. Despite the ups and downs in its fortunes since then (economic sanctions during the war and a post-war shortage of tea due to rationing), it survived and remains as one of Rome's poshest places for enjoying a cup of tea.

La Bevitoria

Piazza Navona 72
Tel: 06 68801022
Open: 11.00-01.00 (Fri & Sat till 02.00)

A friendly little wine bar next to *Dolce Vita* (*qv*). The price at the tables inside is the same as at the bar, but to sit outside costs extra. On balance, the most pleasant bar in the square, with a touch of history in the cellars where the remains of a stadium built by the Emperor Domitian can still be seen. Drink mulled wine in winter.

La Buvette

Via Vittoria 44/47 (Piazza di Spagna)
Tel: 06 6790383
Open: 07.00-20.30
Closed: Sun, 1 week Aug

The studded leather bench seating and bar stools give this a gentlemen's club feel. Not more than a couple of stones' throws from Piazza di Spagna, but the tourists who crowd the Spanish Steps are generally not much in evidence. Last food orders are at 23.00.

Canova

Piazza del Popolo 16
Tel: 06 3612231
Open: 08.00-24.00

Cake shop, tobacconist, bar, restaurant/tea room and, best of all, pavement café. It's a busy place, and one of the smartest in town, done out in modern style, with friendly, efficient staff who wear brass badges on their Canova-labelled waistcoats. Unusually for an Italian joint, they stock French Ricard. Once known for its extreme right-wing clientele, it now attracts aspiring film stars, who come here to be seen (as they do across the square at equally smart arch rival *Rosati*, once the haunt of the intellectual left). Here, you get the late afternoon sun – or you go to *Rosati* to avoid it!

La Casa del Tramezzino

Viale Trastevere 81
Tel: 06 5812118
Open: 07.00-03.00
Closed: Mon pm

South of the river on the main thoroughfare in the Trastevere ('across the Tiber'). The speciality is the eponymous *tramezzino* - a smart Italian word for sandwich, apparently coined by Mussolini during a campaign to ban foreign words. And sandwiches is what they are, all freshly made, as they have been for more than 30 years, and scrumptious in any language. Also ice creams, and hot meals at lunchtime. You can eat outside under parasols with privet hedges in troughs separating you from the pavement.

Antico Caffè Castellino

Via Cesare Battisti 135
Tel: 06 6792404
Open: 24 hours

2000 saw the centenary of an all-day, all-night bar-cum-tobacconist-cum newspaper shop facing the amazing Vittorio Emanuele Monument. Drop in for a coffee or a beer with a sandwich, a pastry, a cold dish or a pizza, or take your pick from the wide range of ice creams.

Chirra Goffredo

Via Torino 133
Tel: 06 485659
Open: 06.30-02.00
Closed: Sun

An amazing wine merchant, but also licensed as a bar, where you can sip a glass of wine with a sandwich while deciding whether to have your Balthazar (16 bottles) of Moët gift-wrapped. They also sell preserves, teas and coffees. The walls are stacked eleven shelves high with wines, aperitifs and spirits.

Dagnino

Galleria Esedra, Via V E Orlando 75
Tel: 06 4818660
Open: 07.00-22.00

A split-level bar where frescoes and mirrors recall the style of a Parisian pavement café of the 1950s. Apart from the bar itself, the terrace, with its own street lighting, is a great place for enjoying one of the first-class Sicilian pastries or an ice cream.

Il Delfino

Corso Vittorio Emanuele 67
Tel: 06 6864053
Open: 07.00-21.00

An atmospheric and historic setting inside the 16th-century Datti Palace for a very smart and permanently busy café-bar. Established in 1938, it offers coffee, beer and a good selection of wines at the self-service bar, while on the eating front sandwiches, grills, pizzas and an extensive cold buffet are the most popular options, with ice cream to round things off.

La Diligenza Rossa

Via Merulana 271
Tel: 06 4881216
Open: 09.00-22.30
Closed: Mon

A little way down the road from Piazza Santa Maria Maggiore, this pretty baroque-decorated building that stands out among plainer neighbours. Alongside the bar stands the popular Red Coach Grill, whose speciality is chickens roasted on a spit over an open fire (*polli cotti a legna*). They also offer a selection of cold dishes. The grill is quite close to the Brancaccio Theatre.

Caffè Dolce Vita

Piazza Navona 70
Tel: 06 68806221
Open: 07.30-02.00

Named after the classic film, although not featured in it, and the name is almost hidden behind luxuriant greenery. Inside are lots of black-and-white photos of film stars and politicians taken with the café's owner. There are a few seats inside, but most customers choose to sit outside under the huge parasols.

Caffè Farnese

Via dei Baullari 106
Tel: 06 68802125
Open: 07.00-02.00

One of the oldest bars in central Rome, in the square just along from the bustling morning food and flower market Campo de'Fiori and opposite the Michelangelo-designed Palazzo Farnese, which now houses the French Embassy. Very good snacks, and therefore very popular.

Il Fico

Piazza del Fico 26/28
Tel: 06 6865205
Open: 08.30-02.00
A prime location in Trastevere known as drinkers' corner (*angolo di bevitori*), where this bar (its name means 'the fig tree') and the *Antico Caffè della Pace* (*qv*) attract some of the smartest and best-known people in show business. Sip a cup of coffee at the bar or mix with the beautiful people toying with an apritif at a pavement table. Good home-made desserts.

Antico Caffè Greco

Via Condotti 86
Tel: 06 6791700
Open: 08.30-20.45
Goethe was a great fan of this historic and very grand café near the Spanish Steps, and other notables passing through the portals include Hans Christian Andersen, Casanova, Wagner and mad King Ludwig of Bavaria. In the early days (it opened in 1760) the majority of the customers were artists or foreign visitors, and at the beginning of the 20th century it was adopted by American visitors. In the 1950s it was finally and formally recognised as a historic institution. Beyond the bar, there is a series of rooms with gilded mirrors, portraits on oil and velvet-upholstered chairs around marble tables; at the far end is a larger room with glass-fronted library shelves.

Bar Gelateria Marani

Via dei Volsci 57
Tel: 06 490016
Open: 06.00-22.00
Closed: Mon
A delightful little bar with a spectacular, secluded, vine-covered garden terrace, sheltered by a high wall, right on the corner of the daily market in Piazza di Osci. Students and San Lorenzo locals are united in their praise of the terrific ice creams and sorbets that are the speciality of Monica Marani's famous place.

Bar del Mattatoio

Piazza Orazio Giustiniani 3
Tel: 06 5746017
Open: 06.00-21.00
Closed: Sun
Mattatoio was Rome's main slaughterhouse from 1891 until 1975, when the vast buildings began to be put to many other uses. In the middle of the square by the main entrance, this down-to-earth bar and tobacconist's kiosk is run with a smile and ready wit by a husband-and-wife team who have been here for years. The early opening time, which once catered for butchers and slaughterers, is now convenient for revellers from nearby clubland who have made a night of it.

Café Notegen

Via del Babuino 159
Tel: 06 3200855
Open: 07.00-01.00 (Sun from 10.30)
The bohemian spirit that was a feature of this area after the Second World War lives on in the basement of Notegen, where there is a stage and seating for political debate, side shows, fringe theatre, even cabaret. On the ground floor the bar is very convivial, selling good coffee, drinks and snacks, and at the back there's a restaurant area. Birreria and pizzeria at night.

Antico Caffè della Pace

Via della Pace 3-4, 5-7
Tel: 06 6861216
Open: 09.00-02.00 (Mon from 15.00)
Times changed a long time ago here at what was once just an ordinary little corner bar. The present owner gave it a makeover and changed it into what is probably the most fashionable bar in the old part of Rome, with cascading greenery and a prime location in the Trastevere. Film stars and other notables come here (or to *Il Fico*, see entry) for drinks or coffees, and often move on to the restaurant in the same premises.
Special Award 2001

Caffè Palombini

Piazzale K Adenauer 12
Tel: 06 5911700
Open: 07.00-24.00 (Sat till 13.00)

One of the leading café-bars in EUR (Esposizione Universale Romana), a vast site which was originally developed for a massive fascist-inspired exhibition due to be held in 1942 but abandoned after a series of arguments and the outbreak of war. Palombini is a favourite meeting place, especially for the young, with its huge patio and garden setting. It gets very busy at lunchtime, when they open the buffet, and on summer evenings you can expect to queue for an outside table. Service is excellent, and they roast their own coffee, blend it and sell it under the Palombini badge.

Café du Parc

Piazza di Porta S Paolo
Tel: 06 5743363
Open: 04.00-03.00

A small kiosk bar specialising in *cremolati* (a creamy kind of sorbet), with tables under tall, leafy trees alongside Viale Piramide Cestia (Pyramid of Cestius). The pyramid was built by the magistrate Gaius Cestius, who admired the tombs of the pharaohs and wanted a miniature one for himself. He was buried here in 12BC. In the adjacent cemetery Keats and Shelley are notable inhabitants.

Café de Paris

Via Vittorio Veneto 9
Tel: 06 4885284
Open: 08.00-01.00
Closed: Tue in winter

The Café de Paris opened its doors in 1956 and was an instant success, benefiting from the post-war revival of Rome as a holiday city, and from the boost the city got from staging the 1960 Olympic Games. Its greatest times came when it was featured in the film *La Dolce Vita*. Brando used to pop in while filming in Rome. Great cakes and a terrific tiramisu.

Caffè Piccarozzi

Piazza della Repubblica 62-63
Tel: 06 4745845
Open: 07.00-24.00
Closed: Sun

A major facelift put a shine back on the stonework of this café, which stands on the north-east side of the vast Piazza della Repubblica. Order a drink and a snack inside or out in the colonnade, where you can enjoy the magnificence of the architecture and watch the world go by in grand, semi-circular piazza with its monumental Fountain of the Naiads.

Rosati

Piazza del Popolo 4/5a
Tel: 06 3225859
Open: 07.30-23.30

Once a favoured meeting place of the intellectual left (Pasolini was a regular), Rosati is a very smart, efficiently run bar with outside tables on the opposite side of the piazza from *Canova* (see entry), opened in 1922 and decorated in the later art nouveau style, with a green marble-topped oak-panelled bar. A two-flight oak staircase takes you to an upstairs restaurant. Piano bar Friday and Saturday evenings in winter. Excellent home baking in the original oven.

Sant'Eustachio Il Caffè

Piazza Sant'Eustachio 82
Tel: 06 6861309
Open: 08.30-01.00

One of the city's most renowned coffee bars, with messages from the world's great and good extolling the quality of its coffee. When at this café, do as the Romans do and join a long queue to be served the tiniest volume of the most intensely flavoured espresso or the most delicious cappuccino, maybe even the *ciocolatto* (coffee, chocolate and cream), or a granita (crushed ice coffee) on a hot day.

Bar Alla Scrofa

Via della Scrofa 104
Tel: 06 6869552
Open: 06.30-20.30
Closed: Sun

A pleasant neighbourhood bar in a street that takes you from the Pantheon up to the Piazza del Popolo just inside the city's old northern gate. It has a couple of tables inside and four outside, and sells good home-made ice cream and snacks. Via della Scrofa (scrofa means sow) has some very grand private residences (*palazzi*) with elaborate courtyards and beautiful fountains glimpsed through enormous gates. The bar celebrated its centenary in 1999.

Gran Caffè Strega

Piazza del Viminale 27-31
Tel: 06 485670
Open: 06.00-24.00

Strega is the Italian word for witch, but in this case it is the name of the familiar Italian liqueur sold here. Tucked away down an alley by the handsome Ministry of the Interior building, this is a very good *pizzeria-birreria* with a real *forno al legno* – wood-fired oven. Brunch is now a feature, and grilled meats are another speciality. There's plenty of room to eat inside and lots of tables under large parasols in the forecourt.

157

La Tazza d'Oro

Via degli Orfani 84
Tel: 06 6789792
Open: 07.00-20.30
Closed: Sun

The sacks and barrels of coffee tell you that La Tazza d'Oro (the Golden Cup) is a major importer of coffee, bringing the beans from, among other places, Jamaica and Costa Rica. In front of you are glass displays of just some of the coffee beans for sale (personal customers, mail order, fax, e-mail). Right next door to the Pantheon and across the square from the Parliament, this is where you'll find Rome's best iced coffee with whipped cream in Rome. This outstanding place has been in the same family since 1947.

Trasté

Via della Lungaretta 76
Tel: 06 5894430
Open: 17.00-02.00
Closed: Aug

Not far from Piazza Santa Maria, whose fountain is a popular gathering place (a sort of Roman Eros), Trasté is a popular and trendy evening spot, heralded from the outside by 'Caffè Sala da Tè' and one of the few places in Rome to specialise in tea! Inside, it is smartly modern, with low, comfortable sofas and tables in the front part which leads to a spacious room with square tables and chairs and the bar itself. A range of infusions is on sale along with the cocktails, draught and bottled beers, cocktails, milkshakes and crêpes both sweet and savoury. Magazines are provided for browsing.

Bar Tre Scalini

Piazza Navona 28-32
Tel: 06 68801996
Open: 09.00-01.30
Closed: Wed

Tre Scalini means 'three steps' and refers to the steps that led up to this long-established bar in Piazza Navona (opposite *Dolce Vita* and *La Bevitoria* – see entries) in the days when Navona was flooded with water in order to hold boat races. Both the races and the steps are now long gone, but the bar still retains its original name and style. Ice creams are a speciality - try the tartufo nero, a rich, rich chocolate variety. Piazza Navona, built on the remains of Domitian's stadium, is the hub of the historic centre of medieval Rome and probably the liveliest square in the whole city, attracting thousands of visitors every day. It's also one of the most spectacular, with three magnificent fountains, including the spectacular Fontana dei Quattro Fiumi, designed and partly sculpted by Bernini. The fiumi - rivers - are the Danube, Ganges, Plate and Nile, representing the four corners of the world.

Il Trimani Wine Bar

Via Cernaia 37b
Tel: 06 4469630
Open: 11.30-15.00 & 18.00-03.00
Closed: Sun except in Dec

The wine bar is an offshoot of the oldest wine shop in the city, just round the corner in Via Goito. The bar offers excellent wines and good snacks, and the shop is vast, and made for browsing, especially as there's no list of the stock.

Caffè Trombetta

Via Marsala 46
Tel: 06 491478
Open: 05.30-24.00

A busy bar opposite the main line railway station, with a big wine section and also a general provisions store – a sort of small supermarket and wine merchant without the trolleys! It's part of a small chain of similar establishments. Bright and light after refurbishment; marble floors, arches and columns.

Da Vezio

Via dei Delfini 23
Tel: 06 6786036
Open: 07.00-20.00
Closed: Sun, also Tue, Wed & Sat between 14.30 & 18.00

A minuscule bar in a little back street not far from the Piazza Venezia (one of the best places in Rome for watching traffic chaos) with just two little tables at the back and a computer with Internet access 'for the comrades' (the communist party headquarters used to be in the next street, and the walls of this little place are covered with photographs and newspaper cuttings of history's best-known left-wing revolutionaries). Documents dating from 1915 have recently been discovered, and the place is now listed among the Bottegi Storici (Historic Shops) of Rome.

Enoteca Antica di Via della Croce

Via della Croce 76b
Tel: 06 6790896
Open: 10.00-01.00
Closed: 1 week Aug

One of Rome's oldest eating and drinking places, dating back to 1842 and still boasting some of the original fittings. The choice of wines by the glass (all Italian) is impressive, and you can enjoy your tipple sitting on a comfortable stool at the bar or at one of the outside tables. One of the chief attractions in the restaurant is an excellent cold buffet featuring rare cheeses from all over Italy

Vineria Reggio

Campo de' Fiori 15
Tel: 06 68803268
Open: 09.00-01.00 (Fri & Sat till 01.30, Sun from 17.00)
Closed: Sun

Located right in the market in an area which has become a popular spot for having a good time, this is one of the best and trendiest of the local bars, offering wines by the glass, at least three draught beers (served with very tasty little canapés) and a wide range of food. It's especially popular in the evening, when the pavement tables are always full. Note the original (16th-century) ceiling. Evening concerts are held from time to time in the square.

Bologna

With a population of half a million, Bologna is the capital of Emilia-Romagna, the gastronomically renowned area that gave the world Lambrusco wine, Parmesan cheese, mortadella and spaghetti bolognese. Not surprisingly, It has some fabulous food shops. Home of one of the world's oldest universities (founded in 1088), Bologna also has one of the finest art museums in Europe, splendid palaces, arcaded walks and leaning towers built by rival families. Many of the grand residences of those old families have been divided up into commercial premises, and it is not unusual to find several different shops, bars and other businesses with the same address. Bologna's café society is very varied, and there are bars and cafés for every occasion, from the grand and sophisticated to the bohemian and studenty.

Bravo Caffè

Via Mascarella 1
Tel: 051 266112
Open: 12.00-15.30 & 19.30-02.00

A nightly jazz bar (with artwork connected with the music) from September to June during the university term, Bravo also opens at lunchtime offering a clientele of students and business people a menu of salads and snacks, something from the wood-fired oven or a dish consisting of pasta, meat and a vegetable with a beer or mineral water. Lots of young people use the bar, but also local business people at lunchtime.

Il Caffè della Corte

Corte Isolani 5/b
Tel: 051 261555
Open: 08.00-21.00
Closed: Sun

A charming place for enjoying croissants and pastries with the morning papers and bowls of nibbles with a drink in the evening. Set in a pretty shaded courtyard a few minutes walk from Piazza Maggiore, it has a bar on one side and a tea room on the other, where concerts of classical music are held on Friday evenings (outside in summer). The courtyard is a further option at this friendly, civilised place.

Godot Wine Bar

Via Cartoleria 12
Tel: 051 226315
Open: 08.00-02.00
Closed: Sun

Wines from around the world are served in a modern wine bar with club-style bar stools and small tables and bench seating along the wall. Jazz plays gently in the background and you are offered tasty little nibbles to go with your drink. At the back is a 60-seater restaurant. They hold regular wine tastings here and stock around 1,000 wines including 25 by the glass which change monthly. Speciality cheeses and salami.

Golem

Piazza San Martino 3/b
Tel: 051 262620
Open: 12.00-02.00
Closed: Mon

What is Golem? In East European Hebrew legend, a creature made by magic with the use of sacred words; in another legend, a powerful creature with 'truth' written on its forehead; to mystics, a creation of the mind that comes about following a festive rite. This arts café with exhibitions of paintings on its walls has called itself Golem partly because this is the old Jewish quarter of Bologna, and partly in the belief that with the power of the idea the café could grow and develop with the creativity of its artistic clientele. More than a café, it's a place to talk, to communicate, to think, to know and to observe. Very nice people, good coffee, drinks and dishes from around the world.

Enoteca Italiana

Via Marsala 2/b
Tel: 051 235989
Open: 07.30-20.00
Closed: Sun

A corner site just off the Via dell'Independenza before you reach the Gran Teatro, selling a broad selection of wines by the glass. Customers both private and commercial come here to buy wines and take a glass, and perhaps a bite from their selection of dry cured meats and cheeses with a roll or some focaccia.

To Steki

Largho Respighi 4/e
Tel: 051 268012
Open: 10.30-23.00
Closed: Sun

A smart Greek wine bar and snackery facing the side of the Teatro Communale. All the 80 excellent wines here are Greek, and the blackboard is in Greek, but the menu cards are in Italian. They serve Paulaner beer and Greek snacks. The inside tables (priority to diners at meal times) are modern, in light beechwood, and there are seats at the bar. Outside are terraced tables where it's pleasant to sit sipping an Italian or Greek coffee. The place has become a favourite with students and the theatre crowd.

Caffè della Via

Via San Stefano 70
Tel: 051 235437
Open: 07.00-20.00
Closed: Sun

A smart daytime coffee place in Belle Epoque style, selling an excellent range of coffees and pastries. This is the media, advertising and design district of town and the professionals in those fields come here at lunchtime and for early evening aperitifs.

Florence

Sometimes called 'The Athens of Italy', Florence is a world leader in the arts, and the birthplace of Dante, Machiavelli and Michelangelo. The city is a treasure-house of Renaissance art, the jewels being the Uffizi Gallery, with works by Botticelli, Leonardo da Vinci, Raphael, Caravaggio, Fra Angelico and Dürer; Brunelleschi's Pitti Palace, now housing several museums; and the Galleria dell'Accademia, where Michelangelo's *David*, carved from a block of Carrara marble, stands behind a glass screen. In the Piazza del Duomo the vast Cathedral of Santa Maria del Fiori, almost austere behind an extravagant exterior, Giotto's bell tower and the Baptistery, with its famous bronze doors by Pisano, show different stages in the development of Florentine art and architecture. The traditional pavement café plays a slightly lesser role here than in some Italian cities, but the tourist will never be short of somewhere to pause for a coffee or an ice cream.

Amadeus
Via dei Pescioni 5/r
Tel: 055 2398229
Open: 07.00-03.30 (Sat & Sun 19.00-02.00)
The Italians and the Bavarians have always had an empathy, especially in the north of Italy, and it is very evident at this Bavarian-style bar in the city centre, two streets from Piazza della Repubblica. Set on three levels, with the feel of a German *beerstube*, it's a great place to meet for a drink, especially on a warm summer's evening.

Enoteca Baldovino
Via San Giuseppe 18/r
Tel: 055 2347220
Open: 12.00-24.30
Closed: Mon, also 16.00-18.00 in winter
Owned by a young Scots couple, David and Catherine Gardner, this is just behind the wonderful Santa Croce church. Under their guidance it has become a busy, cosmopolitan, lively wine bar to complement the trattoria over the road (where you can have full meals - seats for 30 plus a terrace). Wines at this enoteca are sold by the glass and snacks include pizza cooked in a wood-fired oven and salads. Daily specials include the very popular *crostone* - toasted Tuscan bread with a choice of about 50 melted toppings: brie and truffle cream, gorgonzola and honey.

Osteria del Boia
Via Ghibellina 70/r
Tel: 055 2638940
Open: 12.00-01.00 (Nov-Mar from 19.00)
In an old building with high-vaulted brick ceilings, robust walls and arches leading from one room to another (from white to blue to red) customers can sit at simple tables or on stools at the bar and enjoy a warm welcome, an excellent coffee or a glass or two of good Tuscan wine. At lunchtime there's a bargain set menu of a two-course meal and salad with a ½ carafe of wine. In the evening snacks such as crostini and carpaccio fill the gaps.

Caffè Donnini
Piazza della Repubblica 15/r
Tel: 055 213694
Open: 06.00-24.00 (winter till 20.30)
In the square built at the turn of the century in honour of Vittorio Emanuele, a number of society cafés quickly sprang up. Caffè Donnini was among them, and though smaller than when first opened, it remains a Gran Caffè in the old Florentine tradition where you can have an excellent coffee, pastry or ice cream standing at the bar, or sitting at a table inside or out.

Café Gilli

Piazza della Repubblica 39/r
Tel: 055 213896
Open: 07.30-01.00 (winter till 21.00)

Tradition reigns at this renowned old-world grand café with lofty frescoed and moulded ceilings and arched glass doorways leading to several rooms. Inside, the tables have mustard-coloured cloths with cream lace overlays; outside, the cloths are peach-coloured, all very pretty! Sepia photographs of scenes from bygone years abound, and one end of the panelled marble-topped counter has an imposing statue. Best known for its cocktails, Gilli is also a master of all things chocolate, not least some of the super cakes based on old and treasured recipes.

Enoteca de Giraldi

Via di Giraldi 4/r
Tel: 055 216518
Open: 11.00-15.00 & 18.00-00.30
Closed: Sun

The staff at this roomy, cool wine bar are charming and helpful, and the regulars include an eight-strong local choir who often come here after a practice or a performance to dine and then sing for fun. A sheer pleasure, and with the high ceiling the acoustics are great! Giraldi is also a wine merchant and seller of typical Tuscan preserves in jars, and the main counter has a tempting display of meat, cheeses and desserts for sale. The go-ahead owners offer wine-tasting courses, cookery lessons in the splendid Tuscan cuisine and excursions to local wineries.

Giubbe Rosse

Piazza della Repubblica 13-14
Tel: 055 212280
Open: 08.30-01.30

The first of the bars to open when the piazza was built at the turn of the century, Giubbe Rosse is named after the Viennese-style red jackets that the waiters wore in its early years. Long known as a meeting place for artists, intellectuals and journalists, it comprises three rooms: the first is the bar where gentlemen come to read the papers and discuss matters political; the second much brighter room becomes a restaurant in the evenings; the third room is more cosy and intimate. There are also tables out on the pavement.

Harry's Bar

Lungarno Amerigo Vespucci 22r
Tel: 055 2396700
Open: 12.00-24.00 (winter 12.00-15.00 & 18.00-24.00)
Closed: Sun

A famous name, and while this may not be the most illustrious of the Harry's Bars dotted around the world, it's still a great place for passing an enjoyable hour or two. On a fine day you can join the affluent locals on the patio and admire the views of the city across the river – you can just see the Ponte Vecchio. Harry's Club Sandwich, particularly rich with mayonnaise and generous with the chicken and chips, is a meal in itself, served by unfailingly polite, impeccably trained staff. Fresh fish every day. Splendid coffee.

Caffè Italiano

Via della Condotta 56
Tel: 055 291082
Open: 08.00-24.00
Closed: Sun & Aug

Umberto Montano is justly proud of his civilised, elegant and very comfortable Gran Caffè-style establishment in a quiet street behind the Piazza Signoria. Regulars relax with the newspapers in wood-panelled surroundings, or buy wines, liqueurs and coffee (beans or ground) to take home. The cakes are all made in-house, and the chocolate varieties are the tops.

Osteria Caffè Italiano

Via Isola delle Stinche 11-13/r
Tel: 055 289368
Open: 12.00-15.00 & 19.00-01.00
Closed: Mon

A café and restaurant behind the Verdi theatre, in the same ownership as *Caffè Italiano*. For snacking you can sit at an uncovered rough-hewn oak table and drink a glass of wine or two, perhaps with a plate of meats and cheeses. It has very high vaulted ceilings, and enormous French windows open to the street on summer nights to keep the place cool. The bar, along with half the room, has tall oak cupboards, glass-fronted, with back-lit shelves filled with wine bottles. The bar counter is a thick marble preparation area on an antique wooden base housing the refrigerated bottles of white wine, and there's a big brass cauldron filled with iced water and the white wines for sale by the glass. Large wrought bronze chandeliers hang from the ceiling, and the floor is a herringbone pattern of terracotta tiles.

Caffè Concerto Paszkowski

Piazza della Repubblica 6r
Tel: 055 210236
Open: 07.00-01.30

Concerts take place every night at this long-established café, which was originally a beer house. It later became the meeting place for leading politicians, and in 1991 was declared a National Monument. Inside, there is a series of high-ceilinged arched rooms, while the canopied outside seating area is surrounded by privet hedges planted in terracotta holders. Ice creams and cocktails are specialities of the house, and the snacks and pastries are all very tempting. Chocolate is made by owners Gilli. Piano bar in winter.

Caffè La Torre

Lungarno Benvenuto Cellini 65/r
Tel: 055 680643
Open: 10.00-04.00

A pleasant American-style café-cocktail bar across the river in the shadow of the tower in Piazza Giuseppe Poggi. It stays open until very late, offering little dips and nibbles with your drinks. Breakfasts are a big thing here, particularly Sunday brunch, but you can also take lunch, pop in for an aperitif, sit down to a light evening meal after a stroll along the river bank, which is only yards away, or enjoy a late-night drink with some tasty nibbles. La Torre specialises in fresh fruit juices, crêpes and focaccia.

Milan

A bustling business city and the capital of Lombardy. The gigantic Cathedral, plain and sombre behind its flamboyant Gothic exterior, is the city's most imposing building, with 224 statues, 100 gargoyles and some wonderful stained glass. La Scala is one of the world's leading opera houses; and Leonardo's *Last Supper*, in the Church of St Mary of Grace, is probably the most famous mural in the world, recently rescued from the ravages of damp and decay. Sometimes the citizens seem too busy to relax, but there are some excellent cafés and bars, and the usual Italian interest in food - from the region come minestrone, veal escalope milanese, osso buco, gorgonzola and panettone.

Baretto

Via S Andrea 3
Tel: 02 781255
Open: 11.00-01.00
Closed: Sun except spring and autumn fashion weeks
Near the point where Via Sant' Andrea crosses Via Monte Napoleone, Baretto is a smart, club-like bar with wood-panelled walls, buttoned leather-upholstered chairs and bar stools. It's a great favourite with shoppers in the Monte Napoleone, the Bond Street of Milan and home of many of the annual fashion shows.

Bar Basso

Via Plinio 39
Tel: 02 29400580
Open: 08.00-01.15
Closed: Tue
Behind the gargoyled facade is a split personality: one part features elegant part-upholstered chairs and polished tables (relax with the daily newspapers), the other (eating) area all in pine – cladding on walls, tables and benches. 500 cocktails, many using fresh fruit.

La Belle Aurore

Via Castelmorrone
Tel: 02 29406212
Open: 08.00-02.00
Closed: Sun
On the corner of Via Castelmorrone and the tree-lined Via Abamonti, this high-ceilinged café-bar has exposed aluminium duct air-conditioning and walls decorated with posters. Newspapers and magazines for lone browsing, or you can play chess on the boards provided. Specialities: cocktails, aperitifs, home-made desserts.

Biffi

Galleria Vittorio Emanuele II
Tel: 02 8057961
Open: 07.00-01.00

Very grand and very expensive, but the best place for a drink if you also want to be amazed at the vastness of the Galleria, one of Milan's social and political hubs. Many of the shops stay open late, and so does Biffi. On the food front, osso buco is a popular dish.

Caffè Litta

Corso Magenta 25
Tel: 02 8057596
Open: 07.00-21.00

A café dating from the mid-1990s but with the look of a much older predecessor on the site. Inside, it has a conservatory and curved green marble bar with a bottle shelf above, wooden tables and chairs. Pavement tables. Lots of hot and cold snack dishes, sandwiches and rolls. Nice friendly staff in brown aprons serve a clientele of office workers and students from the nearby university.

Orient Express

Via Fiori Chiari 8
Tel: 02 8056227
Open: 09.00-02.00 (piano bar Thur-Sun)

'Nostalgie Istanbul'. Railway buffs feeling nostalgic should steam along to this café-bar in an interesting street of many café-bars to enjoy a drink, perhaps a glass of one of their own-label wines and spirits. At the back, beyond the bar, is a faithful reconstruction of a carriage of the old *Orient Express* in a station at the beginning of the century. The garden is open all year round. At night the street becomes a bazaar with Africans selling leather handbags and carved wood laid out on blankets on the pavement, and South American Indians selling jewellery and knitwear. Popular, too, are the many fortune-tellers reading their tarot cards.

Osteria del Pallone

Alzaia Naviglio Grande/Viale Gorizia 30
Tel: 02 58105641
Open: 11.00-02.00

A football-themed bar at the beginning of the navigable canal. All the cups displayed, at least 40, have been won by the local amateur team, sponsored by owner Mario Farac, himself a former professional player in Serie A (Italian Premier Division). He is football mad and has another café/bar Osteria del Calcetto at Corso Garibaldi 46 (Tel: 02 80 518 65), which displays football jerseys, as well as a bar on the opposite side of the canal called Bar della Stazione, featuring model trains and other railway memorabilia. So whether you get your kicks from football or trains, Mario has a place for you. Three draught and seven bottled beers, evening cocktails, generous salads and cold cuts.

Radetzky Café

Largo La Foppa 5
Tel: 02 6572645
Open: 08.00-02.00
Closed: 2 weeks Aug

The city's thinkers march along to this corner café to enjoy a morning chat, to read the newspapers and to tuck into the excellent *cornetti* and pastries. In the evenings it's very busy with the well-dressed younger set. The full menu changes daily to inclde seasonal produce such as oysters. Good home-made desserts. One side of the room has large round polished tables, the other, small square tables with cloths, and there's a stainless-steel zinc bar counter with a range of at least 30 single malts behind. Classical music in the background.

Il Resentin Caffè

Via Mercato 24
Tel: 02 875923
Open: 12.00-01.30
Closed: Sun

'*Caffeteria, enoteca, bottega delle grappe, birraria, gastronomia, tabaccheria*'. So reads the calling card of this versatile establishment, and the pastry and bread shop next door produces further goodies. The café has two rooms, one with velvet cushions on low bench seating, the other with large polished mahogany tables and chairs. Blues and mood music in the background relaxes you while you read the newspapers - Milan's best-known paper is the *Corriere della Sera*. Note the lovely display of flowers at the bar - and the range of Scotch whiskies on offer! Outside tables. Specialities from the Trentino area including wines and grappa.

Sans Egal

Vicolo Fiori 2
Tel: 02 8693096
Open: 09.00-03.00 (Mon 19.00-02.00)

At the junction with Via Fiori Chiari in a part of town that's well provided with cafés, this one, called a café bistrot, has a smart outside seating area, with trestled railings sheltering it from the street. Inside, behind the bar, are art nouveau-style leaded coloured glass panels and mirrors. At the far end of the bar is a film screen with a silent montage of movie scenes, with background blues music. Cocktails, much more popular in Italy than in the UK, are a speciality. The menu changes daily.

Taverna Moriggi

Via Moriggi 8
Tel: 02 86450880
Open: 08.00-01.00
Closed: Sat pm, all Sun

A very old and very special tavern with a lofty beamed ceiling, an atmospheric bar and a large luncheon room which becomes an overspill for the bar in the evening. The choice for those eating includes a good range of pasta and a fine selection of cheeses displayed on a large oak sideboard. The house wine is made from *fragolo* grapes, which, as the name suggests, are redolent of strawberries. Moriggi's owners grow the grapes in their own vineyards, and there are no labels on the bottles, because under Italian law your own wine is not subject to duty if sold on the premises. Sometimes travelling minstrels play jazz and pass the hat round!

Le Trottoir

Corso Garibaldi 1
Tel: 02 801002
Open: 11.00-03.00

A young person's bar on the corner of Via Tivoli, well-established, quite arty and very popular. It has a deep mahogany bar counter with lots of stools and wooden tables with bench seats downstairs, while upstairs are tables and chairs and provision for nightly live music (very varied: jazz, rock, Celtic folk, guitar). Snacks and full meals are served. They have an excellent selection of malt whiskies.

> "I smoke in moderation. Only one cigar at a time."
>
> **Mark Twain.**

Zucca in Galleria

Piazza Duomo 21
Tel: 02 86464435
Open: 07.30-20.30
Closed: Mon

An impressive arch to the left of the wonderful Duomo is the entrance to the stunning Galleria Vittorio Emanuele II. Immediately on your left through the arch is Zucca, opened with the Gallery in 1867, and recently renovated. Verdi and Toscanini used to drop in on their way back from La Scala at the other end of the Gallery, King Umberto I came because it served the best coffee in the city, and to this day artists, painters, authors, politicians and musicians are numbered among the regulars. There is a room upstairs where you can enjoy a quick meal at midday or Sunday morning brunch. The barmen can make the cappuccino forth into little patterns. One of the specialities is *Rabrabaro Zucca*, a Milanese liqueur with a taste like Campari.

Naples

The double-peaked Mount Vesuvius stands guard over the spectacular bay and this colourful, vibrant city of surprises. The National Archaeological Museum, 16th-century building, is full of finds, particularly decorative wall paintings, from the nearby Roman towns of Herculaneum and Pompeii, overcome respectively by mud and ash by the eruptions of the volcanoes in 79AD. Both are of enormous historical interest, having been preserved almost intact to give a priceless insight into life in the great days of the Roman Empire. The picture gallery of the Capodimonte Palace, in the hills above the city, is a real treasure house, with works by Brueghel, Botticelli, Mantegna, Raphael, El Greco, Titian, Caravaggio and many other great masters. Take the funicular railway up to Vomero for more museums and great views.

Café Amadeus

Piazza Amadeo 5
Tel: 081 7613023
Open: 07.00-03.00

A popular bar in the square at the bottom of one of the funicular railways from the Vomero (the other stations are at Piazza Augusto and Piazza Montesanto). As you walk down the Via Colonna Vittoria towards the historic city centre, note the magnificent church high above you on the left; to the right are steps down to the Via San Pasquale, leading to the waterfront .

Bilancione

Via Posillipo 238/b
Tel: 081 7691923
Open: 07.00-01.00 (winter till 23.00)
Closed: Wed

A serious contender for the best ice creams in all Naples. Their *nocciola* (hazelnut) ice cream has scooped the *Cono d'Oro* (Golden Cone) prize for the past 20 years. And there's a bonus: the view from the bar, which is on the road that climbs out of the Mergellina into the Posillipo and Merliani district, is a splendid one of the Bay of Naples to the port.

Gran Caffè La Caffetiera

Piazza Vanvitelli 10
Tel: 081 5782592
Open: 07.00-01.00

A very smart bar and tea room in the main square in the Vomero, Alta Borghese. You can eat outside under umbrellas immediately in front of the café, where a huge brass cafetière (their logo) is displayed. Across the pavement under some trees are several more tables in a fenced-off area. Tuck into scrumptious desserts and pastries: rum baba, torta caprese with chocolate and almond liqueur, torta Limoncello from Sorrento. There's another chic branch (Tel: 81 7644243) at Piazza dei Martiri 30, and two in Rome (Via Margutta 61a Tel: 06 321 3344 & Piazza di Pietra 00186 Tel: 06 679 8147).

Lo Chalet Ciro de Rosario

Via Mergellina
Tel: 081 669928
Open: 06.45-01.30
Closed: Wed

Rosario Fummo claims to sell the best ice cream in Naples (but there are several others making the same claim!). Under a canopy at the front of the bar are ice cream counters and a refrigerated display of ice creams and cream cakes, and, on the other side of the pavement, tables and chairs under a long canopy.

Caffè Gambrinus

Piazza Trieste e Trento
Tel: 081 417582
Open: 08.00-01.30 (Fri & Sat till 02.30)

Down the years monarchs, intellectuals, poets, painters, sculptors and other notables have passed through the doors of this beautifully decorated café, which claims to have inspired some of the composers of classical Neapolitan songs. To the left of the café is the Piazza del Plebiscito with the 17th-century Royal Palace on one side and the Church of St Francis of Paola, modelled on the Roman Pantheon, on the other. Opposite the café is the Teatro San Carlo, built by Charles lll in 1816, the largest opera house in Italy and one of the world's most distinguished. Gambrinus will be adding brunch to its offerings in 2001.

Caffè Lirico

Via San Carlo 7/a
Tel: 081 413813
Open: 06.00-23.00
Closed: Sun

In a colonnade opposite the entrance to the imposing Teatro San Carlo, Caffè Lirico is a popular meeting place for musicians, musical directors and young hopeful opera-singers. On theatre nights, of course, it throngs with the public. The alternative is to go into the magnificent Galleria to the Bar Brasiliano (Tel: 418 383, open daily 07.00-21.00) where young artists and musicians also gather.

Mario Daniele

Via Scarlatti 104-106
Tel: 081 5780555
Open: 07.30-22.00 (Sat till 24.00)

An elegant bar up in the wealthy Vomero district, known as the Alta Borghese. It also offers good ice cream, excellent pastries and a buffet of hot and cold dishes, served either in a cool room inside or under a canopy on the pavement. They also make their own chocolates and a speciality cake called torrone.

San Remo

Capital of the Riviera di Ponente, a fine old place with all the amenities for the holidaymaker. The best area for exploring is the Old Town - La Pigna (the Fir Cone), with its warren of little streets and alleys. Lovely flower market, lively casino.

La Bouillabaisse

Piazza dei Dolori
Tel: 0184 501571
Open: 12.00-15.00 & 19.00-22.00

A restaurant of character in La Pigna, the old centre of San Remo that is a great place to explore and is gradually being tidied up. Owner Norberto bought and restored the place while at the same time cooking and making friends with visitors from all over the world. In winter there's a real wood fire and grill where he cooks mainly fish.

Caffè Castelli

Corso Imperatrice 17
Tel: 0184 543402
Open: 09.00-03.30
Closed: Wed in winter

A café-bar-restaurant now owned and run by Vincenzo Castelli, whose uncle Dino went to Hollywood in the 50s to seek a career in acting. Before long he opened a restaurant, where all his film star friends became regulars. Around the walls of this San Remo establishment opposite the casino are photos of him with his Cadillac in Hollywood, and the stars who visited his restaurant there. The bar is cool, roomy and comfortable, and there's a terrace of pavement chairs and tables under an awning. Simple snacks are available at all times – cold cuts, frittata and sandwiches – and full meals with advance notice. From 22.00 the mood changes and the café turns into a disco-cum-pub.

Caffè Colombo

Piazza Colombo 2
Tel: 0184 504441
Open: 07.30-01.00
Closed: Sun

San Remo's oldest ice cream parlour, situated in the first square you come to approaching San Remo from the east, at the foot of the historic centre. Little has changed since its opening in 1916 except that it looks cleaner and brighter than in the sepia photos of the time. Pavement tables stand in the shade of the arcade overlooking the square.

Osteria Enoteca Vini d'Italia

Corso Mombello 5
Tel: 0184 591747
Open: 09.00-02.00 (Mon till 15.00)
Closed: Sun

A roomy, comfortable café in the grand style in what is probably the prettiest street in San Remo, with palms and a fountain right in front of the premises. The café is quite new, but all the fittings and furniture are genuine antiques, and even the name is old, taken from a famous bar that existed for many years further up the street but which died some 25 years ago. Snacks include pizzas and typical Ligurian dishes, and there's a large selection of Italian wines.

Siena

An ancient city of the arts built on three red clay hills, and once of great importance in the worlds of wool and banking and a serious rival to the much more powerful Florence. The ravishing Piazza del Campo is the scene of the Palio delle Contrade, a brief but spectacular bareback horserace going back to the Renaissance and held each July 2nd and August 16th between riders from the city's 17 contrade (parishes).
The race takes little more than a minute, but the excitement lasts all day.

Il Palio

Piazza del Campo 47
Tel: 0577 282055
Open: 08.00-03.00 (Nov-Feb till 20.30

The most central of an arc of cafés, bars and restaurants with identical terracotta parasols looking down on the Palazzo Pubblico (a Gothic town hall with Italy's second highest medieval bell tower). The owners plan to double the size of this one in 2001, since they now have four shops in a row. They are all situated on the north side of the brick-paved square, surely one of the most beautiful in the world, and the scene of the thrilling annual bareback horse races. Fine coffee, splendid savoury and sweet croissants and panini filled with prime local produce.

Treviso

The claim is that Treviso boasts the largest street market in Italy – it is said to run for 2km! There is every kind of merchandise on sale – 300 metres at least on both sides are devoted to flowers and plants; then there are kitchenware, hardware and clothes stalls of all kinds.

Hosteria Arman

Via Manzoni 27
Tel: 0422 547747
Open: 08.30-21.00
Closed: Sun

A large, bustling, family-owned market bar that makes its own prosecco and also offers an own-label red wine to enjoy with little snacks.

Bar Muscoli's

Via Pescheria 25
Tel: 0422 583390
Open: 07.00-02.00
Closed: Sun & 3 weeks in Sept

A popular and cheerful wine bar opened in the mid-1970s, facing the fish market, and with the same owners as the fish shop next door. This town abounds with water – canals run right through it, and they have isolated the fish market cleverly, so that when it is swabbed down, the water runs immediately away by the canal. Tables outside in summer.

Trieste

Facing the Adriatic in the far top corner of Italy, Trieste is at the crossroads of Mediterranean and Central European cultures, with a historical legacy that owes much to both. Sometimes dominating its neighbours, at other times taken over by foreign powers, Trieste was occupied three times by Napoleon between 1797 and 1813, and was later part of the Austrian Empire, then an autonomous province under German administration. After the end of World War II, the city was once again occupied until it returned to Italian administration in 1954. Trieste is rich in grand buildings and churches which reflect its history as a melting pot of races and religions. There are many museums, too, and the old Campo Marzio railway station, from which trains once left for Central Europe, now houses a collection of steam and electric locomotives. The city's ethnic diversity is also apparent in its cafés, whose offerings include pastries of Austrian and Hungarian origins and the traditional *rebechin*, meaty snacks to be enjoyed with a glass of wine or beer. The best-known local wine is Terrano, which has been made since Roman times.

Caffè San Marco

Via Battisti 18
Tel: 040 363 538
Open: 07.00-24.00
Closed: Mon

Opened at the beginning of 1914 but destroyed in the war that started soon afterwards. Rebuilt in the 1920s, it soon took its place among the favourite dens for artists, writers and politicians. The coffee tables have witnessed the conception of essays, novels, poems and revolutions: in cafés such as this the most important pages of the history of European culture were written. The interior has a Viennese look, with enromous mirrors, cast-iron tables, black leather armchairs and beautifully restored friezes painted by Marussignon.

Caffè Tommaseo

Riva Tre Novembre
Tel: 040 366 765
Open: 08.00-24.00 (Fri & Sat till 01.00)

A seafront location close to the social and political centre of the city, the massive Piazza dell'Unità d'Italia with the Town Hall at one end. Established in 1848, this was one of the places where the flames of the movement for Italian liberty were spread; since the outset it has been a rendezvous for politicians and business people. The classically-inspired interior, lovingly restored in the 1980s, features mirrors imported from Belgium 100 years ago and the Thonet-style tables and chairs that are a classic symbol of the Belle Epoque café.

Caffè-Bar Pasticceria Torinese

Corso Italia 2
Tel: 040 632 689
Open: 07.00-21.00

Small and charming, a favourite with the people of Turin ever since it opened 80 years ago. The inside is full of cosy little niches, each with its own little marble-topped table that's just about big enough for a couple of cups of coffee. Wood is much in evidence, especially ebony, which gives the interior something of the look of a luxury liner in miniature.

Turin

The capital of Piedmont, a city of almost 1 million inhabitants, Turin is Italy's headquarters of fashion (along with Milan) and cars, with large squares, green expanses, stylish avenues, opulent cafés and Fiat-funded suburbs. Most visitors aim for the Cathedral of St John and the famous Turin shroud, or the Palazzo Carignano, birthplace of Victor Emanuele ll and site of the first meetings of the Italian parliament; car buffs head south to the motor museum, among whose exhibits are the first Fiat (1899), the mighty Itala that won the 1907 Peking-Paris race and the Isotta Fraschini driven by Gloria Swanson in *Sunset Boulevard*. There's also a special section on the development of the car tyre.

Caffè Baratti & Milano

Piazza Castello 27
Tel: 011 5613060
Open: 08.00-20.00
Closed: Mon

Top-quality confectionery is the stock in trade of this elegant and striking café, behind whose facade the amazing bar counter in marble with a bronze panel, the mirrored walls, the mahogany panelling, the chandeliers and the elaborate ceilings are quite breathtaking. Invitingly comfortable seats enhance the pleasure of a visit to this marvellous place, whose chocolate cake *torta Baratti* should not be missed.

Fiorio

Via Po 8
Tel: 011 8170612
Open: 08.00-02.00 (winter till 01.00)
Closed: Mon

The oldest caffè/gelateria in Turin, dating from 1780, and situated among some of the grandest buildings in the city. It soon became the haunt of the rich and famous, but in 1845 it was refurbished under the direction of the sculptor Bogliani, who turned it into a very popular place for the townsfolk. With this new clientele it became known as the Caffè della Confederazione in 1850 and remained such until the turn of the century, when it was taken up again by the grander Torinese, who have stayed faithful to it ever since. It's very grand, and the ice cream is superb.

Mokita

Piazza San Carlo 217
Tel: 011 5628616
Open: 07.00-02.00
Closed: Mon

New owners have kept things as they were at this smart art deco-style café in an equally smart arcaded square filled with elegant shops. Mokita has an undulating bar counter on a dark brown base, two or three tables inside and several in the arcade outside. The speciality here is ice cream, of which there are at least 20 flavours.

Caffè Mulassano

Piazza Castello 15
Tel: 011 547990
Open: 07.30-23.00

The finest craftsmen were involved in the woodwork, carving, gilding, and marbling when the café first opened in the early part of this century, since when it has always been a favourite with both audience and performers at the nearby Teatro Regio. Turin first sampled *bruschetta* and *tramezzini* here in 1925, and both specialities are still very popular, the latter with some amazing fillings such as lobster or swordfish.

Rollplay Café

Piazza Castello 117
Tel: 011 538853
Open: 07.00-21.00 (Fri & Sat till 03.00)
Closed: Wed

Situated in cloisters on the corner (Via Viotti) of a very handsome square, this cafeteria serves a range of dishes, from ice creams to full meals. You can sit outside and admire the magnificent Royal Palace with its two rearing horses at the entrance.

Caffè San Carlo

Piazza San Carlo 156
Tel: 011 532586/5617748
Open: 07.00-02.00

Established in 1828, this elegant and popular café has tables set in the spacious and elegant arcade outside or beyond in the stylish square under parasols in an area afforded some privacy by tall bushes. They specialise in cakes and pastries here, and there's also a restaurant serving both lunch and dinner. But the best snacks come late at night – from 23.45 onwards they make all sorts of crepes with fresh fruit. *Bicierin* is a drink made with chocolate, coffee and cream.

Caffè Torino

Piazza San Carlo 204
Tel: 011 547356/545118
Open: 07.30-01.00 (Sat & Sun 08.00-02.00)

A very smart, grand café-restaurant in the elegantly arcaded San Carlo square. A listed historic building as well as a long-established business, it makes an impact the moment you enter with its marble-topped bar with ornate 19th-century panelling, glass chandeliers and a sweeping staircase leading up from the restaurant, where seafood is a speciality. It's open early for breakfast with sweet pastries, and if you look up at the ceiling you will see lines of verse, maxims for the day. Caffè Torino also specialises in chocolates, prettily packaged in elegant boxes.

Venice

There will never be anywhere in the world like La Serenissima, this magical city built on an archipelago of 118 islets, its buildings supported by millions of larch poles. It fights a constant battle against the forces of nature, with the ground sinking and the water rising. The resident population of around 75,000 is less than half what it was before the Second World War, but 20 million sightseers visit Venice every year. They come to see St Mark's Square with its 15th-century clock tower; the Doge's Palace, former home of the Venetian Republic's rulers and the seat of government and justice; the Bridge of Sighs, connecting the Doge's Palace to the prison where Casanova was once an unwilling guest; and the Rialto Bridge, built at the end of the 16th century with a centre arch tall enough to permit the passage of an armed galley; to take a ride in a gondola or a waterbus (vaporetto); and maybe to sip a Bellini in Harry's Bar; and to get off the beaten track and explore the little alleyways and hidden squares. Major annual events include the regatta on the first Sunday in September, the Film Festival (also in September) and the biennial Modern Art Show.

Bar Accademia Foscarini

Dorsoduro 878/C
Tel: 041 5227281
Open: 07.00 23.00 (winter till 20.00)
Closed: Tue

Two brothers, Roberto and Adriano, run this first-rate sandwich bar next to the Academy of Art, whose gallery houses the finest collection of Venetian art in existence. The ceiling in the brothers' bar is quite astonishing – small, heavily ornate panels in Gothic style - and the second room has windows looking out on to the Grand Canal. The Accademia Bridge leads across the canal into the San Marco district.

Trattoria Antica Mola

Cannaregio 2800
Tel: 041 717492
Open: 08.30-23.00

A canalside trattoria, just across the Ponte dei Ormesini, decorated with photographs and memorabilia relating to gondoliers, some of whom gather here at lunchtime. Renato Bona, a famous gondolier, in whose memory a regatta is held every year in July/August, is remembered here with his oar and its rowlock, mounted as a trophy and presented annually to the victor ludorum of the regatta.

Osteria ai Assassini

Rio Terà dei Assassini, San Marco 3695
Tel: 041 5287986
Open: 11.30-15.00 & 18.45-23.00
Closed: L Sat & all Sun

Using only the best produce from the markets, Giuseppe Galardi provides a different menu each day at his splendid osteria, with fresh fish the Friday speciality. He keeps an excellent range of DOC wines at the bar, and a very good selection of cheeses, pastries and tarts.

Enoteca Boldrin

Salizzada San Canciano, Cannaregio 5550
Tel: 041 5237859
Open: 09.30-21.00
Closed: Sun

From the Rialto Bridge, go along the Salizzada S Giovanni Crisostomo and turn right to find this large modern wine merchant and wine bar, whose impressive list of DOC wines is available by bottle or glass. Also on offer is a selection of *polpette* (deep-fried croquettes), sandwiches, and hot and cold main dishes. Food specialities are prawns, lasagne with rocket and fegato (liver) veneziana. You can eat or drink at the bar or at marble-topped tables.

Osteria alla Botte

Calle della Bissa, San Marco 5482
Tel: 041 5209775
Open: 10.00-23.00 (Wed till 15.00)
Closed: Thur

In a narrow street on the northernmost edge of the San Marco district, a hostelry with a lot of wood in its decoration and wine barrels and demijohns all around. To accompany the excellent wine are some first-rate snacks, including the Venetian dish *kale di granchio* (rice and crabmeat croquettes).

Il Caffè

Dorsoduro 2963, Campo Santa Margherita
Tel: 041 5287998
Open: 07.00-02.00
Closed: Sun

A great place for breakfast, open early for coffee and croissants, and a perfect spot to read the morning paper and enjoy the sun before it gets too hot. Day-long snacks include panini, crostini and tramezzini. In the square, people are bustling about, getting the children off to school, or grabbing a coffee on their way to college or work, or buying groceries and fresh fish. On Thursdays in summer the café hosts jazz and blues concerts from 21.00 to 23.00.

Cantina Do Mori

San Polo 429
Tel: 041 5225401
Open: 08.30-20.30
Closed: Sun

Popular and full of atmosphere, the Cantina, in a 500-year-old building, is a not-to-be-missed wine bar whose walls are hung with scores of copper pans. They serve wonderful tapas-style snacks and an excellent selection of wines to suit all pockets. Apart from a couple of chairs, it's standing room only.

Cantina Do Spade

San Polo 860
Tel: 041 5210574
Open: 09.00-14.30 & 17.30-23.00
Closed: D Thur & all Sun

Cross the Rialto bridge from San Marco into San Polo, and a few little back streets away, through a low arch, is this small cantina (cellar), with wooden walls, wooden chairs and wooden tables. It sells a huge range of wines to accompany simple snack dishes. The cantina has existed since the 14th century and has recently opened up a room where, in the 1700s, Casanova used to entertain his ladies. A secret door leads from the room to his house - useful if an irate husband turned up out of the blue!

Trattoria Corte Sconta

Calle del Pestrin, Castello 3886
Tel: 041 5227024
Open: 12.30-14.00 & 19.30-22.00
Closed: Sun & Mon

A warm, cosy little trattoria hidden away but well worth seeking out. It has a broad, low-level wooden bar counter, low ceilings and comfortable, robust tables and chairs. Excellent seafood, very decent house wine.

Bar Ducale

Fondamente delle Ostreghe, San Marco 2354
Tel: 041 5210002
Open: 07.30-21.00

Facing you as you cross the Ponte San Maurizio is this small, smart bar that started life some 70 years ago as a pharmacy and still retains many of the old fittings. Coffee and pastries, panini and tramezzini.

Caffè Florian

Piazza San Marco 55-59
Tel: 041 5285338
Open: 09.30-24.00
Closed: Wed (in winter), 1 week before Christmas & 1st week Jan

This renowned café first opened its doors in 1720 as Venice Triumphant, and throughout its life it has been the meeting place for artists, poets, writers and politicians (Casanova, Goethe, Byron, Dickens, Dali, Proust et al), as well as a venue for art exhibitions and musical events. There are six luxurious little rooms in different styles with plush velvet seating, marble tables, gilt-framed pictures, splendid frescoes and Murano glassware, and outside seating for around 50 in rows under the porch. A band plays in the summer.

Harry's Bar

Calle Vallaresso, San Marco 1323
Tel: 041 5285777
Open: 10.00-23.00

Home of the Bellini, a beguiling blend of peach nectar and champagne, Harry's Bar attracts visitors from all over the world, with windows looking on to the Fondamenta dei Fontegheto, and a view across St Mark's basin to the Giudecca and the imposing church of St George on its island. Prosecco is a popular alternative to the Bellini, and for solid nourishment there are sandwiches and snacks. The restaurant above is the place where carpaccio was invented. The other Harry's in Venice is Harry's Dolci, Fondamenta San Bagio773, Giudecca Tel: 041 5224844, a café and restaurant with outside tables under canopies by the Giudecca Canal.

Gran Caffè Lavena

Piazza San Marco 133
Tel: 041 5224070
Open: 09.30-00.30
Closed: Tue in winter

A pavement café with a 250-year history. From 1879 to 1883 Richard Wagner was a regular, and reputedly wrote some of his *Tristan and Isolde* and *Parsifal* here. Nowadays a small orchestra plays old Neapolitan songs and more modern Italian numbers.

Bar Ae Maravegie

Dordsoduro 1185, Callo della Toletta
No telephone
Open: 09.00-23.00 (varies!)

Cheap, cheerful and comfortable enough to pause for a cup of coffee, a draught lager or a glass of decent local wine to enjoy with a sandwich.

Osteria al Mascaron

Calle Longa S Maria Formosa, Castello 5225
Tel: 041 5225995
Open: 12.00-15.00 & 19.30-23.30
Closed: Sun

Seafood dishes are a speciality at this lovely old bar and trattoria with wood-beamed ceilings. But if you're not hungry you can still take a table and order a glass or carafe of very drinkable local wine. A cheerful, friendly place that's popular with reporters.

Osteria Al Milion

Corte 1a Al Milion, Cannaregio 5841
Tel: 041 5229302
Open: 12.00-15.00 & 18.00-23.00
Closed: Wed

Tucked away in a tiny square reached through a narrow passage near the Rialto Bridge, a very agreeable hostelry with a charming bar and a capacious dining room. On the walls are lots of framed napkin drawings by the artists who have adopted this place as their own. There are also chairs and tables outside.

Quadri

Piazza San Marco 120
Tel: 041 5289299
Open: 09.00-24.00 (summer till 00.30)
Closed: Mon Nov-Mar

A renowned, very elegant and very happening café-restaurant that has long been a fixture on the Piazza San Marco, with a rollcall of distinguished visitors, including Stendhal, Dumas, Byron, Wagner, Proust and Chaplin. The gilded mirrors and painted panels make a very glamorous setting for enjoying a cup of coffee or chocolate, an aperitif or a cocktail, or you can sit outside in the square to listen to the café's own orchestra playing. A small extra charge is levied for this musical treat. Light snacks are served in the café and a full menu in the second-floor restaurant, where beef, seafood and liver veneziana are among the specialities. For the indulgent there are scrumptious home-made desserts, including double chocolate mousse and *gelato al forno*, baked ice cream with chopped almonds, cream, amaretto liqueur and meringue.
Italy Café of the Year 2001

Hostaria ai Rusteghi

Corte del Pistor, San Marco 5529
Tel: 041 5232205
Open: 09.30-15.00 & 17.00-20.30
Closed: Sun

A grand little establishment in a narrow street, run by a very friendly couple Roberto and his wife Manuella. Good wines, draught beer and coffee are all available, but their specialities are is rustic rolls filled with good cheeses and salami, and wines from Veneto and Friuli.

Enoteca Al Volto

Calle Cavalli, San Marco 4081
Tel: 041 5228945
Open: 10.00-14.30 & 17.00-22.00
Closed: Sun

A wonderful, friendly wine bar with a prodigious stock of wines (some 1,300!) and a splendid cold table. The scene is set by heavy oak tables, benches and stools, and the ceiling is covered in wine labels. The walls are decorated with bits of old furniture, and there is a long piece of prose, politely requesting you not to smoke, which everyone ignores!

Verona

The old part of Verona is set in a curve of the River Adige, along whose banks are produced some of Italy's finest wines. The historic centre, now more or less free of traffic, is focused on the old Roman Amphitheatre, which these days is at the centre of the opera festival which takes place each year in July and August. There is a plethora of tiny streets and alleyways, many of which are not on most maps (but if you can make it to the Via Mazzini someone will probably point you in the right direction). Prominent on the tourist trail are the Art Museum, a striking modern building in the 14th-century castle; the Church of San Zeno Maggiore with its triptych by Mantegna; and Juliet's House (Casa di Giulietta), which is said to have belonged to the Capulets.

Al Carro Armato

Vicolo Gatto 2/a
Tel: 045 8030175
Open: 10.00-15.00 & 18.00-02.00 (but you can get a coffee in the afternoon)
Closed: Wed
A very reasonably priced wine bar whose name means 'armoured car'. The logo is the tank that Leonardo da Vinci designed, and a model made from his drawing stands on a sideboard in the dining room. All sorts of locals come here – old and young, working class and professionals – to enjoy a drink and a snack with a newspaper in the daytime calm. In the evening things can get a little more lively, particularly on Tuesdays in winter, when live jazz makes the place jump.

Osteria Mondo d'Oro

Via Mondo d'Oro 4
Tel: 045 8032679
Open: 10.00-14.30 & 17.00-22.00 (summer open all day)
Closed: Mon (but Sun instead in May & Jun)
Is it a wine merchant? Is it a delicatessen? Is it a restaurant? Is it a bar? All four! Tucked away in a pedestrianised area off the Via Mazzini, it has an extensive range of wines by the glass and a chilled display of cheeses, cooked meats and dried sausages to buy to take home, to snack on the premises or to combine with a meal in the restaurant. Outside tables.

La Toga

Via Scudo di Francia 3
Tel: 045 597945
Open: 10.30-15.00 & 18.00-24.00 (summer till 04.00)
Closed: Tue
La Toga (full name La Bottega del Vino) is a 15th-century building owned by a partnership called Societa La Toga. This is where the gentlemen of Verona come to discuss the world and its woes, and to fill in their betting slips. Founded in 1890, it is a wine bar and restaurant, its ornate exposed beams inscribed with good advice as to why you should 'drink wine and let water work the mill'. Big bowls of little dry biscuits and grissini sit on the old oak tables in the bar area, where scores of wines are sold by the glass with a different glass for each type of wine (some magnificent *balons* for the better reds). Next to the bar counter is a chilled display of antipasti – cheeses, cooked meats and salamis, and various salads. If the gentlemen are here, where are the ladies? Probably shopping, as La Toga is just off Via Mazzini, Turin's answer to Oxford Street, and the main market is also very close in Piazza d'Erbe.

Netherlands

Telephone Code: 00 31

With the exception of Malta, this is Europe's most densely populated country. A large percentage of the land is below sea level (the highest point in the country is the Vaalserberg Hill at 321m), and the country's history tells of a constant struggle against the sea, with engineers using incredible skill and ingenuity to preserve and extend the land with dunes and dykes and pumping stations that work round the clock. Holland is probably best known for its flowers, providing over 50% of all the cut flowers and potted plants sold throughout the world. The village of Boskoop is perhaps the largest garden centre in the world but all over the country there are festivals and exhibitions and auctions.

The great masters of painting did much to make the country famous, starting with Hieronymus Bosch and reaching a dazzling peak in the 17th century with Franz Hals, Rembrandt, Ruysdael and Vermeer. Beer and gin (once known in England as 'Hollands') are the national drinks, but there's also a long tradition of drinking coffee, particularly in Amsterdam's much loved Brown Cafés, so called because of their dark brown interiors.

Amsterdam

A city of 160 canals crossed by 1,400 bridges, the liberated capital of a liberated country, with a long and rich history and a round-the-clock whirl of social and cultural activity. It's an easy place for the sightseer, and boat tours are an excellent way of seeing; cycling is what most of the locals do, a cheap alternative to the efficient service provided by the metro, trams and buses. The works of the great Dutch and Flemish masters hang prominently in Amsterdam's Rijksmuseum, while Van Gogh has a museum to himself. Other places to visit include Ann Frank's House and the state-of-the-art Holland Experience. Sightseeing soon generates a thirst and Amsterdam is as well supplied as almost any city in the world with cafés and bars. These range from the famous Brown Cafés with their nicotine-stained walls to grand establishments with terraces, literary cafés and alternative bars.

Aas van Bokalen

Keizergracht 335
Tel: 20 623 0917
Open: 17.00-01.00 (Fri & Sat till 02.00)
An unpretentious Brown Café in a pleasant canalside setting, with music from the 70s to the 90s - a place for everyone. Food is served until 22.30.

Backstage

Utrechtsedwarsstraat 67
Tel: 20 622 3638
Open: 10.00-17.30
Closed: Sun
A very well-known and very theatrical coffee bar-boutique, owned by a larger than life character who was formerly a well-known cabaret entertainer and appeared in over 30 countries in partnership with his late brother. The walls and ceiling are covered in dazzling pop art, cartoons and photographs of the brothers in action. The clientele ranges from local residents to tourists and show business people.

Café Ebeling

Overtoom 52
Tel: 20 689 1218
Open: 11.00-01.00 (Fri & Sat till 03.00)

Features of the bank that previously occupied the premises have been adapted for its current role - for example, the toilets are downstairs in the old vault. The café itself is on two levels: the ground floor is a circular reading station with newspapers and comfortable sofas, and upstairs is the bar area with the kitchen behind it. A wide variety of coffees, teas, wine and beers is on offer, as well as some light meals and snacks served until 17.30. At the far end of the long bar is a games area with pool table, pinball machine, chess and backgammon boards.

Café Americain

Leidskade 97
Tel: 20 556 3000
Open: 12.00-23.00

The café, an outpost of 1930s America, has retained many of its best features, including the vaulted ceiling, original light fittings, some extraordinary tile murals and superb stained glass. Long reading tables make it the place for a civilised chat, a quiet study or a leisurely sweep through the international newspapers over a cup of coffee. The café has a separate entrance in the renowned American Hotel, designed by Willem Kromhout in 1902.

Benelux Special Award 2001

de Kleine Karseboom

Nieuwendijk 51
Tel: 20 624 9251
Open: 10.30-01.00 (Fri & Sat till 03.00)

A lovely old corner café with an inviting white wooden facade, lace curtains and pot-plants in windows. There is often a guest beer on tap and a limited range of bar snacks is available throughout the day.

Koepel Café

Kattengat/Hekelveld
Tel: 20 621 2223
Open: 11.00-01.00 (Fri & Sat till 02.00)

A tourist café in the Renaissance Hotel with a covered terrace that opens up when the weather is warmer. It's a very convenient stop-off for a quick drink before leaving for the railway station just around the corner; snacks and full meals are also served. Koepel means 'dome' and refers to the dome on the church building next door.

De Kroon

Rembrandtplein 17/1
Tel: 20 625 2011
Open: 10.00-01.00 (Fri & Sat till 02.00)

A theatre bar when it opened 100 years ago, De Kroon takes a natural history museum as its rather bizarre decorative theme. Skeletons, animal skins, stuffed birds and butterflies are mostly displayed in glass cabinets built into the large horseshoe-shaped bar, but other ghoulish artefacts, including some fantastic snakes preserved in jars, are just mounted on the walls. Great fun for a drink and a bite to eat or just a cup of tea or coffee. It occupies the same building as several TV and radio stations, so it's very popular with media people.

Du Lac

Haarlemmerstraat 118
Tel: 20 624 4265
Open: 11.00-02.00 (Fri & Sat till 03.00, Sun till 02.00)

Once a bank, now a beautiful grand café done out in art deco style with greenery and objects of all kinds, from bottles and model cars to crocodile skins. Good range of drinks and snacks to enjoy in the conservatory, on the raised gallery or tucked away in one of the snugs. They no longer have live music on Sunday; instead there's a DJ for R&B Thursday, Friday and Saturday.

Café Luxembourg

Spuistraat 22-24
Tel: 20 620 6264
Open: 09.00-01.00 (Fri & Sat till 02.00)

Large, atmospheric Luxembourg has established itself as one of the best cafés in Amsterdam, through attention to detail, an excellent breakfast and attentive service by young, attractive staff. Food is served from opening time to 23.00 (midnight Friday and Saturday), and the vast choice runs from breakfast with scrambled eggs with smoked salmon to dim sum, Luxemburgers, club sandwiches and veal croquettes. With abundant comfortable seating inside and more out on the pavement, it's a popular meeting place for large groups of friends embarking on a big night out, but during the quieter daytime hours, racks of newspapers are available to those who have just popped in for a cup of coffee or a quick snack.

Het Molenpad

Prinsengracht 653
Tel: 20 625 9680
Open: 12.00-01.00 (Fri & Sat till 02.00)
Peaceful by day, when a discerning crowd come to read the papers and enjoy a glass of wine with classical music and the monthly-changing exhibitions of work by local artists. Later on, however, local arts students fill the dark, narrow place and the atmosphere and music become a lot more upbeat. This is also the venue for tastings and meetings organised by the local wine society. Light lunches; full evening menu.

Nieuwe Lelie

Nieuwe Leliestraat 83
Tel: 20 622 5493
Open: 14.00-01.00 (Fri & Sat till 02.00)
Monthly exhibitions of artwork hang on the walls of a corner bar-café with tall windows, heavy brocade curtains and just enough light to make out the quirky assortment of objects dotted around the place. All the usual beers and spirits are on offer, plus orange juice and special Jordaan liqueurs produced in the local brewery. Light snacks and cold meats. Billiards and chess. Live music at the weekend - Flamenco or Klazmer (Yiddish).

Ovidius

Spuistraat 139
Tel: 20 620 8977
Open: 09.30-21.00 (Sun from 10.30, Thu till 23.00)
A beautiful café serving great coffee, super sandwiches and light lunches and suppers. Next to a shopping mall, this bright and airy modern place spread over three floors boasts some fabulous window seats, both in the ground-floor bar area and upstairs in the gallery. It's very popular with shoppers and stays open later on Thursday to cope with the late-evening mall visitors.

Papeneiland

Prinsengracht 2
Tel: 20 624 1989
Open: 10.00-01.00
A cosy, relaxed Brown Café in a corner of the Jordaan, with the hubbub of the nearby market every Saturday and Tuesday. Inside, the beautiful tiled fireplace, worn wooden benches and stools, and heavy velvet curtains on brass rails, are lit by the many little lamps and candles. Sandwiches and drinks.

De Prinsessebar

Haarlemmerstraat 105
Tel: 20 624 01 06
Open: 11.00-01.00 (Fri & Sat till 02.00)
Closed: Wed
In business for 120 years, a family-run Brown Café with a loyal contingent of locals. The atmosphere is friendly, and the miniature models of traditional Dutch homes, which are set into alcoves around the room, are a unique feature. Some snacks are available - perhaps pancakes or bacon and eggs - but this is first and foremost a drinking place. Billiard table.

De Tuin

Tweede Tuindwarsstraat 13
Tel: 20 624 4559
Open: 10.00-01.00 (Fri & Sat till 02.00, Sun from 11.00)
One of the best of the Jordaan bars, dark and lively, set among dozens of little boutiques in a trendy shopping street. The walls are practically covered with posters and flyers for musical and theatrical events around town, while the ladies and gents toilets are identified by life-size nude paintings of a man and a woman on the door. A great place to enjoy a coffee with an apple tart or a beer with olives and nachos, maybe with a game of chess or backgammon.

Twee Prinsen

Prinsenstraat 27
Tel: 20 624 9722
Open: 10.00-01.00 (Fri & Sat till 03.00)
A particularly friendly bar with a large following of locals. The decor is very traditional, with plenty of dark wood and light brown wallpaper, and this is a pleasant place to enjoy one of the many local beers on tap with a light snack or a baguette. Heated outdoor terrace.

Vergulde Gaper

Prinsenstraat 30
Tel: 20 624 8975
Open: 10.00-01.00 (Fri & Sat till 03.00)
An intimate and inviting café with a low, marble-topped bar lit by 1930s-style lamps and tables made of oak. Pistolettes, hot from the oven and with a choice of 20 fillings, are the lunchtime fare, while in the evening they serve sausages, toasties and various other snacks.

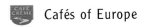
Wildschut

Roelof Hartplein 1-3
Tel: 20 676 8220
Open: 09.00-01.00 (Fri till 03.00, Sat 10.30-03.00, Sun 09.30-01.00)

This is a popular art deco-style venue for lunching businessmen for lunch or informal meetings during the day. It becomes livelier at night, when a well-dressed office set flocks here to do some intensive unwinding. This is also a popular choice with families for a snack meal at the weekend. Meals are served from noon till 22.00. Terrace.

Eindhoven

Duke Hendrik l of Brabant first put Eindhoven on the map, granting the right of freedom, self-government and the administration of justice, as well as a weekly market. The first steam engine came in 1828, sowing the seeds for the industrial boom that was to come. Gerard and Anton Philips arrived in 1891 with their light bulb, the brothers Van Doorne started with DAF in 1928, and today Eindhoven is a young, vibrant town which has expanded from its industrial past into becoming a leader in research, education and high technology. And PSV isn't a bad football team.

Grand Café Berlange

Kleine Berg, 16 5611 JV
Tel: 040 245 7481
Open: 12.00-02.00

A terracotta-fronted grand café with its three sets of double doors, located in a quiet, narrow street just off the main shopping area. It's a popular place with young folk, who leave their bikes outside and meet for an excellent Cook & Boon coffee or a glass of freshly squeezed orange juice. Comfortably spaced tables lead through to a stage where live music is regularly played on Monday evenings and all day Sunday. Beyond, through French windows, is a pretty garden terrace.

Carousel Café-Restaurant

Markt 35 A 5611
Tel: 040 245 3890
Open: 09.00-23.00/24.00 (weekends till 01.00/02.00, Sun from 11.00)

On the main market square, the name is the theme. The globe-lit interior is bedecked with fairground horses on poles and gypsy caravan carvings and paintings. The front part has round tables and wicker chairs and extends on to a terrace under an awning and on into the square under huge blue umbrellas. Right next to these is a fully working carousel for children. At the back is a restaurant.

Grand Café Queen

Markt 7 5611
Tel: 040 245 2480/2873
Open: 11.00-24.00 (weekends till 02.00/03.00)

The Queen's interior is quite baroque - a cupola supported by a wall of stained glass below which is ornately carved woodwork. One of many cafés standing side by side in the mainly pedestrianised square, this mainly attracts the younger crowd.

Tomas Café

Stratumseind 23 5611EN
Tel: 040 246 5231
Open: 11.00-01.00 (Thur till 02.00, Fri till 03.00, Sat till 04.00)

Once the home of the Eindhoven Men's Choir, Tomas has a solid mahogany bar, high ceiling and plaster-panelled walls. As you enter, you pass under the balcony (now the restaurant) into the main auditorium, which is lit by crystal chandeliers. Up ahead you can make out what was the stage, now set with comfortable armchair furniture. The staff wear jeans and grey shirts bearing their logo. Sitting at one of the large, highly polished tables you can enjoy a coffee, beer or glass of wine with the newspapers provided, and take a snack - perhaps a toasted sandwich or a pastry.

Trocadero

Stationsplein 15 5611AB
Tel: 040 244 9016
Open: 10.00-23.00 (Sun from 12.00)

Opposite the station, and therefore a popular spot with travellers, this is a Parisian-style restaurant with a far from French kitchen: snacks like nasi goreng reflect the country's connection with Southeast Asia. This dish is a sort of oriental bubble & squeak, using any left-overs with fried rice as an alternative to the proper recipe. The interior is on two levels, with the bar on high, a set of tables in the window and a terrace of tables outside. Its brasserie style offers eating and/or drinking throughout opening hours.

De Vooruitgang

Markt 11 5611ES
Tel: 040 243 3995
Open: 10.00-03.00 (Sun & Mon 12.00-01.00, Tues 10.00-02.00, Wed 10.00-01.00, Thur 10.00-02.00)

In a building dating back to 1890 in the old market square, the interior of this grand café has two startling spiral staircases, the main one, of steel, just inside the door. The other is of wood and is completely enclosed by little windows. The decor visits the 1950s, 1960s and 1980s, getting modern the further in you go; an old Daf car (remember them?) is parked inside. A wide variety of snacks is available in the café, and a more formal menu in the upstairs restaurant. Regular DJs or live entertainment.

The Hague

Once the hunting lodge of Count Floris IV of Holland, this green, elegant city is now home to the country's seat of government, various international bodies and one of the world's premier picture galleries: Mauritshuis, the Royal Picture Gallery, contains works by Holbein the Younger, Rubens, Rembrandt and Vermeer. Just outside town is a great family attraction in the shape of Madurodam - a four-acre site filled with miniature replicas of 150 of Holland's most famous buildings, as well as houses, windmills, canals and countryside. Also cars and trains, boats and planes - and at night the whole thing is lit by 50,000 tiny lights.

Ca L'Emile

Maliestraat 16
Tel: 70 365 54 00
Open: 16.00-01.00 (Fri & Sat till 01.30)

There is a distinctive Spanish flavour to the architecture in this part of town, but this is a typically Dutch bar with good beer and excellent snacks. On some Sundays there is live jazz music, which is definitely worth checking out, as are the toilets, which are wallpapered entirely with sheets of music!

Taveerne de Resident

Denneweg 58
Tel: 70 364 8788
Open: 17.30-24.00

A friendly, cosy bar in a picturesque part of town crammed with small shops and restaurants and close to the main square and a pretty canal-side avenue. There is a good selection of beers and wines at very reasonable prices, and a variety of snacks both hot and cold. The spare ribs are what the bar is best known for, and people come from all over the country for them.

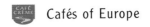

Maastricht

European treaty signing put this charming little place on the map, but it was very well established even in Roman times. The capital of Limburg province, it lies in the south of the country by the Belgian border; the French influence is strong.

Grand Café 'in de Moriaan'

Stokstraat 12
Tel: 43 321 1177
Open: 12.00-24.00 (Sun 14.00-22.00)

A café with a grand name, with the distinction of being the smallest in the whole of the Netherlands and the oldest in the street by the oldest square in the country. This charming place, which has a large terrace, is full of local people with the occasional visitor from Germany and Belgium. A full range of drinks, beers, teas and coffee and a range of sandwiches is on offer along with their speciality onion soup, with salads in summer (till 9.30).

Café in den Ouden Vogelstruys

Vrijthof 15
Tel: 43 321 4888
Open: 09.30-02.00

The Old Ostrich is a wonderfully cosy café with a tiled floor, and wooden walls adorned with signed photographs of past and present famous customers and regulars. Efficient, friendly service from smartly attired waiters wearing their emblemed ancient ostrich ties. The main lunchtime fare is excellent ham or cheese sandwiches served on black bread, and one of the speciality drinks is Emperor, a Maastricht beer.

Rotterdam

The world's largest port, whose storm surge barrier - 2 miles long - is an amazing piece of modern engineering. Most of the city has an uninspiring concrete and glass look, but it *does* have a soul, and it also has a wonderful collection of paintings (Bosch, Franz Hals, Rembrandt, Ruysdael, Rubens and the Impressionists) in the Boymans-Van Beuningen Museum. Away from the centre, Delfshaven adds a picturesque dimension. It's the historic part of the harbour, from where in 1620 the Pilgrim Fathers set sail for England to join the *Mayflower*. Outside the town are the famous Kinderdijk Windmills, 19 mills built in the 18th century along the canals. Their working days are long past, but they remain a great tourist attraction, particularly on Windmill Days. The great humanist Erasmus was born in Rotterdam and has given his name to the University.

Café 't Bolwerk

Witte Huis 1c, Gielderskade 3011
Tel: 10 414 21 42
Open: 11.30-04.00 (Fri & Sat till 06.00)

A large, handsome café overlooking the Old Harbour, across which you can see groups of modern buildings of various architectural styles, including the extraordinary cube houses designed by Piet Blom (one of these is open to the public). This is a serious meeting place for café-goers, either prior to going up town to discos, cinema or theatre, or for a meal from the simple but varied menu.

Henkes'

17 Voorhaven 3025
Tel: 10 425 55 96
Open: 11.30-24.00

One of the best bar-brasseries in town, Henkes' stands on the site of the famous Henkes gin distillery, which the family set up in 1824. The ship SS *J H Henkes*, which used to be moored outside, has been moved to another berth. To eat: anything from a light snack or salad during the day to a three-course dinner.

Oude Sluis

7 Havenstraat 3024
Tel: 10 477 30 68
Open: 12.00-01.00 (Fri & Sat till 02.00, Sun from 14.00)
There are some 40 beers to choose from at this corner site with two rooms and a covered balcony that overlooks the lock between Coolhaven and Achterhaven. A few years after opening in 1912 it acquired some Rubens-style scenes in plaster relief depicting customers playing cards, throwing dice or just leaning on a barrel smoking pipes. Simple wooden chairs are set at granite-topped tables, and the notably friendly atmosphere makes this a great place to relax with a beer, a snack and a newspaper.

Sijf

115 Oude Binnenweg 3012
Tel: 10 433 26 10
Open: 10.00-01.00 (Sun from 11.00, Fri & Sat till 02.00)
A modern café with a traditional look, on the north side of the pedestrianised Oude Binnenweg. A long pine bar leads to a split-level dining area at the back. It's popular with young people who come for the beer and wine and to enjoy a very generously served pork rib snack at the bar.

Le Vagabond

99 Nieuwe Binnenweg 3014
Tel: 10 436 52 93
Open: 12.00-02.00 (Fri & Sat till 03.00)
A butcher's shop until World War II, it has been a bar ever since and is well known in the music world, with a DJ on the odd Saturday and live music on Sunday. Small as it is, it has charm with its wood-panelled bar counter and jumbled assortment of pictures and ads on the wall. Outside, ivy grows up the wall and a large tree shelters the pavement tables. Only light snacks are served – toasted sandwiches of chorizo sausage and cheese. Once a month, on a Thursday, there's a cocktail night. Each year on the birthday of Queen Beatrix 5,000 or more people congregate here on roller blades - the bar is the start and finish of the day's run.

Utrecht

A major cultural, commercial and religious centre with the country's largest university, a colossal shopping centre, industrial fairs, an annual festival of ancient music (late August/early Septrember) and abundant museums and castles. The Old Canal (Oudegracht) runs through the middle of the town. Ferrequinologists should make tracks for Maliebaan station and the fascinating railway museum, whose stars are more than 60 steam locomotives.

Brasserie Domplein

20 Domplein 3512
Tel: 30 232 28 95
Open: 08.00-01.00 (Fri & Sat till 04.00)
The sandwiches are hard to beat at this brasserie, which is nearly always busy at lunchtime, and seriously busy at lunchtime, which can last four or five hours. Besides the sandwiches there's a selection of tapas and fish dishes, washed down with Brand beer on tap. All sorts come here, as it's close to the Cathedral and the centre, and because it offers good value for money. Very friendly staff, with smart uniforms of blue T-shirts and blue aprons. A striking decorative feature is a ceiling painting of the Cathedral surrounded by angels.

De Luifel

35 Neude 3512
Tel: 30 231 16 32
Open: 12.00-02.00 (Fri & Sat till 03.00)
An ancient Brown Café (vintage 1606) where students come to drink and snack. Over the years bric-à-brac has been added to the walls – enamelled signs and adverts from France, a saxophone, a French horn, an old gramophone, even a child's rocking horse hangs from the ceiling. It's a *taperij*, meaning a place with beer on tap, and here they offer Vos, Wieckse and Heineken. Plenty of choice on the menu, with fries and salads to accompany the dishes.

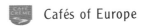

De Morgenster

323 Oude Gracht 3511
Tel: 30 234 32 06
Open: 15.00-02.30 (Sat & Sun from 11.00)
A quiet 'thinkers' café on a corner near the bottom of the Old Canal that divides Utrecht from top to bottom. Lots of newspapers and magazines to read and snacks to nibble.

Oudaen

99 Oude Gracht 3511
Tel: 30 231 18 64
Open: 10.00-02.00
Tall windows, enormous exposed beams on the lofty ceiling, a very grand fireplace and an elaborate tableau reaching up to the rafters. That's the scene at Oudaen, which is usually very busy with couples and groups sitting in leather-upholstered chairs at candle-lit oak tables. There's a long, broad, blue-red granite bar top on the right and a quarry-tiled floor with raised timber dais at either end of the room. Drinks and little snacks.

Eetcafé de Poort

2 Tolsteegbarrière 3511
Tel: 30 231 45 72
Open: 11.00-02.00 (Sun & Mon till 01.00)
A large café, popular with all ages for lunch, dinner and all points between, at the bottom of the Oude Gracht where it meets the canal that goes round the city. There's a stack of board games – everything from Monopoly to backgammon and chess – and lots of newspapers and magazines. On the walls are an assortment of musical instruments and photos of jazz musicians. In the summer when it's fine people mostly want to sit on the spacious terrace overlooking the canal.

Norway

Telephone Code: 00 47

Norway is one of the least densely populated countries in Europe (a little over 4 million inhabitants) and boasts the most northerly town in the world: this is Hammerfest, which stands at latitude 70° 39' 46". Its streets were the first in Europe to be lit by electricity. The Vikings were among the world's earliest explorers, a tradition carried down to modern times with such as Amundsen, Nansen and Thor Heyerdal. Ibsen, Grieg and Munch made major contributions to the world's treasury of literature, music and painting, and in recent years Grete Waitz dashed on to the scene as the world's leading lady marathon runner.

Oslo

A dramatic setting for Norway's capital city, at the end of a fjord, surrounded by hills and forests. Places to visit include the National Gallery, one of whose rooms is devoted to Edvard Munch. His most famous painting, *The Scream*, hangs here, while some 20,000 paintings, prints, letters and assorted documents are on display in the Munch Museum, purpose-built to house the collection bequeathed by the painter just before his death in 1944. On the Bygdøy Peninsula are the Viking Ship Museum and the Kon-Tiki Museum, where Thor Heyerdal's balsa wood raft and his papyrus boat Ra ll are the stars of the show.

Café Amsterdam

Universitetsgate 11, 0164
Tel: 23 35 42 45
Open: 11.30-00.30 (Fri & Sat till 02.30, Sun from 13.00)
Part of the Quality Savoy Hotel, the café is lofty and spacious, but nevertheless quite dark, with an abundance of stained oak. Twenty and thirty-somethings meet here in the evenings when mainstream jazz plays; there are posters on the walls and papers to read. A wide range of draught beers, including Newcastle Brown, Hoegaarden, Leffe, Murphy's and Heineken, jostle with local brews Aass and Frydenlund. Snacky things to eat.

Arcimboldo

Wergelandsveien 17
Tel: 22 69 44 22
Open: 11.00-24.00 (Thur till 01.00, Fri & Sat till 03.00)
Closed: Sun
Cafeteria to the 'Artists' House' Kunstnernes Hus, a fashionable art gallery founded in 1930. Popular with showbiz and media folk, it's a great place for people-watching as well as picture-viewing, and there's a fine view across to the gardens of the Royal Palace. Daily changing menu of straightforward dishes.

Grand Café, Grand Hotel Driftselskap AS

Karl Johansgate 31, 0101
Tel: 22 42 93 90
Open: 06.00-23.00

In the main street leading from the castle into town stands the venerable and aptly named Grand Hotel, whose elegant rooms are the smartest in Oslo. In its renowned café a large modern painting takes the eye in the bar, but it is the painting on the far wall that is so well known. Painted in 1928 by Per Krohg, it depicts many of the habitués of the 1890s: the then owner Kristian Fritzner is surveying a scene which includes Edvard Munch, Henrik Ibsen, two army officers, several journalists and many other notable patrons of the day. In the centre of the room is a mouthwatering hors d'œuvre table groaning under a wonderful choice of traditional dishes. Outside are old-style tables and chairs where the punters can watch the world go by or bury their heads in the daily paper.

Scandinavia Special Award 2001

Kafé Celsius

Radhusgate 19, 0158
Tel: 22 42 45 39
Open: 11.30-00.30 (Fri & Sat till 01.30, Sun 13.00-21.30)
Closed: Mon in winter

Built in 1629, this is one of the oldest buildings in Oslo and was once the Town Hall. A café for many years, it's a popular haunt of artists and is flanked by galleries, one for the work of young artists. A long bar incorporating the kitchen leads out in one direction to a cosy sheltered courtyard surrounded by mature planting, and in the other to two further spacious rooms (one non-smoking). At lunchtime and on Sunday the music is classical, while in the evening it's more Piaf and traditional café style. The lunch menu (sandwiches, salads, omelettes, pasta) runs until 14.30; the choice in the evening is similar but more elaborate, with some added fish dishes. To accompany, or to enjoy on their own, is a wide range of red and white wines from around the world.

Café Hemingway

Ovre Slottsgate 10, 0157
Tel: 22 33 06 68
Open: 11.00-01.00 (Fri & Sat till 03.00, Sun 13.00-24.00)

Owned by brothers Erik, Run and Stig, Café Hemingway (photographs of the writer hang on the walls) is a spacious, air-conditioned café with lots of standing space on the parquet floor by the bar and comfortable seating at dark pine tables. Glass doors open out on to the pavement, where there are some wooden slatted deckchairs in the pedestrianised street. It's good to note that they serve beer from the Norwegian brewery, Aass, from Drammen, a small independent family concern whose excellent products are becoming harder to find; on Wednesdays the NOROL, Norske Olvenners Landsforbund (Association of Norwegian Ale Sellers) is on the premises, and, after 17.00, simply by joining this Club (free!), you can enjoy half-litres of their three brews at a much discounted rate. Christmas time they produce a special ale which often wins the top prize for its excellence. Snacks and light meals include baguettes, salads, grills, brunch and cakes, with coffee, tea and wines by the glass if you don't want beer. The downstairs area is rented out as Rock Inn, with live rock music.

Café Luxembourg

Nedre Slottsgate 2, 0153
Tel: 23 10 73 00
Open: 15.00-24.00 (Wed & Thur till 01.00, Fri & Sat till 02.00)
Closed: Sun

Slightly out of the way, but still in the city centre, this roomy café gets quite a lot of its clientele from the attached hotel, whose entrance is in the next street. (The café is not open in the morning, so the hotel 'borrows' it for breakfast.) The new English chef has brought a touch of the old country to some of the snacks, but otherwise it's Norwegian open sandwiches, fish soup, lasagne, burgers and mozzarella, tomato and basil salad. Teas, coffees, wines by the glass.

Theatercaféen, Hotel Continental

Stortingsgaten 24/26, 0117
Tel: 22 82 40 50
Open: 11.00-23.00 (Sun 15.00-22.00)

With its own corner entrance in the family-run Hotel Continental, the Viennese-style Theatercaféen opened in 1909, a year after the National Theatre across the road, and has been in the same family ever since. Modernised by a second generation manager in 1949, it was faithfully restored to its early style by his disapproving daughter, who meticulously replicated the furnishings and fittings of the original; the only actual artefact from 1909 is a mirror from the inner sanctum. The café has always attracted Oslo society and celebrity, particularly from the arts; some 70 of their portraits hang on the walls. Some come to relax with a newspaper on one of the settees, others for animated discussion or to celebrate a success or an anniversary; some pop in for a quick drink, perhaps with an open sandwich, while others settle down to a full-blown repast of classic Norwegian dishes that ends with excellent pastries.

3 Brodre (Three Brothers)

Ovre Slottsgate 14, 0157
Tel: 23 10 06 70
Open: 11.00-01.00 (Wed-Sat till 02.00)

A former hat and glove shop whose ceiling has painted glass panels of branches with autumn leaves, an eye-catching feature dating from 1897. The old counters are still there, and the tiled floor, with cast-iron radiators standing on it, the wall paitnings and the glass chandeliers could all be of the same vintage. Things have changed since last year: downstairs is now a Mexican restaurant, while upstairs is a piano bar every evening except Sunday. This is located in the main shopping and entertainment area of town, so the clientele is very varied.

A Touch of France

Ovre Slottsgate 16, 0157
Tel: 22 42 56 97/23 10 01 65 (booking)
Open: 15.00-23.00 (winter from 16.30)
Closed: Sun

A delightful location in the old quarter of the town near the Sackershus Slott, a Renaissance castle that replaced a medieval fortress. The ground floor was a shoe shop until 1991, but D'Artagnan, the gourmet restaurant upstairs, is an older part of the business, having been on the go for over 20 years. A Touch of France is popular with a 40-something clientele, who come for anything from a beer or a coffee to a dish from the classic French menu. Simply decorated in cream and burgundy, the large downstairs room opens on to pavement tables in the pedestrianised street. Waiters are dressed traditionally in white shirts and aprons, and black ties and waistcoats.

Portugal

Telephone Code: 00 351

The sea is the greatest influence on England's old ally and trading partner, and Portugal's position on the Atlantic coast gave early explorers more than a head start in their quest for the New World. Her finest days followed the discoveries of Henry the Navigator (1394-1460), when explorers founded what was to become a large and far-flung colonial empire stretching to Africa, South America and the Far East. Much of the coastline is unbroken beach, and the Algarve, which covers the whole of the southern region, has been a popular holiday destination for 30 years. Inland, beautiful, lonely landscapes are broken by delightful little villages and market towns, usually with a number of cheap and cheerful cafés, where a cup of coffee or a glass of something stronger is often accompanied by an excellent pastry. Portugal is the world's seventh largest wine producer and is of course best known for its port. Port is the national drink, *fado* the national singing style. You should sample both in fairly small doses. The Portuguese are almost all very friendly and they're kinder to their bulls than the Spanish – both nations emphasise skills, elegance and courage in their bullfights but in Portugal they don't kill the bull.

CAFÉ CRÈME

Lisbon

The delightful city of Lisbon is built on seven hills at a point where the River Tagus opens into a wide bay. Its ancient name was Olisipo, perhaps meaning 'delightful little port', perhaps from the legend that it was founded by Ulysses. The old part of the city, the Alfama, is a maze of narrow streets, many of them steep and sometimes slippery, but there are also broad avenues, peaceful parks and a busy harbour. Walking can be very tiring here, but there are some very agreeable alternatives, including leisurely tram rides and boat trips along the Tagus estuary. Much of the city was destroyed in 1755 by a terrible earthquake followed by fire and tidal waves, but enough medieval buildings survive to interest the historian or sightseer. The major museums house notable art collections and two museums are devoted to more esoteric subjects - coaches and carriages, and the wonderful painted tiles (*azulejos*) for which Iberia is renowned. The Coach Museum, home to numerous mainly 18th-century royal carriages, is part of the magnificent Manueline monastery of Belem (Bethlehem), from where Vasco da Gama set sail for India in 1497. Lisbon is the home of the mournful *fado*, which you can hear being performed by a woman with accompanying guitarists in many of the restaurants, bars and clubs. The most notable exponent of *fado*, Amalia Rodrigues, died in the autumn of 1999, an event that was marked by three days of national mourning.

Antiga Confeitaria de Belem

84-92 Rua de Belem
Tel: 21 363 8077/8
Open: 08.00-23.00

A unique pastry shop-cum-café with a 150-year history, famous for its little tartlets with cinnamon-flavoured custard, sold by the hundred packed in tubes. The rooms are decorated in tiles up to at least a metre high, with here and there an elaborate mural in tiles depicting scenes of Belem. Really worth a visit to feast your eyes and your palate.

A Brasileira

120-122 Rua Garrett
Tel: 21 346 9541
Open: 08.00-02.00

The most renowned of Rua Garrett's many beautiful old coffee houses, A Brasileira has been a meeting place of poets and other literary figures down the years. A notable feature is a bronze of Fernand Pessoa, the poet, which sits at a table with an empty chair for visitors to join him! Elaborately decorated in art nouveau style, it first opened its doors in 1905 and quickly eclipsed the intellectuals' other favourite haunt, *Martinho da Arcada*. Inside, through the arch and one of the three green-painted doorways, you'll find busy tables on the left and a long bar counter on the right, with panelled walls and mirrors. Outside, the pavement tables are almost constantly occupied, but it's worth waiting for one to watch life passing by on this affluent street.

Portugal Café of the Year 2001

British Bar

52-54 Rua Bernadino Costa
Cais do Sodre
Tel: 21 342 2367
Open: 07.00-24.00
Closed: Sun

On the left as you enter this civilised place is a bar with a brass top and rail and wood panelling, and behind the bar there are mahogany cabinet style shelves with bottles of various ports, sherries, whiskies and other spirits. There's nothing very British about the place, but expats who live along this coast like to drop in for a small libation when coming up to town or while waiting for a train from the station almost opposite.

Cerca Moura

4 Largo Portas do Sol
Tel: 21 888 0298
Open: 11.30-02.00 (Sun till 21.00)

From the centre take the 28, one of the splendid pre-WW1 trams that are still doing yeoman service, to Largo Portas do Sol, where you get a magnificent view of S Vincente Church, and down to the sea over the rooftops and the church of S Ingracia de Fora. Opposite is this attractive little bar built into the rock foundations of the massive walls of St George's Castle. Take a coffee or cool refreshing beer or some vinho verde and if you're hungry a light snack at one of the pavement tables, or in the little salon dug under the exposed rock.

Chiadomel

105 Rua de Santa Justa
Tel: 21 347 4400
Open: 10.00-00.30

This little café has one of the best views of Lisbon from its perch at the top of the Santa Justa Elevador, the extraordinary lift built by a pupil of Gustav Eiffel at the turn of the century. From here you can see down to the Rossio, St George's castle, the port and, behind, the shell of the church. The Elevador takes you from the town centre and lifts you into the smart Chiado and Bairro Alto areas but if you climb another two flights you arrive at this platform with chairs and tables, waiter service, and the prospect of coffee, a cool beer and snacks such as sandwiches, rolls etc and ice creams.

Doca de Santo Esplanada

Doca de Santo Amaro - Alcantara
Tel: 21 396 3522
Open: 12.30-03.00 (weekends till 04.00)

A capacious and very comfortable modern café in the shadow of the third longest suspension bridge in the world. At the entrance are four huge umbrellas set among palm trees and on the left a terrace bar. Up some solid wooden steps is the main bar, well ventilated and air-conditioned, leading to a mezzanine set with basket chairs and tables. The long, V-shaped stainless-steel and glass bar counter displays tapas-type snacks, and there's an à la carte menu. During the summer months it gets very busy, and at the weekends it is packed and stays open almost till dawn.

Gambrinus

25 Rua das Portas de Santo Antao
Tel: 21 342 1466
Open: 12.00-01.30

An exclusive, clubby bar-restaurant in a pedestrianised street just north of the Rossio. The long bar is immediately inside this entrance and beyond are three lofty dining rooms and another entrance into a little square (Largo de Santo Domingos) and the main fire station for Lisbon. The bar is in teak, as are the panelled walls, a decoration effected some 35 years ago and beautifully maintained ever since. Service here is the best in town, and while the bar is really for drinking they'll lay up a place for you if you feel like a snack. There's a dress code - no shorts, especially in the evening. Seafood is the main speciality of the restaurant.

Special Award 2001

191

Martinho da Arcada

3 Praça do Commercio
Tel: 21 887 9259
Open: 07.00-21.30
Closed: Sun

The oldest café in Lisbon, situated in a square built after the great earthquake of 1755. The café and its elegant restaurant are beautifully decorated in blue-and-white tiles which in themselves are worth seeing, but more than that is the atmosphere. A favourite haunt of intellectuals and men of letters, it is busy from early breakfast to dinner time. Excellent coffee and pastries in the morning, sandwiches and appetising rolls, à la carte in the restaurant next door.

Café Nicola

24-25 Praça D. Pedro IV
Tel: 21 346 0579
Open: 08.00-20.00 (restaurant 12.00-16.00, 19.00-23.00)
Closed: Sun

Opened in 1929 and decorated in art deco style, Nicola is a spacious café on the main square in the Baixa district. The frontage is very distinctive and used effectively as their logo - an imposing marble arch carved in scrolls, bearing bold capital letters NICOLA supported by two stylised tapering square pillars at each end and two Ionic pillars in the middle. Out in the arcade are basket-seated chairs under sunshades where you can take your coffee or aperitif and perhaps glance through the newspaper. Good Portuguese wine list; steaks with their 'secret' sauce a speciality.

Passeio d'Avenida

Avenue de Liberdade, Praça Central next to Cinema Condes
Tel: 21 342 3755
Open: 08.00-02.00 (Sat 03.00)

On the east side of a broad leafy avenue is this very good restaurant in a single-storey glass-sided permanent structure like a pavilion. In the front there are some eight or ten pavement tables, while at the other end are the kitchen and an open-air bar. Beyond are set three ranks of cloth-covered tables and elaborate white wrought-iron chairs leading to a bandstand and dance area for the nightly live music. Ice creams are a speciality.

Pastelaria 1800

7 Largo do Rato
Tel: 21 388 2631
Open: 06.00-22.00 (Sat 20.00)
Closed: Sun

Down by the polytechnic and medical science faculty of the university (see *Real Fabrica*), Pastelaria was built in 1857 and restored in 1924. It has all the modern requirements of a first-class patisserie (all the pastries are made on the premises) while retaining its decorative arch, tiled interior and facade. Very popular in the morning, it also serves light lunches and suppers but closes 'early'.

Pavilhao Chines

89-91 Rua D. Pedro V
Tel: 21 342 4729
Open: 18.00-02.00 (Sun from 21.00)

Owner Luiz Pinto Coelho has an amazing private collection of pottery, bronzes, militaria, pictures and paintings crowded into seven large interconnecting rooms that include two bars. The chairs are comfortably upholstered and the tables ornate with decorative marquetry. The bar counters are teak with rosewood panels supporting the tops elaborated with more marquetry and the walls are decorated in damask - but the eye doesn't at first see that backdrop to the truly astonishing collection. The bar-café offers 40 types of tea, 100 cocktails, Portuguese wines and special sandwiches. The glasses are elegant blue-based flutes, the china blue and white. Almost everything is elegant and antique - even the washbasins in the lavatories. Classical and Portuguese music, professional service by staff in blue waistcoats and bow ties.

Real Fabrica

275/283 Rua da Escola Politecnica (ao Rato)
Tel: 21 387 2918
Open: 08.00-02.00
Closed: Sun

A large, well-used student cafeteria spread over two floors. Students are a thirsty bunch and here the beer is stored in enormous cylinders over the bar; each holds some 2,000 litres and lasts about a fortnight. The kitchen can be seen beyond the bar through wide stone and brick arches. The space is increased by a peninsular marble-topped horseshoe bar area, and a large glass display cabinet shows the pastries, sandwiches and snacks available down here; a full menu is available upstairs. Half a dozen pavement tables.

Café Rosso

53-61 Rua Ivens
Tel: 21 343 2671
Open: 09.00-02.00

Approached from either Rua Ivens or 19 Rua Gambetta, this is a peaceful café tucked away in a courtyard. It's spacious and modern inside, and there are comfortable seats in the courtyard sheltered by umbrellas away from the traffic. Enormous sandwiches head the list of snacks.

Oporto

Portugal's second largest city (Porto to the Portuguese) gained worldwide recognition through giving its name to the country's national drink. The wine cellars, on the left bank of the Douro, are an absolute must for any visitor. The magical Douro itself is spanned in Oporto by three amazing bridges, the all-metal Maria Pia railway bridge designed by Gustave Eiffel, the spectacular Luis 1 road bridge with a two-tiered roadway, and the Arrabida road bridge that crosses the river in a single span of nearly 900 feet.

Majestic Café

112 Rua Santa Catarina
Tel: 22 200 3887
Open: 09.30-24.00
Closed: Sun

A remarkable art nouveau café, declared a national monument by the Ministry for Archaeology and Architecture. It was immortalised by the national poet Antonio Ferro in 1922, when it was very much the venue of intellectuals and men of letters. In the winter there's a resident piano player, while in the summer the pavement tables in front and the terrace at the back are more popular than inside. The elaborate plasterwork and framed mirrors are beautifully restored, as are the elegant suspended ceiling lights, and the furniture is either original or faithfully reproduced. There's a good list of Portuguese wines, and among the specialities on the menu are cod Oporto-style, bass, hake, squid, and duck in port wine.

O Muro

87-88 Muro dos Bacalhoeiros
Tel: 22 208 3426
Open: 12.30-02.00

Along a narrow path on top of the wall overlooking the old customs area and in front of the old terrace houses of the port you come across this very relaxed café, converted from two of those houses. A few tables on the path outside afford a splendid elevated view across the Douro river to the bodegas of the big name port wine producers. Inside, the pretty, narrow bar and its tables are looked down on by a large iron chandelier, and assorted artefacts hang haphazardly on the walls. The atmosphere is casual and very laid back as people sip their drinks and chat. The cuisine is traditional.

Postigo da Ribeira (do Carvao)

24-34 Rua Fonte Taurina
Tel: 22 200 4539
Open: 18.00-02.00
Closed: Mon

In the old part of the centre of town in a narrow back street near the river is this spacious bar/snack bar/restaurant on a split level. Original huge stone blocks form the walls and floor, and the arches and pillars over the open-plan kitchen. Three large iron posts with life-size street lamps give the impression of being outside while still enclosed. The wines on offer, all Portuguese, are sold by the carafe. Snacks are served on wooden platters - mostly seafood (their speciality) such as monkfish, lobster, grilled fish and seafood risotto but also tripe, cheese and chorizos. Another popular order is *liposta a Merandeza*, a half-kilo steak served with a special sauce. There's often a party atmosphere, with live music at the weekend and at holiday times.

Confeitaria Xodo

662 Rua do Bon Jardim
Tel: 22 332 5160
Open: 07.00-20.00
Closed: Sun

A very busy local café behind the Trindade station: excellent espresso, *galao* (coffee with milk served in a glass), pure pulped juices and a bar. They also offer substantial snacks such as the Portuguese speciality *bacalhau* (salt cod) with rice, savoury pies and cooked-to-order omelettes. Best of all are the wonderful pastries to eat in or take away. Sit at the bar or at the street window on a tall stool, or around a small table. Friendly service for all ages, including young children.

Spain

Telephone Code: 00 34

The Spanish landscape is enormously varied, with a vast coastline, stretches of arid, sun-parched semi-desert, lush green hills and a criss-cross of mountains. The people are equally varied, and Spain's history comes vividly to life in its remarkable art and architecture, from prehistoric cave paintings in Cantabria and Levante through Roman arches, aqueducts and amphitheatres to Moorish mosques, Gothic, Renaissance, Baroque, Bourbon and some wonderful and extraordinary modern constructions like Gaudì's fanciful cathedral in Barcelona and the stunning art museum in Bilbao. Religious festivals and the bullfights are high on the list of national priorities; the latter, known as La Fiesta Nacional and originally a sport practised on horseback by the aristocracy, remains an occasion of excitement and colour. Spaniards of all ages love their cafés, which for many are almost another room in the house - or a series of rooms, one for breakfast, another for lunch, a third for pre-dinner drinks.

Madrid

Spain's artistic heritage is as rich as any and Madrid's Prado is one of the world's greatest art galleries, with major works by masters such as Goya, Velazquez, El Greco and Titian, as well as modern pieces. Europe's highest capital is a bustling, cosmopolitan city that's constantly on the move, but there are also plenty of places for getting away from the bustle. Best of the many well-kept open spaces is the former royal park Retiro, in the heart of the city close to the Prado, with shady avenue and formal gardens, open-air exhibitions, superb statues, and a lake with rowing boats. Madrid has a night life that's almost as busy as its daytime, and when the museums and galleries and parks and shops are closed the bars and cafés and restaurants take over until the wee small hours. The cafés and bars, of which there are at least 17,000, are places of universal appeal to the people of Madrid, whether quiet, humble neighbourhood haunts, elegant lounges or see-and-be-seen open-air terraces on one of the grand boulevards.

Café de los Austrias

Plaza de Ramales
Tel: 91 559 8436
Open: 09.00-02.30 (Fri & Sat 11.00-03.00, Sun 17.00-02.00)
More modern than its turn-of-the-century look would suggest, this is a popular, convivial café, with an attractive wooden bar, marble tables, old prints of royalty on the walls and not a trace of the nunnery that once occupied the site. There's a particularly good ambience towards midnight as everyone congregates for drinks. Good selection of gourmet coffee, drinks, tapas and pinchos.

Café Central

Plaza del Angel 10
Tel: 91 369 4143
Open: 14.00-01.30 (Fri & Sat till 03.30)
An attractive, high-ceilinged café-bar just off the bustling Puerta del Sol. A full range of coffees, teas, drinks and snacks is available all day, and it's crowded throughout the late evening with people who come to enjoy the live jazz , probably the best in Madrid, in a sophisticated and buzzy atmosphere. The jazz is played from 22.00 to midnight.

Café del Circulo de Bellas Artes

Calle Alcalá 42
Tel: 91 521 6942
Open: 09.00-01.00 (Fri & Sat till 03.00)

A spacious, airy café with a pavement terrace, one of the most stylish and popular places to meet for a drink and a chat. Overlooking Calle Alcalá, the capital's longest street, it is part of a varied and prestigious arts centre that includes exhibition halls, galleries, a library, a theatre and a concert hall that stages frequent performances of contemporary music. Good tapas accompany the drinks.

Café Comercial

Glorieta de Bilbao 7
Tel: 91 521 5655
Open: 07.30-01.00 (Fri & Sat till 02.00, Sun from 10.00)

A treasured institution with a lofty chandeliered ceiling, heavy wooden tables, mirrored walls and pillars. It has long been one of the city's most popular meeting places, constantly busy with a complete cross-section of locals and visitors and a civilised, intellectual atmosphere. Earnest conversation shares time with chess and draughts and the newspapers, and there's Internet access in the upstairs bar; resident pianist Friday and Saturday evenings. Classic eats: churros with coffee or hot chocolate, good tapas and a three-course menu of the day.

El Espejo (restaurant)

Paseo de Recoletos 31
Tel: 91 308 2347
Open: 10.00-02.00 (Fri & Sat till 03.00)

Fashionable, classy, civilised, relaxing: El Espejo was created in 1978 in predominantly art nouveau style, with mirrors, bar and exquisite tiling echoing the period; it has a black-and-white tiled floor, marble-topped tables with ornate metal legs and red upholstered bentwood chairs. A variety of tapas/starters and a large selection of drinks and speciality coffees is always available, or if you prefer choose the restaurant at the rear in the same elegant style - specialities include merluza rellena (stuffed hake) and biscuit de almandres (almond cake).

El Espejo - El Pabellon del Espejo (cafeteria)

Paseo de Recoletos 31
Tel: 91 319 1122
Open: 10.00-02.00

El Pabellon, on the doorstep of El Espejo, is a beautiful glazed pavilion, complete with marble slab floor, huge chandeliers and an ornate marble-topped wooden counter with mirrors that takes the eye as you enter. Coffees, teas, beers and wines are always available, as are tapas and tostadas (Spanish canapés) from the bar. A cosmopolitan mix of people visits this wonderful café in all seasons and in summer, when it more than doubles in size with its outside park terrace, it really is *the* place to be in Madrid.

Los Gabrieles

Calle de Echegaray 17
Tel: 91 429 6261
Open: 12.30-02.30

The facade of this sometime biscuit shop and brothel hides a truly remarkable interior, clad almost throughout in the most exquisite Andalusian glazed tiling, depicting 19th-century scenes of drinking, shopping and purveying of various goods. The food stops at 18.00, when the place starts to take off for the night, the bars heaving with a young, convivial, well-heeled crowd. On Tuesday nights a flamenco concert starts at 21.00.

Café Gijón

Paseo de Recoletos 21
Tel: 91 521 5425
Open: 07.00-01.30 (Sat till 02.00)

A bastion of Madrid's café culture for 120 years, the place where the tradition of *tertulia*, the gathering of friends to discuss a certain topic, often literary, held sway. Gijón attracts a constant stream of local business people, journalists, writers, artists and visitors from all over the world. It remains the definitive literary café and each year awards a prize for the best short story. You gather for drinks at the bar, situated to the left as you enter, or sit at one of the tables for waiter service. The main restaurant is downstairs (paella a speciality), but a good range of tapas and snacks is always available at the bar.

Café Manuela

San Vicente Ferrer 29
Tel: 91 531 7037
Open: 16.00-02.30

Story-telling (*cuentacuentos*) and poetry nights are a highlight of Café Manuela, a lively, vibrant place with a unique atmosphere that owes a lot to its plush late-19th-century Alfonsino decor: marble floor, cream and beige walls, red divans, wooden counter and marble tables. The evenings are multi-lingual, with tales told in English and French as well as Spanish, and there are also debates on topics of art and literature. Saturday nights are given over to live traditional Spanish music.

Nuevo Café Barbieri

Calle del Avemaria 45
Tel: 91 527 3658
Open: 15.00-02.00 (Fri & Sat till 03.00)

Coffee is a speciality (about 20 varieties to choose from) at a beautiful café that is the embodiment of faded grandeur. The interior is one which is difficult to leave - it would be easy to spend the whole day there. The room is supported by lovely 19th-century columns and these, along with the beautiful curved bar, the elegantly fading mirrored walls, the seductive lighting and the reams of voluptuous red velvet, make it easy to imagine that you are in an old-time music hall or some other equally romantic setting. Sumptuous cakes are on offer, accompanied by the coffees, teas and stronger liquor. For the solo visitor, newspapers to read or an interesting youngish crowd to mix with.

Café de Oriente

Plaza de Oriente 2
Tel: 91 541 3974
Open: 08.00-01.30 (Fri & Sat till 02.30)

With the Royal Palace opposite and the Opera House just round the corner, this grand and stylish café keeps exalted company. Antiques and paintings are liberally scattered around, and there's plush red seating, with white lace antimacassars, and wooden-framed mirrors complete with coat racks. In the summer the action moves out on to the canvas-canopied terrace. It's a popular place at any time of day, from breakfast right through to a late-night drink; tapas and pizza are served to the end, and there's a full restaurant down in the vaults.

Spain Café of the Year 2001

Taverna del Real

Plaza Isabel II
Tel: 91 559 6922
Open: 11.00-00.30 (Fri & Sat till 01.30)

Opposite the opera house, this lively little bar counts many opera-goers and performers among its large and loyal following. Through the narrow entrance, the bar opens up into a larger rear room with an upstairs bar area and a downstairs plant-filled garden room. Sawdust is strewn on the marble floors, and the place is always busy with people coming for drinks and coffees. Specialities: beer, vermouth from the barrel, tapas, shellfish, rice dishes.

Café de Ruiz

Calle Ruiz 11
Tel: 91 446 1232
Open: 14.00-03.00

A comfortable, atmospheric café with an appealing interior of fin-de-siècle furnishings, lots of wood, old mirrors and lamps, tiled floor and large windows. Fruit juices, splendid milk shakes (batidos), coffees, hot chocolate and ice creams are available in an extensive choice, with or without alcohol, and there's ham, chorizo, cheese and paté for snacking. Debates cover astrology on Tuesday, poetry and literature on other days.

Salon del Prado

Calle del Prado 4
Tel: 91 429 3361
Open: 14.00-02.00 (Fri & Sat till 03.00, Sun till 01.00)

An elegant, civilised, even genteel setting for the mainly young crowd that gathers to enjoy a coffee (plain, Russian, Irish...) or something stronger while listening to the evening's entertainment, which could be anything from comedy to chamber music. Canapés come free with the drinks.

La Sastrería

Hortaleza 74
Tel: 91 532 0771
Open: 10.00-02.00 (Sat & Sun from 11.00, Fri & Sat till 02.30)

A two-tiered café in yellow and blue, with interesting and amusing decorative features from its previous incarnation as a tailor's shop. Staff, dressed in a modern design based on old tailors' costumes, complete with tape-measures as lapels, are courteous and helpful, gliding around the large room for table service, or you can help yourself from the busy bar area. Coffee varieties include Irish, Turkish and Viennese. Hot food at lunchtime; sandwiches and cold snacks in the evening.

Barcelona

The capital of Catalonia, and Spain's densely populated second city, Barcelona is rapidly becoming a rival to Paris for a short break. Its beauty and vibrancy are irresistible, and its architectural attractions run the gamut from traces of Roman occupation to the amazing works of Gaudì. Spain's most famous architect, Antoni Gaudi I Cornet (1852-1926) is being assessed for canonisation, though the verdict is not expected imminently, as he joins a list of more than 3,000. His two best known projects are the incredible Sagrada Familia Cathedral and the sprawling wonderland of Parc Güell, which was intended to be a fashionable residential area for a few wealthy families. The eccentric and obsessed Gaudi worked on the grandiose Cathedral project for 42 years, from 1884 until the day he was run over and killed by a tram on the Gran Via. It remains unfinished, but work continues towards its completion. 2002 has been designated the Year of Gaudi. Joan Miró also left his mark on the city, and the Miró foundation, inaugurated in 1976, is well worth the trip up Montjuïc mountain. Rambling is the recommended way to see this exciting city, or join a guided walking tour any Saturday or Sunday morning at Plaça de Catalunya. La Rambla is one of the most vibrant and exciting streets in the world, containing museums, shops, markets, bars, cafés and restaurants. Even more than in Madrid, there's a buzzing nightlife, and the thought of an early night should not even cross the mind of the serious tourist. If you're ever stuck for a topic of conversation, try football, and if you're a real aficionado, make the Barça Museum your goal: the exhibits include the 1992 European Cup, won at Wembley against Sampdoria, and all kinds of football memorabilia.

Café del Born Nou

Plaça Comercial 10
Tel: 93 268 3272
Open: 09.00-02.30 (Thur-Sat till 22.00)
Closed: 25 Dec, 1 Jan & Easter

A favourite haunt of painters, musicians and architects, this spacious café opposite the old Born market has high ceilings, a wooden floor and surrounds, and wide glass doors that open on to the terrace. Regular art exhibitions and monthly live musical evenings.Newspapers for solo visitors. The menu has expanded with the kitchen.

Laie Libreria Café

Pau Claris 85
Tel: 93 302 7310
Open: 09.00-01.00 (Sat from 10.00)
Closed: Sun

An art-exhibiting café on the first floor of a large book-store with a wooden floor, tiled passageway and bar, and a series of inter-connecting rooms with an outside area. It serves speciality teas, infusions and exotic coffees to a young, arty and literary clientele, who enjoy a browse through the newspapers and magazines provided. Breakfast, buffet lunch, afternoon tea, à la carte dinner with a Mediterranean flavour. Live jazz nights take place between February and September, with special requests from the audience.

Mauri

Rambla Catalunya 103
Tel: 93 215 8146
Open: 09.00-14.00 & 16.00-21.00

In a beautiful building dating back to 1886, Mauri is a popular place with ladies who lunch; it is situated at the upper end of the Rambla Catalunya, in the elegant Eixample area. It is part shop and part café, whose counter tempts with a mouthwatering array of delicious up-market snacks, including caviar and foie gras sandwiches, croquettes and pastries; coffee, tea and cold drinks are waitress-served. The shop sells all sorts of goodies including home-made chocolates. Handy for tourists visiting Gaudí's nearby Casa Milà and for shoppers visiting the design emporium Vinçon. Almost opposite is another Mauri at 102, with an original elaborate painted ceiling.

El Meson del Café

Calle Llibreteria 16
Tel: 93 315 0754
Open: 07.00-23.00
Closed: Sun

Close to the Cathedral (dedicated to the city's patron saint, Eulàlia), and just off the Town Hall square, this splendid little coffee shop and bar has a history going back 90 years and the original coffee machine is a proud part of the decor. Other original features are wooden panels depicting street life in turn-of-the-century Barcelona. Super speciality coffees include one with double cream and whisky, and home-made *churros* (deep-fried pastries) sell like hot cakes. They also make their own chocolates from the purest ingredients. Fast, efficient service.

Café de l'Opera

Ramblas 74
Tel: 93 317 7585
Open: 08.00-02.30 (Fri & Sat till 03.00)

Picasso, Miró and Dali are among the many notables to have passed through the doors of this elegant, long-established café, the best of the many on the Rambla. Today's clientele revolves around shopping during the day and the Opera at night. At street level is a long marble bar with an ornate plaster ceiling and mirrors engraved with female opera figures; upstairs, green-painted wall panels, mirrors and crystal lamps take the eye. Specialities include 12 different types of coffee, 300 teas, and, of course, hot chocolate with *churros*, the perfect nightcap as well as the perfect start to the day. In warmer months the outside tables are great for people-watching.

El Paraigua

2 Pas de l'Ensenyança
Tel: 93 302 1131
Open: 08.30-02.00 (Sat 18.00-03.00)
Closed: Sun

A bar on two levels, tucked away through an archway off Ferran; it used to be an umbrella shop, which is how it got its name. Upstairs, open for breakfast onwards, is art nouveau, while the evening basement bar, where you can sip cocktails or a whisky to classical music, has stone-vaulted ceilings in baroque style. Well worth a visit for the decor alone, but you'll also be rewarded with a warm welcome and courteous service.

El Pi Antic

Plaça Sant Josep Oriol
Tel: 93 301 7191
Open: 10.00-24.00

This large double-fronted café-restaurant started life in 1571 as a small palace, other parts of which can be seen through the courtyard next door. Large stone arches span and support the traditional wooden ceiling, and the black-and-white marble floor and pink marble-topped tables create a cool atmosphere in which to take a coffee or snack in the summer. A pianist plays in the evenings on Saturday, Sunday and Bank Holidays, and the café is used by both locals and tourists exploring the Gothic quarter. Specialities are paella and Catalan dishes.

Els Quatre Gats

Carrer Montsió 3-bis
Tel: 93 302 4140
Open: 08.00-01.00 (Fri & Sat till 03.00, Sun 17.30-01.30)
Closed: 1st 3 weeks Aug

Picasso had his first show at this historic building, which was designed in 1897 by Puig I Cadafalch. Other leading figures from the world of art, including Miró and Utrillo, made it their regular haunt, and the paintings on the walls, which are reproduced on the table mats, date from the early 1900s. A fine place to meet for a glass of wine or one of their speciality coffees, and if you bring an appetite there's a restaurant at the back that specialises in Catalan cuisine. This is the room where the original owner, Pere Romeu, presented puppet shows and other performances. Piano and violin evenings.
Special Award 2001

Salambo

Calle Torrijos 51
Tel: 93 218 6966
Open: 12.00-02.30 (Fri-Sun till 03.00)

A modern café with a 30s' look, decorated in shades of terracotta with a wooden floor and wooden slatted bench seating. It offers a good range of snack food and speciality drinks, served by friendly young staff. The menu is seasonal, with a vegetarian section.

El Tio Che

Rambla del Poble Nou 44-46
Tel: 93 309 1872
Open: 10.00-01.00 (Fri & Sat till 03.00). Winter 09.00-13.00 & 16.00-22.00 (Fri-Sun till 23.00).
Closed: Wed in winter

A family gelateria on a pedestrian street near the beach, started in 1912 by current owner Alfonso Iborra's great grandfather. *Horchatas*, made with *chufa* nuts, are a speciality – in summer some are made without sugar for diabetics – or try the *leche merengada*, milk with sugar and cinnamon, and the home-made ice creams (30-odd flavours). Tapas and *bocadillos* are also served, and at Christmas thay make special *turrones* (nougat). The parlour is decorated in a typical Valencian style with white ceramic walls, and outside there are two terraces with marble-topped tables and blue parasols.
Visit the website: www.eltioche.com

Bilbao

A sprawling, industrial city, very friendly, with one of Spain's most important art galleries; and plenty of bars and restaurants in the old quarter on the east bank of the Nervión. The place goes wild during the fiesta in the second half of August, when the streets are filled with bars and music and dancing.

Bar Basque

3 Astarloa
Tel: 94 424 2621
Open: 10.00-22.00
Closed: Sat & Sun
Just off the main street of Bilbao's shopping centre, this Belle Epoque-style bar has been serving shoppers, shop staff and office workers since the 1970s. Tapas are served until 16.00, after which it's drinks and canapés only, with a list of speciality cocktails. Spot the brass snake that winds its way up one of the pillars, and the silk on the walls above the panelling.

Café Bar Bilbao

6 Plaza Berria (Plaza Nueva)
Tel: 94 415 1671
Open: 07.00-23.00 (Fri till 24.00, Sat 09.00-24.00, Sun 09.00-14.30)
One of a number of delightful old cafés in an enchanting arcaded square in the old part of town. It has an all-marble horseshoe bar in one room and tables with waiter service in the other. The bar is loaded with an amazing array of tapas, among which ham croquettes, stuffed peppers, *jamon* and fried cuttlefish are specialities. The atmosphere here really buzzes and the staff dash around to keep up with the orders.

Café Boulevard

3 Paseo de Arenal
Tel: 94 415 3128
Open: 07.30-23.30 (Fri & Sat till 02.30, Sun from 11.00)
1871 saw the founding of Café Boulevard, which has remained a popular meeting place down the years. Nowadays it has a neon-lit frontage that looks a bit like a cinema and a vast, elaborately decorated interior with marble, gilt and lots of mirrors. Coffee, breakfast cake, deep-fried snacks.

Café La Granja

3 Plaza Circular
Tel: 94 423 0813
Open: 07.00-24.00 (Sat & Sun 09.00-02.30/03.00)
One of three roomy old cafés under the same management, La Granja is an easy walk from the Arenal Bridge and the old town, Casco Viejo. Its main clientele is office workers in the morning, shoppers at lunchtime and a young, lively crowd in the evening.

Café Iruña

Jardines de Albia, Berastegui 5
Tel: 94 423 7021
Open: 07.00-01.00 (Fri & Sat till 02.30)
Still going strong after nearly 100 years, Iruña overlooks the gardens and the monument to A Trueba. It has two bars, very different but both eye-catching. The first has revolving doors, a chandelier and a mosaic-decorated floor. Pass through a door to the right of the semi-circular bar and you enter a startling room with walls tiled in blue, white and yellow and tiled panelled tableaux advertising sherry and brandy from various producers. Here, at the long horseshoe bar, the locals swap news, sip their drinks and nibble their tapas.

Serantes

16 Licenciado de Poza
Tel: 94 443 5006
Open: 07.30-00.30 (Sun 10.00-01.00)
Seafood is king here, with first-rate oysters, cockles, mussels, crayfish, deep-sea prawns and a local crustacean called *percebes,* all to be enjoyed as snacks at the bar or as meals in the upstairs restaurant. The other speciality is *Jabugo* cured ham, pork and sausages. Spain has a cuisine that happily mixes fish and meat without a blink so it's no surprise that they've got it spot on here.

Victor Montes

8 Plaza Nueva, Casco Viejo
Tel: 94 415 5603/7067
Open: 10.00-24.00 (Sun till 15.00)
Café-restaurant, delicatessen and wine merchant in the arcades of a picturesque square in the old quarter. The elaborately decorated façade suggests quality, and you certainly get that here. The glass-fronted cabinets display a wonderful selection of wines and spirits, and the tapas prepared in the deli include not only ham and pork but goose, duck, salmon and even caviar. Pavement tables.

La Viña

10 Calle Diputacion
Tel: 94 415 5615
Open: 08.00-22.30
Closed: Sun

A wine bar in the shopping district, with legs of cured *jamon* hang over the bar and racks of wine bottles behind it. There's plenty of room to stand at the bar, and the rest of the room is set with marble-inlaid wooden tables with ornate pedestals and matching octagonal stools. Other food specialities include foie gras, a refined cured ham called *Cecina*, chorizo, tuna, salmon, anchovies and cheese, which can all be enjoyed in house or bought at the shop at one end; and there's a very good *viña real* among the numerous wines available by the glass.

Granada

Moorish monuments are a stunning feature of this wonderful city, which soon has visitors under its spell. Granada's most famous building is the Alhambra, a remarkable fortress built by Muhammed I in the 13th century atop a wooded hill, from which the Sierra Nevada can be seen in the distance. The festivities of Holy Week are popular with locals and tourists alike - indeed, tourism is a mainstay of the area's economy.

Gran Café Bib-Rambla

3 Plaza Bib-Rambla
Open: 08.00-02.00

A Gran Café in classic art nouveau style. The original cast-iron pillars still support the ceiling (now lowered to accommodate air-conditioning), and there are leaded glass lights over the shelves and a grand circular centrepiece on the ceiling. Coffee, wines by the glass, sandwiches and salads are always available, but the real speciality is ice cream, with 24 flavours on display. Seats are set outside in the shade of a tent.

Chikito

9 Plaza del Campillo
Tel: 958 223364
Open: 12.00-16.00 & 19.30-23.30 (terrace open in summer 12.00-24.00)
Closed: Wed

An excellent tapas bar and restaurant that attracts a wide cross-section of Granadians. The bar has numerous *jamon* hanging from the beams, while on the counter is a mouthwatering array of little snacks, with seafood a speciality - mussels, roe, clams, baby squid. This area opens out on to the square, where you can sit in the shade and enjoy a glass of wine or a cool beer with your snack. Chikito has been a favourite meeting place down the years of the leading figures of music and literature; on the outside wall a plaque commemorates the period of the *tertulias del riconcillo* between 1915 and 1929 when Manuel de Falla and Federico Garcia Lorca would come to the bar to discuss literary topics. They won a prize for merit from the town council for services to tourists and patrons.

Pilar del Toro

12 Hospital de Santa Ana
Tel: 958 223847
Open: 09.00-03.00

Originally a grand mansion, and later a hospital, this is now a café-bar-restaurant of distinction. Great oak doors, ten feet high and three inches thick, lead into the bar area with a broad marble-topped counter under a beamed ceiling; beyond this is a cool, glass-covered courtyard where cane chairs are set at black coffee tables round a fountain. There's also a small salon off the bar, and down some steps into the Plaza Nueva is a sheltered terrace where you can watch the world go by while enjoying a glass of wine or a cool beer with a few tapas; or a coffee with a complimentary little cake.

San Sebastian

'The Pearl of Cantabria', an elegant seaside resort with two glorious beaches. Luxury is the watchword of this renowned holiday spot, which first became fashionable in the 19th century when Queen Maria Christina of Hapsburg started to spend the summers here. The main sights, including the baroque Church of Santa Maria, are in the atmospheric old quarter.

Casa Alcalde
19 Calle Mayor
Tel: 943 42 62 16
Open: 10.00-23.00
Closed: Mon
The tradition here is food from the land: *jamon* (ham) of course, but also chorizo and stuffed vegetables, cheeses and olives. The long, low-ceilinged premises are packed out from early evening when glasses of wine flow - glasses that could probably hold half a pint but are only filled about an inch, and glass that's so thin it's amazing that they don't break. The walls here are hung with framed photos and posters of bullfights and bullfighters. And hanging from the beams are a score or more *jamon*. Waiter service at tables at the back.

Iturrioz
30 San Martin
Tel: 943 42 83 16
Open: 08.00-23.00
Closed: Sun
A very busy café in the modern centre of town, serving a large selection of beers and good house wines. At lunchtime, shoppers and shop staff drop for lunchtime snacks of sandwiches, rolls and tapas. A cheerful, happy place with friendly, helpful staff.

La Casa del Jamon
13 Calle Oquendo, corner of Avda de la Libertad
Tel: 943 42 15 91
Open: 08.30-24.00 (Sat from 09.30)
Closed: Sun
'Ham House' is a split-level café in the modern centre of San Sebastian. In the gallery hang rows of *jamon*, each labelled as to origin, weight and price. At street level is the charcuterie and ice cream dispensary, and steps take you down to the horseshoe bar where you can take drinks and tapas. Beyond is a counter for selling wines and fortified wines, which are displayed on shelves reaching up to the ceiling.

Oquendo
8 Oquendo, Donostia
Tel: 943 42 09 32
Open: 08.30-01.00
Tradition and style are evident at Oquendo, where much of the original 1924 decor has survived. The bar is smart in black and cream, with simple marble-topped tables and bentwood chairs and a restaurant area beyond. Hams, chorizos and salamis hang on the wall behind the bar, while the walls on the public side are adorned with framed posters of concerts of classical music and music festivals. Smart female staff wear black with white aprons.

Casa Vergara
21 Calle Mayor (Parte Vieja)
Tel: 943 43 10 73
Open: 11.00-24.00
Closed: Wed in winter
Newly renovated, this is a great place for seafood in the old part of San Sebastian in the shadow of the elaborately decorated Church of Santa Maria. In Vergara's window is displayed a selection of fresh seafood - much of it alive - crabs, lobsters, prawns, mussels, cockles, etc. The place is packed from early in the evening as customers squeeze their way up to the bar to order a drink and a snack, or make their way to the back where there's waiter service. They recently won a prize (Label Basco) for their tapas.

Seville

Old quarters with narrow streets; carriage rides round lovely parks and gardens. The capital of Andalusia, this is one of the world's most beautiful cities. Its Cathedral is the largest Gothic building in the world, the third largest church in Europe (beaten only by St Peter's and St Paul's), and houses the tomb of Christopher Columbus. The Giralda (climb to the top and the view will take your breath away) is the tower of the 12th-century mosque which was there before. Holy Week, with its colourful processions, and the Feria soon after are times of great excitement and huge religious fervour. The city is the spiritual home of flamenco, whose influence can be experienced in the many little cafés (*tabloas*) serving copas and tapas.

La Alberiza

6 Betis
Tel: 95 433 2016
Open: 13.00-16.00 & 21.00-24.00
Closed: Mon
A shrine to sherry and ham, La Alberiza is a traditionally styled building with dark green-shuttered windows and high beamed ceilings. The sherry barrels are stacked solera-style around two walls of the bar, behind which is the kitchen and beyond that a formal restaurant serving excellent seafood dishes. But the main action is in the bar, where whole cheeses stand on the counter, legs of *jamon* hang from the ceiling and barrels on the flagstoned floor provide a resting place for your glass.

La Andaluza

14 Garcia de Vinuesa
No telephone
Open: 12.00-16.00 & 20.00-02.00
Surely one of the smallest and cheapest bars in all Seville, and certainly one of the oldest, having started life on its corner site in 1887. Chorizo and ham are the food staples, while from the barrel or from Vinicola Hidalgo you can sample an excellent oloroso or a moscatel. Decorating the shelves behind the bar are miniature hooded figures of Holy Week processionists.

Bar Belmonte

24 Calle Mateos Gago
No telephone
Open: 08.00-00.30/01.00
A busy tapas bar, popular with the young of Seville, with some tables and chairs set out under shady trees in a narrow street in the Old Town behind the Cathedral. Beer is very popular here, and a jug of sangria is always ready in the fridge. Some of the wines and sherries are kept in blue-and-white pottery coolers on the bar counter.

Bar Commercio

9 Calle Lineros
No telephone
Open: 08.00-19.30
Closed: Sun
In the commercial centre, as its name suggests, this bright, welcoming bar dating from 1904 specialises in cold meats. Have a look at the decorative tiles, especially on the bar counter support, the whole length of which is an advertisement for a fino brandy.

Meson SJ

1 Calle Castelar
Tel: 95 421 5862
Open: 07.30-24.00

Named after Jamon SJ, the house ham, this popular place has a horseshoe bar with pink-red brick, wrought-iron enclosed balconies with the underside tiled in blue ceramic, and a two-storey conservatory clinging to the front. Ham is the speciality, along with pork sausages and cheeses, and so popular is the ham that a member of staff is delegated full time to slicing - and he certainly has his work cut out. A demanding and discerning clientele of 40-somethings are looked after by ever-helpful waiters in smart green jackets braided with the letter 'J'. Have a look at the ceramic tableaux depicting stylised porkers and amusingly entitled 'Pigs'. Previously called Meson Sevilla Jabugo.

Giralda

1 Mateos Gago
Tel: 95 422 7435
Open: 09.00-24.00 (Sun from 10.00)

Blue, white and bronze tiling decorates this popular and durable bar-restaurant, where a list of tapas is chalked up on a blackboard; the chalk is also used to mark up your order on the well-lacquered mahogany bar top. Marble pillars support a vaulted ceiling, and there's a hum of activity as the waiters tend to chattering customers sitting at the marble-topped tables. Outside, aluminium tables and chairs are set on the pavement. If swordfish is on the menu, try it.

Bodega Santa Cruz

1 Calle Rodrigo Caro
No telephone
Open: 07.00-01.00

A great sawdust bar for locals and an occasional smattering of tourists. This is the place for local gossip, a drink and some good cheap tapas. It's got soul, and it's cheerful enough to put a smile on even the most miserable face!

Bodegon Torre del Oro

15 Santander
Tel: 95 421 4241
Open: 07.00-24.00/01.00

In a 15th-century building two minutes from the bull-ring the old bar area is hung with tresses of garlic and haunches of *jamon*, and the height of the ceiling and the paddle fans keep the place cool in even the hottest weather. Photographs of famous bullfighters clutter the walls and professional barmen in black bow ties are always attentive. A favourite among the tapas is cod's roe and mayonnaise with a glass of fino.

Valencia

Spain's third largest city, on the Costa del Azular, home of paella and to a sadly declining number of traditional cafés on and around the main square. The great annual festival - Las Fallas - of bonfires, bull-fighting, dancing and carnivals takes place in March, but there's a holiday atmosphere for a large part of the year, and the coastline north and south contains many of the most popular resorts.

El Generalife

5 Calle Caballeros
Tel: 96 391 7899
Open: 08.00-18.00 & 20.00-01.30
Closed: Mon & Tue
A popular place with both locals and tourists tucked away in the corner of the Plaza de la Virgen with its sumptuous basilica and opposite the Palacio del Generalidad (a 15th-century palace that is the seat of local government). The café-restaurant is on two levels, with some tables in the square outside. Popular with tourists and office workers. Good menu plus daily specials.

Mare Nostrum

85 San Vicente Martir & Plaza Ajuntiamento
Open: 08.00-01.00
Valencia's answer to the traditional Gran Café. There are two branches in the city, one in a side street near the station, the other at the narrow end of Plaza Ajuntiamento. Excellent coffee (the best in town) comes in a host of different ways to accompany pastries and sandwiches, and the hot chocolate is very good, too. Both places are spacious and well-ventilated, with lofty ceilings and stacks of sacks and barrels printed with the names of coffee plantations around the world.

Cafeteria Noel

Av Marquez de Sotelo 4
Tel: 96 352 9494
Open: 07.30-23.00 (Sun from 09.00)
In a side street off the main square, this fine old cafeteria has probably one of the longest bar counters in Spain. Customers drop by to take refreshment and enjoy one of the fine sandwiches, bocadillos or perhaps delicious chapata filled with salty anchovies drenched in rich olive oil, and for hungrier souls there is also an à la carte menu. Two coffee grinders are clearly labelled *suave* and *fuerte* (mild or strong), a sensible choice! A second, equally large counter on the other side offers a large range of patisserie, charcuterie and wines to take home, and if you feel that luck is with you go up to the first floor and buy a lottery ticket from the old office.

Valladolid

The lively capital of the province of Castille and Leon on the central plateau north of Madrid, Valladolid was for centuries the seat of the kings and queens of Spain. There's a serious tradition of drinking coffee here as well as quaffing the wines that are produced nearby. The university, founded in the 15th century, is in the middle of town, and during term time the students give a great lift to the café scene.

Café Continental

Plaza Mayor
Tel: 983 370618
Open: 08.00-03.00
To the left of the impressive Town Hall (1908) in the corner of the largest square in Valladolid is Café Continental, for many years a popular meeting place - comfortable and roomy inside, with additional tables on the arcaded pavement and out in the square under large parasols. Their Illy coffee is the great thing here, a 100% arabica served in many different ways, from corto to americano, with brandy or with whisky ice cream. Snacks include tortillas and croquetas, and a selection of cakes is baked daily.

Café Epoca

38 Calle Nunez de Arce
Tel: 983 399507
Open: 08.00-01.00/02.00 (Sat from 09.00, Sun 10.00-24.00/01.00)
Coffee and cocktails are both best-sellers at this popular student bar with reproduction Belle Epoque decor opposite the College of Santa Cruz which Cardinal Mendoza founded in 1479. The university staff also drop in during the day for breakfast, a snack or a light lunch, while the younger set tend to take over in the evening.

Lion d'Or

4 Plaza Mayor
Tel: 983 342057
Open: 09.00-03.00 (Fri & Sat till 04.00, Sun 11.00-02.30)

In another corner of the main square (see *Café Continental*) to the right of the Town Hall, this elegant café was established in its present form in 1979 but sports many artefacts from a much earlier period, including ornate furniture, elaborately framed mirrors and a wall clock. The lighting is also vintage, and the impressive bar has a marble top, brass rail and mirrored mahogany panels. Behind the bar are large coppers dispensing coffee and hot milk. You can also get a beer or a glass of some of the very good local wine. Staff are friendly and professional.

La Miña

7 Correos
Tel: 983 333008
Open: 11.00-16.00 & 19.30-00.30
Closed: Tue

A popular bar, long and narrow, in a pedestrian street just off the main square. The high ceiling with exposed beams supports elaborate brass chandeliers, and the timber bar and exposed brickwork give a warm and friendly atmosphere that is matched by the welcome from smart, professional staff. At the far end is the kitchen, where you can watch the preparation of tempting looking dishes bound for the dumb waiter and the upstairs restaurant. Excellent wines from the Duero.

La Tertulia

6 Pasaje Gutierrez
Tel: 983 396904
Open: 08.00-01.00 (Fri & Sat till 02.00)

Two narrow streets east of Plaza Mayor are connected by a stunning glass-roofed gallery, among whose shops and boutiques is this elegant little café where you can get a snack throughout the day to accompany a coffee or a glass of wine. Sit at the bar or one of the tables inside, or marvel at the art nouveau splendour from a chair outside.

El Tostadero del Buen Café

Calle de Santuario
Tel: 983 295040
Open: 08.00-01.00
Closed: Sun in Aug

A small chain of air-conditioned cafés serving an impressive range of 22 coffees and 30 teas or infusions. They also serve beer and spirits, cakes and sandwiches, and you can buy packets of your favourite blend of coffee to take home. They have a clever little motto, which goes 'Coffee comes like this: black as the devil, hot as hell, sweet as love, and pure as an angel'. Other Tostaderos are at 5 Plaza del Cano Argales, Calle Conde Ansurez and Centro de Ocio Parque Sol.

Sweden

Telephone Code: 00 46

The Swedes are peaceful, tolerant, industrious and efficient, and their contributions to the world arena include the Nobel prizes, instituted by Alfred Nobel in 1896 and awarded annually for outstanding achievement in the fields of physics, chemistry, physiology or medicine, literature, economic sciences and peace. The practical Swedes also gave us Ikea furniture, the Tetra Pak, the monkey wrench, the cream separator, the Celsius scale and the ombudsman. And Abba. Coffee is usually good in Sweden, and the cities and towns all have a fair sprinkling of cafés and bars where you can get a coffee (often with a free refill) or a drink, and a snack. On the food side, Sweden's best-known gifts to the world are gravad lax and the renowned smörgåsbord, an appetising array of open sandwiches with myriad toppings.

Stockholm

The original settlement was founded in 1252, and Stockholm has been the country's capital since 1436. Spread over 14 islands and surrounded by water so free of pollution you can fish and swim in it, Stockholm is one of the world's cleanest capital cities. The area officially called Norrmalm is known by Stockholmers as City and is where all the main shops are found. East of that is the wealthy area of Ostermalm with its grand avenues and houses. Over any of several bridges to the south is the Old Town called Gamla Stan, which lies on an island behind the Royal Castle (now used as offices and for formal occasions rather than the monarch's residence). Characteristic of the Old Town are the narrow streets, small premises and the renowned 'glass ceilings'. On the western end of Djurgarden is the Vasamuseet, where the 17th-century warship *Vasa* is housed. The top-heavy *Vasa*, pride of the fleet of King Gustavus Adolphus, sank on her maiden voyage in 1628, and lay in the harbour silt until 1961, when it was raised almost intact and restored with great skill and patience to its pristine state.

Engelen/Kolingen (downstairs)

Kornhamnstorg 59b (Gamla Stan) Box 7065, 103 86
Tel: 8 20 10 92
Open: 16.00-02.00 (downstairs till 03.30)
A corner site bar with live music every night except Monday, when it's the turn of stand-up comedians. The bar leads to a blackjack table, to a restaurant in an elegant room, and to downstairs, which is a real rabbit warren - another bar, more blackjack tables, cloakrooms etc. House wine is sold by the bottle but you only pay for what you drink. The cheerful, energetic staff, always eager to help, are used to dealing with demanding crowds. Steakhouse-style food.

Gamla Stans Bryggeri

Skeppsbrokajen, Tullhus 2, Gamla Stan
Tel: 8 20 20 65
Open: 14.00-01.00 (Fri & Sat till 03.00, Sun till 23.00)
A micro-brewery in an enormous, very well-appointed shed on the quayside known as Customs House 2. Its main output is unfiltered beer, which is therefore acceptably cloudy. Above the central bar made of substantial oak (the brewing takes place in the very centre) is a pair of roll-back roof panels; oak is grown abundantly around Stockholm and in Sweden generally, though many hectares were lost in August 1999 in a dreadful fire in southern Sweden. This place gets really busy at the time of the Water Festival (an event to compare with Semana Grande in Spanish cities), when a live band entertains in great style, but it's also popular in the winter when the terrace is dismantled and the action is all inside.

Café Gateau

Sturegallerian, Stureplan 2
Tel: 8 611 65 93
Open: 08.00-18.00 (Sat 10.00-17.00, Sun 11.00-17.00)
A bakery-cum-cafeteria-style café in a smartly maintained shopping mall. The bakery shop is on the ground floor and the café is up a sweeping stair in the gallery overlooking the shop and the shoppers as they move from boutique to boutique. The pastries are excellent, as is their deli-type lunch, and the coffee is Illy. Wine (Spanish/Italian/German) and beer, both draught and bottled, are also on offer. You can cut your own slice of crusty twisted loaf to go with, perhaps, a bowl of gazpacho, a popular summer choice. In the winter season (October-May), when it's dark and cold outside, this place is packed and a resident piano player entertains.

Grand Verandan

Blasieholmshamnen 8, Blasieholmen
Tel: 8 679 35 86/717 00 20
Open: 07.00-11.00 for breakfast, 12.00-15.00 (Sat & Sun 13.00-16.00) for lunch, 18.00-22.00 for smorgasbord. Bar open 11.00-02.00 (Sun 12.00-00.30)
The terrace of Stockholm's leading luxury hotel is renowned for its smorgasbord, and there's a fine view across the water (Norrstrom) to Gamla Stan and the official Royal Residence. Other offerings include an à la carte menu and two- or three-course fixed-price menus. The cuisine is very traditional, with gravad lax, smoked eel, roe, herring, reindeer; halibut and lobster in a cream sauce; raspberries and raspberry ice cream. The surroundings of this grand hotel, designed by Frenchman Regis Cadier in 1874 and used by the Nobel Prize winners each December, are quite formal, and there is a dress code in the restaurants.

Duvel Café

Vasagatan 50, Norrmalm, 111 20
Tel: 8 23 48 20
Open: 11.30-01.00 (Mon and Tue till 24.00, Sat from 17.00)
Closed: Sun
New owners at the former Greitz, Stockholm favourite close to the Oscar and Vasa theatres, the station and many of the top hotels. First established in 1895 as Klosterhof, a beer room and restaurant, it has two bars and a highly talented new chef cooking Belgian-style.

Hard Rock Café

Sveavagen 75, Norrmalm, 113 50
Tel: 8 16 03 50
Open: 11.00-23.00
A huge corner site, with a terrace under awning, and inside, a big black American convertible built-in over the bar, a Harley Davidson over the merchandise shop, famous guitarist's instruments around the walls, and lots more to take the eye. The food is traditional American bar-b-q ribs, chicken, burgers, salads and sandwiches; the drink, draught beer in three measures - 28cl, 40cl and a 170cl pitcher; 17 varieties of bottled beer, coffee, and half a dozen wines by the glass. "Love All - Serve All" is the motto, and the oldy songs come one after another. Live music is performed on a new stage once a week.

Café Kristina

Vasterlanggatan 68, Gamla Stan, S-111 29
Tel: 8 20 80 86
Open: 11.00-22.00/23.00, Sun 13.00-22.00
This was once Queen Kristina's session room, built in 1625 and restored internally in 1904, externally in 1947. After several varied incarnations it is now a rather grand café, somewhat larger than many of the properties in this cramped island centre of old Stockholm, and run as an Italian hostelry. The floor has no doubt been changed several times down the years, but the panelled ceiling could be turn-of-the-century. Enter from the street, where there are a few terrace tables, into the bar area, beyond which are two rooms (one non-smoking), separated by one huge pillar supporting a somewhat distorted beam. Interestingly, if you ask for a glass of wine in Sweden you are commonly brought a glass of water as well, much as you would with an espresso in Italy.

Mandus

Osterlangatan 7, Gamla Stan
Tel: 8 20 60 55
Open: 17.00-24.00
A small café/bar only a stone's throw from the Royal Palace, playing music in various styles from Latin American to Marlene. Three white and three red wines are sold by the glass, and the food is good: fish specialities, mussels, reindeer, ox fillet, goat's cheese, gravad lax, chanterelles. There are a couple of tables outside, several inside and seating at the curved bar where the patron surveys his domain. Tourists get into every nook and cranny in Gamla Stan, but here there's mainly a very friendly mixed crowd of regulars.

Martini

Norrmalmstorg 4, 111 46
Tel: 8 440 38 80
Open: 11.00-24.00 (Wed & Thur till 02.00, Fri & Sat till 03.00, Sun 13.00-23.00)
An Italian-style café/restaurant with a terrace, but with a Swedish feel and Swedish cuisine. The place to be is either on the terrace in summer, or at the large bar in the centre of the room. Theatre suppers are a regular feature. This is the centre of Stockholm's downtown, where all the best shopping and entertainment is found. People of all ages come here, as couples or to meet as a group, to enjoy a good glass or coffee, or to sip a cocktail. On Friday and Saturday a DJ starts spinning at 23.00.

Café Mix

Sibyllegatan 2, Stockholm
Tel 8 660 0625
Open: 11.00-16.00 (Sat 11.00-17.00)
Closed: Sun

This was once the Royal Bakery, sandwiched as it is between the Kungliga Dramatiska Teatren and the Royal Stables, and it is the oldest building in this part of town. It was nearly knocked down in the 1970s to create a new car park, but it was mostly rescued when its history and antiquity were pointed out; by then, the original ovens had already been destroyed. The back part of the building is the Music Museum, where its Friends hold classical concerts in the winter season, hence the resident piano. Snacks run from jacket potatoes and crêpes to lasagne and moussaka. No smoking inside.

Mosebacke Etablissement

Mosebacke Torg 3, Sodermalm, 116 46
Tel: 8 55 60 98 90
Open: 17.00-01.00 (Thur-Sat till 02.00)

Located at the back of one of the oldest theatres in Stockholm, this place was established in 1985, and it now has a restaurant with a dance floor and stage. But its best attribute is the great views over the rooftops of Gamla Stan, across the water to the Grand Hotel, Strandvagen's grand houses, Skeppsholmen and the funfair at Djurgardsstaden. Breakfasts are served from the kiosk on the terrace, lunch at the grill. Saturday and Sunday brunch with live jazz. At night there's an entrance fee to go inside to listen to or dance to live music or DJs starting at 22.00 and going on until closing time.

Operabaren

Operahuset, Karl XII:s Torg, 111 86
Tel: 8 676 58 07/08
Open: Café 11.30-03.00 (Sun from 13.00) Bar 12.00-01.00 (Sun 17.00-24.00)

A haunt of royalty and stars of the worlds of theatre, music and tennis, and a place of several names, depending on which part you choose: the opulentissimo Operakallaren restaurant, Operabaren, Café Opera (one of the city's top night spots), Bakfickan. Matsal is the main dining room, Nobis the wine cellar. The first parts opened in 1787, but the café dates from 1895, and the bar from 1904. The cafe/brasserie/bar/bistro has a spectacular ceiling painting by Vicke Andren and huge crystal chandeliers, while the rest has a contemporary look. At midnight it becomes a disco, but during the earlier parts of the day it is equally popular for lunch, tea or an early supper. The bar has changed little since its opening; the decor is art nouveau and the refined atmosphere that of a gentleman's club. Young, intellectual Stockholmers regularly meet here.
Scandinavia Café of the Year 2001

Ortagarden

Ostermalmstorg
Tel: 8 662 1728
Open: 10.30-21.30 (Sat 11.00-20.30, Sun 12.00-20.30)

For the past 20 years this has been a vegetarian café in the 140-year-old City-owned Saluhallen market, which has a preservation order. The owner, a lady of a certain age, chooses the vegetables herself to produce the freshest of seasonal menus and is highly regarded among the traders downstairs; indeed, she has published a fully illustrated hardback recipe book. Ortagarden is a great favourite with users of the market, but even out of market hours it attracts a regular local clientele who come here to enjoy live piano Monday, Tuesday and sometimes Sunday) while they sup or snack. Coffee is the traditional filter variety.

Café Riche

Birger Jarlsgatan 4, 114 14 (Norrmalm-Sture)
Tel: 8 679 68 40
Open: 11.00-03.00, bar from 17.00
Bar (Pachanga), Veranda, Theatergrill, Club, Butik: this is still the fashionable quarter where the well-heeled come for luxurious pampering. The bar is an elaborate zinc-topped affair, where tapas-style snacks are sold - naturally, the head of a bull graces the wall. The Veranda, or terrace, has high-backed wicker basket chairs (and smart little ashtrays). The restaurant, which offers a full à la carte menu, is partly in a glassed-in area of the terrace and partly inside. The staff give the bar a real Latin American feel, assisted by the music and the cocktails to complement the *jamon*. This place really hops at night - and that means dancing on the bar!

Stampen

Stora Nygatan 5, Gamla Stan
Tel: 8 20 57 93/86
Open: 19.00-03.00
A smoky, swinging jazz club spread over two floors; upstairs is funky, with all sorts of artefacts hanging from the ceiling - mostly jazz instruments, but also the odd rocking horse (for rock music?). There's a good list of wines, many available by the glass, and a wide variety of beers and spirits. Sometimes, like during the Water Festival, there is an entrance charge.

Sundbergs Konditori

Jarntorget 83, Gamla Stan, 111 29
Tel: 8 10 67 35
Open: 08.00-19.00 (summer till 23.00)
In a 500-year-old building in a pretty little square, this charming patisserie/café was established by Johan Ludwig Sundberg in 1785 in the reign of King Gustav III. Renowned for its coffees, teas and hot chocolate, it has also earned an almost legendary name for its pastries, sweets and liqueurs. The interior has retained all its period charm, notably in the 'glass' ceiling, a feature of the old houses of Gamla Stan, and in the Venetian glass chandelier. Outside, in the largely pedestrian cobbled square, is a roped-off area with cane chairs and tables, while inside is a display counter on one side and tables on the other, with a huge copper coffee urn among the cups and saucers on a table in pride of place under the chandelier. A great favourite with both locals and visitors to the city.

Vau De Ville

Hamngatan 17, Norrmalm, 111 47
Tel: 8 611 25 22
Open: 11.30-01.00 (Fri & Sat till 02.00, Sun 13.00-01.00)
A busy corner bar/restaurant in brasserie-style, with a cheerful welcome from French staff, and free access where a lot of the 'smarter' places have three or more bouncers and charge an entrance fee at the weekends. Green chequered table cloths, globe lighting - only the zinc bar top is missing! The clientele are much as you'd find in Paris; in fact you could be forgiven for thinking you were there. Of course the cuisine is French, too.

Vette-Katten

Kungsgatan 55/Klara Norra Kyrkogatan 26, 111 22
Tel 8 21 84 54/20 84 05
Open: 07.30-20.00 (Sat 09.00-17.00, Sun 12.00-17.00)
The smartest cake shop in town, established in 1928, with two changes of ownership since - the last in 1979. Years ago artists would come here to eat on credit, often trading their work for something to eat. Now the smart set come here for their pastries and bread (very delicious they are too, and so are the chocolates!). Originally, the only entrance was in Kungsgatan, but having expanded over the years (the last addition 12 years ago), they now have three entrances in two streets.

Karlstad

Karlstad stands on the estuary of the River Klarälven and the shores of Lake Värnen, which freezes over in winter. It is a summer holiday resort and a university town of some 9,000 students, and also hosts several festivals, notably the water festival, Hamnfestival, at the end of July/beginning of August. The town is famous for its good weather and all sorts of outdoor sports, from fishing and sailing in the summer to skiing and skating in the winter. It is known for its restaurants and local dishes like 'nävgröt porridge with bacon, salmon, elk meat and whitefish roe.

Café Royal
Järnvägsgatan 10
Tel: 54 15 51 20
Open: 08.00-20.00 (Sat & Sun 09.30-18.00)
Like so many cafés in so many countries, this was once a bank; it was acquired four years ago and converted into this grand café. You enter through the imposing front door and lobby to be greeted by an array of wonderful sweet and savoury pastries, all prepared on the premises. Under the high ceiling supported by ornate, robust pillars, and hung with crystal chandeliers, are brightly coloured bentwood chairs on a polished wood floor. It's in the centre of town, so all sorts of folk come here for refreshment, to relax and talk, or just to recover from shopping.

Örebro

Örebro, one of Sweden's largest cities, with a population of just under 125,000, lies on what is called the Scandinavian King's Road, Oslo-Stockholm-St Petersburg. A meeting point for trade since the Middle Ages, it crossed the River Svartän by a gravel ford until a bridge was built that gave the town its name. It is dominated by its photogenic 700-year-old Castle Vasaborg, which overlooks the bridge. Further along the riverbank is the well-known village of Wadköping, built in 1965 to preserve the traditional timber houses that were once in the town centre.

Slottkrogen
Örebro Slott
Tel: 19 13 42 69
Open: 18.00-23.00
What could be more delightful than a cool beer on the terrace of what is probably the most picturesque castle in Sweden, in the sunshine overlooking the river? Dating back to the 13th century, it has seen some memorable times. Jean Baptiste Bernadotte was elected King of Sweden here, and it is said that the ghost of Engelbrekt, the rebel leader murdered in 1436, wanders about with his head tucked underneath his arm. There is a full restaurant inside the castle, and in the summer a glass-sided tented bar by the walls, with more tables outside under broad white parasols. Concerts are also held here.

The Bishop's Arms
Drottninggatan 1
Tel: 19 15 69 20
Open: 15.00-24.00 (Fri & Sat till 02.00, Sun from 17.00)
In 1854 a great fire in Örebro destroyed, among many other places, the hotel that had been on this site since the 17th century. Local money was raised to build the present one, built entirely of local materials and completed in 1860. Another fire in 1909 damaged part of the building and its restoration included an extra storey; it has remained thus ever since. The Bishop's Arms specialises in single malt whiskies and also has a good range of beers or coffee to enjoy inside at the bar or on the terrace outside.

Wadköping Café
Torget, Wadköping
Tel: 19 30 73 70
Open: 11.00-17.00
Once a tin foundry house built in 1780 and located in Örebro town centre, the home and workshop of the tin-founder, it is now a working café. In the mid-1960s the centre of Örebro was cleared to make way for shopping areas and better housing for the growing population. The pick of the old timber houses were saved from destruction and moved to this new site to form a village. All the buildings are lived in and worked in as a sort of living museum. They include a smithy, a wealthy merchant's house, a grain store, a linen-weaver's home and a glove-maker's home, as well as this café serving coffees, wine and beer, snacks and full meals; apple cake is a speciality.

United Kingdom

The millions of visitors who arrive in Britain each year discover an amazing variety of scenery, major seats of religion and learning, magnificent cathedrals and churches, castles and stately homes, stunning city architecture and everywhere a tangible sense of history and culture. The heritage of pomp and pageantry is jealously preserved against the inexorable worldwide slide into uniformity, and the cultural scene is highlighted by marvellous museums and art galleries (the Tate Modern, on the Thames in London, has proved an instant huge success); important festivals of music and theatre supplement top-quality performances throughout the year in almost every town and city. The British might not admit to many eccentricities, but they are there in glorious abundance: until Brussels sprouts a further crop of legislation, we will continue to enjoy our pints, to drive our cars on the left, travelling miles and burning gallons, and to hop on and off the backs of the wonderful old Routemaster buses, still going strong after 40 years. The café culture that is sweeping the world is particularly strong in Britain, with hundreds of outlets opening each year, offering an attractive alternative to the British pub in responding to the desire of people of all ages to socialise and relax with friends in casual surroundings without breaking the bank.

London

Since the first century AD, when the Roman Emperor Claudius founded a settlement on the banks of the Thames, the river has been the lifeblood of London, and river trips combine the traditional sights and modern developments like Docklands and the mighty Thames Barrier. There are several brand new sights on the riverscape: the Millennium Dome, visited by millions but not enough millions; the giant ferris wheel called the London Eye or Millennium Eye; and a famously wobbly pedestrian bridge crossing the Thames from below St Paul's to the acclaimed Tate Modern, one of the world's largest and finest modern art galleries (actually 84 galleries!) housed in the former Bankside power station. On dry land, tourists throng the squares and the historic buildings, while Londoners and those in the know enjoy the surprising number of wide open spaces, from the Royal Parks in the heart of the city to Hampstead Heath, Greenwich and Epping Forest. Lovers of the performing arts have a huge choice of theatres, concert halls and popular music events; sports fans can have a field day, and the centre of the capital buzzes until well into the night. The coffee bar boom continues unabated, with new outlets springing up daily, matching strides with the new juice bars and the apparently inexorable rise of the fast food outlets. But the traditional pubs and wine bars and cafés are still very much part of the social scene, while for a true taste of high society afternoon tea in the foyer of a grand hotel remains a uniquely English treat.

All Bar One

1 Liverpool Rd, Islington N1
Tel: 020 7843 0021
Open: 12.00-23.00 (Sun till 22.30)

One of the smaller sites in the growing chain, with an overhead ordering system clicking its wandering path through the suspended lights and ventilation ducting to the kitchen. Huge wall mirrors enhance the sense of space, and the robust horseshoe bar with its brass furniture displays the wines in bins behind - many sold by the 250ml glass. As business people and shoppers lunch, Ella could be singing *Summertime* even if *Baby It's Cold Outside*. The menu on blackboards offers tasty small, medium and big plate meals, sandwiches and the fresh soup of the day.

There are more than 40 ABOs in London, and a dozen more spread around the country.

L'Antico

564 King's Rd SW6
Tel: 020 7371 9536
Open: 09.00-23.00 (Sun from 11.00)

In the western stretch of King's Road, among fabric, art and antique shops and some trendy bars, L'Antico is a bright little annexe of Italy with a cheerful customer base of expat Italians. In the morning it's coffee and croissants, and from noon onwards a menu of pizzas and a list of daily specials, from bruschetta and pasta of the day and some excellent, simply prepared fish dishes, takes over.

The Arches

7 Fairhazel Gardens NW6
Tel: 020 7624 1876
Open: 12.00-23.00

A splendid little café-restaurant-cum-wine bar where all sorts of bits and pieces, from swords to model planes, old cameras to street signs (including The Arches from the City of Westminster) and old photos of the area burst out of every corner and hang from every inch of wall-space. The serious, extensive and ever-changing wine list is the work of enthusiastic owner Harry Gill, who likes to offer his customers the opportunity to try wines that could be beyond their pocket by imposing the gentlest of mark-ups. He also keeps some fine cognacs and armagnacs, a good selection of bottled and draught beers and the usual varieties of teas and coffees. There's a bar menu of snacks and light bites, and full meals can be enjoyed in the restaurant downstairs. His customers, many of whom have become his friends, come from far and wide to enjoy the company, the ambience, the wine and the food.

UK Special Award 2001

Balans West

239 Old Brompton Rd SW6
Tel: 020 7244 8838
Open: 08.00-01.00 (Sat till 02.00)

One of a chain of four informal, gay-friendly restaurants with an uncluttered modern look and an all-day menu in contemporary style. This branch has seats for 85, including a glassed-in conservatory that's sunny by day and intimately candle-lit by night. The breakfast/brunch list run from traditional English to blueberry pancakes by way of burrito (spiced scrambled eggs with grilled cheese, tomato salsa and sour cream in a toasted flour tortilla). The rest of the menu is also a mini-tour of the world's cuisines. To drink, coffee galore, a long list of wines, seven champagnes, cocktails and pitchers of Pimms, Sangria, Long Island Iced Tea, Woo-Woo and Mai-Tai. Pavement tables.
Also at: Balans Soho 60 Old Compton St, Soho W1 Tel: 020 7437 5212
Open 08.00-05.00 (Fri & Sat till 06.00, Sun till 02.00); Balans Knightsbridge 239 Brompton Rd SW3 Tel: 020 7584 0070; Balans Kensington 187 Kensington High St W8 Tel: 020 7376 0115 Open: 08.00-24.00.
And one in Miami!

Café Baroque

33 Southampton St WC2
Tel: 020 7379 7585
Open: 12.00-24.00
Closed: Sun

A civilised spot that really lives up to its name on the last Tuesday evening of every month, when live Baroque opera and more familiar arias are performed by mainly professional singers. Throughout the day you can relax to taped classical music in the bar with a cup of really good coffee, a drink and some excellent tapas-style snacks. There's a good wine list, with two dozen available by the glass. In the first-floor dining room modern British and European cuisine is served lunchtime and evening, including pre- and post-theatre menus.

Bluebird Café

350 King's Rd, Chelsea SW3
Tel: 020 7559 1000
Open: bar 12.00-23.00, café 09.00-22.00 (Sat till 21.00, Sun till 18.00)

Firmly established on the gastronomic scene, the King's Road outpost of the Conran empire is a combination of restaurant, café, bar, food market, flower market and kitchen shop, all housed in a handsome building that was, when built in 1923, Europe's largest motor garage. The café, with seats for 60 and as many more outside on the forecourt (but you still might queue), proposes croissants, home-made scones, biscotti and a tempting list of dishes from the food market, from the day's pasta special to wood-roast vegetables and grilled herb sausages with mash and onion gravy. A popular venue at all times, and great for Sunday brunch.

Blue Mountain

18 North Cross Rd SE22
Tel: 020 8299 6953
Open: 09.00-18.00 (Sun from 10.00)

A delightful little café in a former dairy in East Dulwich. Of the various dining rooms, some are distressed rustic, others bright and modern; the back room has large mirrors, while the top room has a Greek theme; there are also some outside tables in the garden and on the pavement. Breakfast is served from 09.00 till noon, and among the favourite daytime snacks are 'melts' served in a baguette with salads. There's a notable patisserie counter, and the cappuccino is spot on. Blue Mountain is a great favourite with families: children's portions can be provided on request, and high chairs are available.

Café Bohème

13 Old Compton St, Soho W1
Tel: 020 7734 0623
Open: 08.00-03.00 (Thur-Sat 24 hrs, Sun 09.00-23.30)

Intimate and usually quite loud, with something of the look and feel of a Parisian brasserie and round-the-clock service Thursday to Saturday. Look in for anything from a coffee to a full-scale meal (and the latter won't set you back more than a tenner). A perennially popular place which attracts the whole spectrum of Soho characters, after-office drinkers and visitors to this permanently bustling part of town. Pavement tables get even closer to the full Soho experience.

Café Brera

Ground Floor, Cabot Place West, Canary Wharf E14
Tel: 020 7512 9191
Open: 07.00-20.00 (Sat & Sun 10.00-18.00)

This lively Italian-style bar, tucked in the entrance hall of Cabot Place shopping complex, serves the best coffee in the area, plus fresh ciabatta sandwiches (choice of at least a dozen varieties), salads, excellent Maison Blanc patisserie, and beers, wines and spirits. On sunny days the chairs and tables spill out on to Cabot Square. New Café Brera, with a huge terrace and great river views, is at Hanover House, Westferry Circus E14 Tel: 020 7512 9575. Another Brera is housed in the Lyric Theatre Hammersmith, King St W6 Tel: 020 8741 9291.

La Brioche

238 West End Lane NW6
Tel: 020 7431 8175
Open: 08.00-22.30 (Mon till 19.00)

Brioche, baguette, croissant, and especially bruschetta are the order of the day here. Breakfast can be simple and French with patisserie, or something more substantial like the full English or smoked salmon and scrambled eggs on bruschetta. And there are some excellent pastries, tortes and cakes, all on display in the cabinet as you come in, to enjoy with a very good Piazza d'Oro espresso. Wines by glass or bottle. Generally this is a quiet, contemplative place, with unobtrusive background music playing, newspapers and magazines to read, a place to write a chapter or two of your life story, or at least a letter home..... but on Fridays there's live music, when the owner on guitar is accompanied by two more and a bass, and it's time to party and dance. And at the weekend it's packed, with everyone trying to get a seat.

Browns Restaurant & Bar

82-84 St Martins Lane, Covent Garden WC2
Tel: 020 7497 5050
Open: 12.00-24.00

A handsome building housing a 320-seat restaurant and bar on the ground floor. It is open for lunch, afternoon tea, pre- and post-theatre suppers and dinner. The main menu is very diverse, ranging from hot sandwiches through salads, pasta, classic main courses like salmon cakes and steak, mushroom & Guinness pie to moreish puddings. To drink, a good list of bottled beers, and around 40 wines (a dozen available by the glass) as well as some sparklers. The building was formerly Westminster County Courts, and the upstairs courtroom, complete with the bench and judges' chairs, is an atmospheric setting for parties or functions.

Also at:

47 Maddox Crt W1 Tel: 020 7491 4565 (last food orders 22.00; closed Sun)

8 Old Jewry EC2 Tel: 020 7606 6677 (last food orders 22.00)

Hertsmere Rd E14 Tel: 020 7987 9777 (last food orders 21.45)

3-5 Kew Green, Richmond Tel: 020 8948 4838 (open 12.00-11.30, Sat from 11.00, Sun till 22.30)

201 Castelnau SW13 Tel: 020 8748 4486 (open 12.00-23.00)

Chamomile

45 Englands Lane NW3
Tel: 020 7586 4580
Open: 07.00-18.30

Specialities here are the wide range of coffees, the delicious home-baked pastries and the all-day breakfasts. Four pavement tables under a blue awning are popular when the weather's fine, while inside, the tables are quite close to each other, but the high ceiling gives a sense of space. Beyond the counter, a notice board with local information leads to a narrow smoking area at the back. Lunchtime snacks: soup, pasta, savoury pancakes, omelettes, jacket potatoes; also sandwiches and a takeaway menu. Four reds and four whites from France and the New World in ½ bottles, and a range of healthy juices. It's amazing how time flies with the pleasure of a Segafredo espresso or caffe latte and the *Times* crossword.

Chelsea Kitchen

98 King's Rd SW3
Tel: 020 7589 1330
Open: 11.30-23.30 (Sun 12.00-23.00)

Let's do the time warp again. In complete contrast to the trendy shops and bars that are its neighbours, this 60-cover Italian-run café in the Stockpot fold offers good old-fashioned eating at bargain basement prices in modest, homely surroundings. Shoppers and locals drop in for anything from a cup of coffee to a full-scale meal, and there are not many places in London where you can round things off with jelly and ice cream!

Corney & Barrow

1 Leadenhall Place EC3
Tel: 020 7621 9201
Open: 09.00-22.30 (Wed-Fri till 23.00)
Closed: Sat & Sun

Two of the best-known institutions meet in the City: Corney & Barrow at Lloyds of London. Beneath the New Exchange with the guts on the outside, the long-established wine importers Corney & Barrow sell early morning snacks, sandwiches, hot light dishes and cakes to be washed down with excellent coffee, beers from Sweden, Germany, the UK and Japan, or something from their long wine list. A constant tide of business people ebbs and flows through the doors, some for a hasty refreshment at the bar, others in meetings casual or intense. There are nine other branches in the City, plus one at 9 Cabot Square, Canary Wharf (Tel: 020 7512 0397) and one at 116 St Martin's Lane WC2 (Tel: 020 7655 9800). Opening times vary between 07.30 and 09.00, and half have fitted kitchens that allow them to offer a more extensive menu.

The Counting House

50 Cornhill EC3
Tel: 020 7283 7123
Open: 11.00-23.00
Closed: Sat & Sun

A rare chance to see the inside of one of the City's old bank buildings, given up by Lloyds Bank in early 1997, and now a Fuller's house. A domed skylight and chandeliers, a gallery and old pictures and mirrors look down on the banking floor and an ornate central bar set about with oak tables and leather-bound chairs under the gallery. Good drinking (London Pride is an excellent pint) and decent snacking attracts the City crowd. Food served until 20.00.

Café in the Crypt

The Crypt of St Martin-in-the-Fields, Duncannon St WC2
Tel: 020 7839 4342
Open: 10.00-19.30

Those in the know give thanks for this cool, civilised retreat from the hubbub of Trafalgar Square. Soft lighting and gentle classical music set a soothing tone, and the tombstone- and flagstone-covered floor and the brick arches provide a setting with a difference for the regulars and the tourists who refresh themselves with a cup of tea or a glass of wine and a snack or one of the daily-changing hot specials. Good value is a hallmark of this establishment, whose profits go towards the maintenance of the church above.

Daquise

20 Thurloe St, South Kensington SW7
Tel: 020 7589 6117
Open: 11.30-23.00

An apparent fixture in a changing world, this fully licensed restaurant and café serves Continental and Polish specialities in old-fashioned, slightly down-at-heel surroundings. Coffee and excellent home-made cakes in the late morning give way at lunchtime to the main menu of simple, satisfying dishes like stuffed cabbage, goulash pancakes or hunter's stew, with sweet pastries and puddings to round things off. A special lunchtime set menu offers particularly good value for money. After years of threat from redevelopment, this much-loved local in the same block as South Kensington underground station seems to be in the clear for a few years at least.

Dartmouth Arms

35 York Rise NW5
Tel: 020 7485 3267
Open: 11.00-23.00

Once a pub, now a café bar that's quickly become very much part of the local community. Forthcoming events are displayed on a scroll hanging near one of the windows on a corner site in a residential area between Kentish Town and Highgate. Competitions, games, festivals and jazz regularly feature. On the food front, an imaginative menu typically includes spinach and mushroom soup, oysters, roasts, and tarte tatin, and on Sundays a particularly good late breakfast selection. Good wine list and a variety of ales. Coffee is the splendid Illy, and there's a rack of daily papers for customers to read.

Café Delancey

3 Delancey St, Camden Town NW1
Tel: 020 7387 1985
Open: 09.00-23.30 (Sun till 22.30)

A few steps off bustling Camden High Street, Café Delancey is a long-established, long-hours local stalwart with wooden floors, pot plants and some outside tables on the pavement and in an internal courtyard. Everything on the menu is available all day, starting with coffee and croissants with the daily papers and ranging via salads, deep-fried camembert with calvados jelly and croques ('Delancey' has mozzarella, tomato and crushed olives) to hearty favourites such as eggs and bacon or sausages and onions with the Delancey signature rösti, rack of lamb, or entrecote with a peppercorn sauce. Three-variety chocolate mousse is a delicious way to end a meal, a tempting alternative to the tangy lemon sorbet.

The Deli Bar

117 Charterhouse St, Clerkenwell EC1
Tel: 020 7253 2070
Open: 09.00-20.00 (Wed, Thur & Fri till 23.00, Sat 11.00-23.00)
Closed: Sun

A modern bar and deli in a listed building that was once part of the parish church property. The vicinity has a long tradition of charitable deeds, and in the back room are three 19th-century rolls of honour recording the benevolence of some parishioners to others, which it is the owner's duty to keep on the wall. The ground floor is a bar, with some tables outside getting a glimpse of the mid-afternoon sun. Long and narrow, the bar leads through to that comfortable back room. On the menu are titbits like olives, cornichons, anchovies, pecorino and salami served with Sardinian bread, pasta, salads and sandwiches, all beautifully prepared and very tasty. All the wines are Italian. The walls are decorated with modern art by a group of local artists who take it in turn to show for a month.

Dominique's

218 West End Lane NW6
Tel: 020 7435 3703
Open: 08.00-23.00

For 15 years Dominique's has been providing all-day refreshment to the denizens of West Hampstead. Italian-owned, it offers a variety of breakfasts - traditional English, smoked salmon with eggs benedict - and an array of cakes and pastries for a morning break. Other options on the menu include sandwiches, salads, simple lunchtime dishes and a more elaborate evening list. Marble-topped tables are set invitingly on the broad pavement, with a notice urging passers-by to step inside. The tall wooden folding doors lead into a spacious room where newspapers are available; the walls are hung with the work (for sale) of local artists. Reasonable wine list. A peaceful spot in the week, but packed at the weekend.

El Vino Martin Lane

6 Martin Lane, off Cannon St EC4
Tel: 020 7626 6303
Open: 09.00-20.00 (Fri till 21.00)
Closed: Sat & Sun

Beck's, Steinlager, Budvar, Bishop's Finger, a very extensive wine list at excellent prices, espresso and filter coffee. Visited by City types throughout the day and into the evening (practically no tourists), this wood-panelled City institution, established in 1879, serves first-class sandwiches and sweet things such as cheesecake or fruitcake - excellent with coffee and a glass of port, madeira or dessert wine. Upstairs, displayed under glass, is part of a fireplace that celebrated the declaration of peace after the American War of Independence. Cellar restaurant open for lunch. Other El Vinos are at 47 Fleet St EC4 Tel: 020 7353 6786; Bastion Highwalk, 125 London Wall EC2 Tel: 020 7600 6377; and 30 New Bridge St EC4 Tel: 020 7236 4534.

Euphorium Bakery Bar Restaurant

203 Upper St, Islington N1
Tel: 020 7704 6909
Open: café 08.00-17.00, bar 12.00-14.30 & 18.00-22.30
(Sun 09.00-15.30)

Evolved over five years, Euphorium is now a café, bar and restaurant as well as a bakery. The café on the left displays its mouthwatering patisserie, and beyond it is the bar with its zinc-topped tables, and the restaurant at the back. On fine days there are some dozen tables in the garden. Among the wines are a sparkler from California, three white wines and two reds available by the 175ml glass, notably a viognier and a Firesteed barbera; and by the half bottle and bottle are, for example, a chablis and a chateauneuf. Restaurant food ranges from leek and potato soup or caesar salad to chicken tagine, osso buco and grilled snapper.

Fifth Floor Café

Harvey Nichols
Knightsbridge SW1
Tel: 020 7235 5000
Open: 10.00-22.30 (Sun 12.00-18.00)

After a major shop, those in need of refreshment head for the heights and this bright, chic café, which shares the floor with a restaurant, bar and food market. All the food is seasonal and fresh, and the Mediterranean-inspired menu changes constantly; the cakes, served with the popular 'Fifth Floor Tea' from 15.30 to 18.00, are home-made. A variety of coffees is available, many freshly ground on site. Outside tables on the rooftop terrace. Children are welcome, with high chairs available for tiny tots not quite ready to swap plastic spoons for plastic money.

Florians

4 Topsfield Parade N8
Tel: 020 8348 4060
Open: 12.00-23.00 (Sat & Sun from 11.00) restaurant 12.00-15.00 & 19.00-22.00

The partners owning this congenial café/bar/restaurant came to England some years ago, and having gained experience in the London restaurant/bistro scene, they set up here in November 1989. Their weekend breakfasts are very good (eggs, Italian sausage, bacon, cannellini beans and garlic Toscano bread £4.50, eggs benedict, fishcake with a seafood sauce and fried potatoes £3.50, washed down with a Drury espresso, orange juice, a Bucks Fizz or a Bloody Mary). The bar is always popular for a drink and a snack. This is at the front; past the kitchen is the restaurant at the back with a small terrace that's popular in the summer. The regions of Italian cuisine are very distinctive, and the menu here draws on the traditions of both owners.

Gill Wing Café

300 St Paul's Rd N1
Tel: 020 7226 2885
Open: 09.00-23.00

An oasis at Highbury & Islington Corner, some distance from the busy restaurant area of Upper Street running all the way down to the Angel. English-owned but French-run, this café offers genuine French pastries, cuisine and wine. Michael endows this busy junction with a certain French flair, drawing customers who come to browse through the papers over a croissant and coffee, or lunch Parisian-style (but with a roast on Sunday), or enjoy a simple evening meal. Snacky items on the menu include croques monsieur et madame, omelettes and chicken with mayo in a warm baguette. Michael plays good jazz music as a background during the day, and from Wednesday to Saturday he opens up the basement for live jazz groups. The cream-coloured walls, the art nouveau lights and the bentwood chairs set at marble-topped tables produce a delightful ambience into which all types and ages are attracted.

Est. 1926

Konditor & Cook

Young Vic, 66 The Cut, Waterloo SE1
Tel: 020 7620 2700
Open: 08.30-23.00 (Sat from 10.30)
Closed: Sun

With its own bakery on the premises, this bright, lively café attached to the Young Vic theatre sells a great range of superb cakes and pastries. The breakfast menu, served until 11.30 (till noon on Saturday), runs from toasted brioche, croissants and *pain au chocolat* to scrambled eggs and smoked salmon and the full English. The main menu is available from noon to 20.00 and offers the likes of smoked haddock with poached egg, asparagus and mascarpone ravioli and cider-braised guinea fowl with Bramley apples; the enjoyment level stays high to the last, with those lovely pastries served with organic ice cream or spring-water sorbets. To drink: coffees, teas, Belgian hot chocolate, juices and smoothies, beers, three white wines and two reds by bottle or glass, champagne by bottle or half bottle. The glass conservatory-style frontage is a real sun-trap in this excellent place, where the posters on the walls change with the current Young Vic productions.

LED

171 Farringdon Rd EC1
Tel: 020 7278 4400
Open: 08.00-24.00 (from 10.00 Sun)

Or should it be RED, judging by the colour scheme? Sandwiched between the fire station and the well-known Gazzano Italian deli (it's a little outpost of Italy hereabouts), with a red awning over the window, this is a meeting place for the young, a pre- and post-club venue. The speciality is fresh fruit cocktails with names like HINRG (with apples, carrot, celery and milk), to enjoy over a newspaper or listening to disco sounds. Snacks include baguettes with imaginative fillings like venison sausage, ham and spinach, or focaccia with tomato, mozzarella and basil pesto. A glass of Oxford Landing is £2.50. Good coffee.

Bar Italia

22 Frith Street W1
Tel: 020 7437 4520
Open: 24 hours

A real Soho institution, where London meets Italy at any time of day or night for coffee, snacks, pastries and Serie A on the big screen.

Jerusalem Tavern

55 Britton St EC1
Tel: 020 7490 4281
Open: 11.00-23.00
Closed: Sat & Sun

Named after the Priory of St John of Jerusalem and once part of it, this historic tavern dates back to the 14th century. Now owned by one of the smallest independent breweries in the UK, St Peter's in Suffolk, it retains its old-world interior with its wooden floors, original fireplaces, panelled or glassed partitions, curved windows, an oddball assortment of chairs and tables and wall mosaics depicting the seasons. The beers are naturally the speciality, including fruit beer, wheat beer, porters and a good stout. Also available are three red and three white wines by the glass and espresso coffee. Sandwiches (toasted in the evening) and speciality sausages (excellent lamb and mint) provide the solid fuel. Pavement tables.

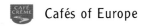

Lomo

222-224 Fulham Rd SW10
Tel: 020 7349 8848
Open: 12.00-23.30 (Sun 12.00-23.00)

A classy modern take on the tapas bar by the people who brought us the successful Lola's restaurant in Camden Passage. Here in SW10, bang opposite the Chelsea & Westminster Hospital, the decor is stylishly modern, with stools perched at the bar and around very small round tables, and four larger, lower tables with more relaxing banquette seating at the back. The menu deals in high-class tapas-style snack dishes, including salt cod brandada, open steak sandwich, garlicky sizzling mushrooms, ditto sizzling chicken, patatas bravas, ham and potato croquetas, cold meats and pretty, leafy little salads. Good value, particularly the 12.00-17.00 deal. Sunday brunch. Well-chosen wines, strong on Spanish, and including the wonderful Pedro Ximenez sherry, which has been described as liquid Christmas pudding. Happy hour (drinks) from 17.00 to 21.00.

Le Metro

28 Basil St SW3
Tel: 020 7589 6286
Open: 07.30-23.00
Closed: Sun

An ideal bolthole for weary shoppers, this cool, stylish, air-conditioned brasserie and wine bar is located in the basement of L'Hotel, next to and in the same ownership as the Capital Hotel. Continental and English breakfasts are served until 10.30 and from noon onwards the main menu comes on stream to tempt with appetising modern creations such as crab, potato and spring onion toasts, or tomato risotto with broad beans and rosemary. There's a great wine list, divided by style, with a large number available by the glass. The afternoon tea ritual is observed from 15.30 to 17.30.

Café Mode

57 Endell St WC2
Tel: 020 7240 8085
Open: 08.00-22.00 (Sat 10.00-20.00)
Closed: Sun

An excellent place to pause in Covent Garden, with a lively atmosphere and friendly, clued-up staff. A light, lemon-coloured back room and a cave-like basement room are the setting for good-value, high-class Italian-style snacks, toasted sandwiches, salads and cheeses. Drink beer, wine or coffee. Pavement tables.

Mona Lisa

417 King's Rd, Chelsea SW10
Tel: 020 7376 5447
Open: 07.00-23.00 (Sun 09.00-17.30)

Take a trip to the World's End and this most egalitarian of cafés, where the plastic-clad tables are usually full from early in the morning till late into the evening. The dishes on the long all-day breakfast menu are excellent fuel before a day's work or for a lunchtime pit stop, and there's a lengthy list of filled rolls and sandwiches for quick snacks. Elsewhere on the long menu are a few other true Brit dishes such as fried cod or steak & kidney pie, but the main thrust is Italian, with big portions of pasta (the parmesan is freshly grated at the table) and classics of the chicken valdostana and liver with butter and sage variety. Good composite salads, too, and always ask about Pepe's specials. Usually smoky, always fun, with affable, hard-working staff, Mona Lisa is one of the few places where a down-to-earth bacon buttie with brown sauce can be found sharing a table with a classy sea bass and a balsamic-dressed salad.

Café Mozart

17 Swains Lane N6
Tel: 020 8348 1384
Open: 09.00-22.00

Scrumptious Viennese pastries, cheesecake and strudel, dumplings, goulash, chicken schnitzel: all good choices at a long-established Austrian café that's a favourite with local solos and families and anyone who's worked up an appetite with an invigorating walk on nearby Parliament Hill. They also do an all-day cooked breakfast. No smoking inside. Tables outside on the broad pavement.

Picasso

127 King's Rd SW3
Tel: 020 7352 4921
Open: 08.00-23.00 (Sun till 22.30)

A popular Italian café among the trendy clothes and shoe shops on busy King's Road, with some tables out on the pavement, packed with snackers from early in the morning till late at night. English and Continental breakfasts start the day, and over the long lunchtime tables are reserved for those who are eating. The menu offers sandwiches, pasta, risotto and daily specials, and there's always a good choice of cakes and pastries. Picasso is next door to the Harley-Davidson shop.

227

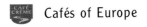

Portrait Café

National Portrait Gallery, 2 St Martin's Place WC2
Tel: 020 7312 2465
Open: 10.00-17.30 (Sun 12.00-18.00)

A photogenic café in the National Portrait Gallery, with a glass ceiling and a display of black-and-white photographs. The food is first-class, whether it's a generously-filled sandwich, an inventive salad or one of the super cakes and pastries. Coffee, cold drinks, and organic wine by glass or bottle.

Putney Bridge Bar

The Embankment SW15
Tel: 020 8780 1811
Open: bar 12.00-23.00

A striking wedge-shaped bar and first-floor restaurant running along the river bank just below the bridge, which is prettily lit at night. The downstairs area is a bar with a snack menu of simple little luxuries like salted almonds, smoked salmon, caesar salad and foie gras. Sit outside on the planked terrace for the full 'river' effect; without knowing it you might see the Athens gold-medallists breezing along the Thames.

St John

26 St John St, Clerkenwell EC1
Tel: 020 7251 0848/4998
Open: bar 12.00-23.00 (Sat from 18.00) restaurant 12.00-15.00 & 18.00-23.00
Closed: L Sat & all Sun

A one-time smokehouse, the chimneys still intact, has been combined with a Georgian town house to become a flagship of British meat cooking, in which all known parts of the pig except the squeak have at some time found their way on to the main menu. The look of the place is bright and functional, with a concrete floor, plain white walls and industrial furniture lit by long, suspended enamelled lamps and a skylight. Trevor Gulliver's wine list always includes some interesting bin ends available by the glass, and Fergus Henderson's menu delights and surprises with unusual offerings like potato soup & cured pork belly, ox tongue with turnips, or shark with leeks and aïoli. For snackers there's a separate section with a terrific all-day bar menu in the same vein; they have their own bakery on the premises, producing some of the finest bread in London. The logo of St John is a pig sectioned off by type of cut: with a week's notice you can order a whole suckling pig, and with no notice at all you can buy a copy of Fergus's cookbook *Nose to Tail Eating - a Kind of British Cooking.*

Sausage & Mash Café

268 Portobello Rd W10
Tel: 020 8968 8898
Open: 11.00-22.00
Closed: Mon

Large S & M symbols in frosted glass announce this great little café sandwiched between takeaways opposite Portobello Green Arcade and virtually under Westway. The name says it all, for this is *the* place to come for a hearty meal of sausage and mash. The sausages come in eight varieties, including Cumberland, creole smokey, wild boar with juniper and vegetarian Glamorgan; there are three kinds of mash - regular, celeriac and green pea - and three gravies - madeira and thyme, roasted red onion and Guinness. If you opt for the £7 deal you can select any three sausages with your choice of mash and gravy, which means that, choosing three different sausages each time, you could have 504 meals here without placing the same order twice. And that's without the special sausages of the week and the other options on the menu, which include baguette sandwiches and salads. Ice creams or the home-made pud of the day to finish; coffees, teas, juices, sodas and beers to drink. A fun place with young, friendly staff.

Smithy's Wine Bar & Restaurant

Leeke St WC1
Tel: 020 7278 5949
Open: 11.00-23.00 (Sat till 18.30)
Closed: Sun

A compulsory stop on any true wine-lover's tour of London, this building was once a main depot of the London General Omnibus Company, dating from the days when the buses were horse-drawn. The old ramp that led to the stables climbs over the real charcoal grill, and the floor is still wood-block, grain-up, and laid in a brick pattern. Converted as recently as 1982, the bar has a great range of beers on draught and by the bottle, but the *pièce de résistance* is the astonishing wine list of over 200 wines from all over the world, listed on blackboards around the bar, and nearly all available by the glass (175 or 250ml). Snacks and bigger dishes are listed on another blackboard and can be ordered throughout the day. Everything comes fresh from the markets to be prepared and sold the same day. Seafood is a speciality.

Stockpot

18 Old Compton St, Soho W1
Tel: 020 7287 1066
Open: 11.30-23.30 (Sun 12.00-23.00)
Generous portions of decent basic food at rock-bottom prices. That's the allure of the little group of Stockpots (plus *Chelsea Kitchen* - see entry), where the starters start at £1 for soup, spaghetti bolognese is £2.50 and the mains are nearly all under £4 - cottage pie with two veg, tuna fishcake with salad and chips, grilled liver and bacon, a large cheese and apple salad. To finish, how about a nostalgia trip with jelly and cream, banana split or golden syrup sponge pudding with custard? This Soho branch has doors that open on to one of the buzziest and most cosmopolitan streets in Soho.
Also at:
40 Panton St SW1 Tel: 020 7839 5142
6 Basil St SW3 Tel: 020 7589 8627
273 King's Road SW3 Tel: 020 7823 3175
50 James St W1 Tel: 020 7486 9185

The Troubadour

265 Old Brompton Rd SW5
Tel: 020 7370 1434
Open: 10.00-23.00
A marvellous, atmospheric Earls Court café that stands out from run-of-the-mill rivals with its unique and unchanging bohemian appeal. A large band of regulars has stayed loyal down the years, and first-time visitors will love the period feel, the clutter of vintage coffee pots and musical instruments, and the extensive menu of home-cooked snacks and more substantial dishes. Downstairs (with a licence till midnight) is a room that acts as a theatre for the live entertainment that takes place almost every night, anything from poetry reading and stand-up comedy to all kinds of music. Starry visitors down the years include Bob Dylan, Jimi Hendrix and Paul Simon. The little garden at the back is a boon in summer.

Patisserie Valerie

66 Portland Place W1
Tel: 020 7631 0467
Open: 08.30-18.00
Closed: Sun
Part of the renowned small chain, this outlet has a distinguished setting in the rejuvenated and imposing building (opened by King George V) of the Royal Institute of British Architects. Situated up an art deco marble staircase on the first floor, with an outdoor terrace, the café occupies an area beside one of the exhibition halls as well as having tables scattered around the mezzanine landing. A row of handsome standard lamps is a notable feature. The morning menu (breakfasty items, snacks, super gateaux) is available until 11.30 (all day Saturday), while the 'regular' menu might include such delights as Thai crab and salmon fishcakes, wild mushroom and sun-dried tomato risotto and a pasta dish of the day. To accompany morning coffee or afternoon tea it's hard to resist the tempting array of high-quality patisserie in the display cabinet. The Institute houses various exhibitions open to the public.
Also at: 105 Marylebone High St W1 Tel: 020 7935 6240
This is Patisserie Valerie at Maison Sagne, opened in the 1920s by Monsieur Sagne, a notable Swiss chocolatier and patissier. The café features some splendid murals.
Open: 07.30-18.45 (Sat from 08.00, Sun 09.00-17.45)
215 Brompton Rd SW3 Tel: 020 7823 9971
8 Russell St, Covent Garden WC2 Tel: 020 7240 0064
250 years of history at what was previously Boswell's Coffee House. It first opened its doors in 1752 as a tea house, and it was here in 1763 that the diarist Boswell met Dr Johnson.
44 Old Compton St, Soho W1 Tel: 020 7437 3466
Open: 07.30-21.45 (Sun 09.00-17.45)

Wok Wok Café Bar & Restaurant

67 Upper St, Islington N1
Tel: 020 7288 0333
Open: 12.00-23.00 (Sun till 22.30)
Split level and on two floors at the front, Wok Wok offers an express lunch that typically includes ribs and hoi sin sauce plus a starter for around £6. Very drinkable house wine from South Africa is £2.60 a glass (actually a stemless goblet). When in café mode, snacks include prawn crackers and rice crackers, but also for unadventurous Westerners cake or muffins to go with an espresso. In bar mode, with house wine or one of the others by the glass, try spring rolls, fish cakes, or chicken satay to dip in a spicy sauce, and to eat with disposable chopsticks if you wish. This is one of six Wok Woks in London, and there are also branches elsewhere.

Bath

The grace and elegance of the 18th century are embodied in the beautiful stone buildings that are such a feature of Bath, but the city and its springs were renowned even before Roman times. It was the Romans who developed the city and turned it into a major spa resort, but its present look is largely the work of the two John Woods, father and son, who used the local honey-coloured stone to create a handsome new city. Pulteney Bridge, lined with little shops, is the work of Robert Adam. Bath is a very busy place, the most visited city in Britain after London, and is full of shops, restaurants, cafés and bars.

Batys

Old Post Office, York Buildings, George St
Tel: 01225 331532
Open: 11.00-23.00 (Sun 12.00-22.30)
Taken over in 1998 and opened in November of that year, Batys was once, as the address and the words on the wall indicate, a post office. One of three around the country, it was initially owned by Greenalls, and is now in the ownership of Scottish & Newcastle. Operating as a brasserie, it offers a full menu throughout the day (as a condition of its licence, though it is not compulsory to eat). It is a spacious, laid back and comparatively quiet place to go during the day, but it gets more boisterous in the evenings. Daytime shopping mothers and prams (wheelchair access) are welcome, while later in the day it is popular with the twenties and thirties crowd.

Browns

Orange Grove
Tel: 01225 461199
Open: 08.00-23.30 (Sat from 11.00, Sun from 12.00)
This was a police station until about 1993, when the law moved to bigger premises. Left locked up for five years until Browns took it over, it opened its doors again in April 1999. The use of the cells at the back now allows customers freedom to come and go as they wish! One of the cells is now a private dining room, with the original doors and even some of the prisoners' graffiti. Upstairs there's a gallery and a cocktail bar, and at the back a large terrace for summertime sipping. A favourite haunt of the Bath smart set.

World Café

130 Crouch Hill Crouch End N8
Tel: 020 8340 5635
Open: 09.30-23.00 (Sun till 22.30)
The World is blue, or at least this corner of it on the outside. The tall windows look out on to terrace tables on the broad pavement. Breakfast is served from opening time to 15.00, while the café menu kicks in at noon and runs till 19.00, and the dinner menu runs from then until last orders at 22.15. For snacks and the sweet of tooth there are pastries, tarts and flans. The blackboards list wines and beers from around the world: wines from France, Spain, Italy, Chile, Australia and South Africa, beers from Belgium, Italy, Spain, Portugal, Turkey, Czech Republic, Australia, Jamaica and Japan! Crowded on fine days at the weekend, inside and out, with locals chatting, grazing or reading the papers over a drink.

Café Fromage

John St
Tel: 01225 313525
Open: 08.30-17.00
Closed: Sun

Carlo Cazzulini, Cazz to his regulars, runs this busy café situated above a cheese shop in the centre of Bath. Climb the narrow staircase up to a small but airy room which overlooks the street to sample Cazz's delicious home cooking with a cappuccino or a glass of house wine. The six tables and two bar stools are served by Cazz, his wife Fiona and friendly staff. This is very much a family affair and Giulio, Cazz's father, often prepares the soups using fresh seasonal vegetables. Daily specials could include sauté of Bleu d'Avergne with avocado, croutons and a mixed leaf salad with sweet basil dressing, or grilled flat mushrooms filled with stilton and walnuts. The selection of six farmhouse cheeses is another popular choice. Croissants, pastries and baguettes start the day. The walls are hung with colourful and varied works by local artists. The prices here are extremely reasonable, so Café Fromage is a popular meeting place; if you a short wait for a table it will be well worth it.
Review submitted by Annie Wild

Green Park Brasserie

Old Green Park Station, Green Park Rd
Tel: 01225 338565
Open: 10.00-23.00 (Fri & Sat till 24.00, Sun & Mon till 15.00)

Opened some eight years ago, Andrew Peters' family-friendly brasserie/café is open all day except Sunday & Monday afternoons & evenings (though there is talk of re-opening at 18.00 on Mondays for salsa dancing; no food will be available). The station fell under the Beeching axe and was empty and disused for a long time. A few years ago Sainsburys opened a store (free parking for two hours where the trains once ran) and there is a market where the main concourse once was. The brasserie occupies the Victorian station building, and in the corner opposite the bar is a library with internet station, where you can travel the world without having to wait for a train!

Pump Room

York St/Stall St
Tel: 01225 444477
Open: 09.30-16.30 (summer till 17.00)

A beautiful, opulent and lofty room built in the late 18th century and the haunt of fashionable people who came to take the remedial waters for which Bath had been renowned since Roman times. With crystal chandeliers, giant Corinthian columns and a view down into the steaming Roman baths, this is a very elegant place for taking refreshment. Lunches only are served between 12.00 and 14.30, light snacks at other times, and a choice of traditional afternoon teas, one with clotted cream. One of the specialities is the Bath bun, a sweet bun with currants and lemon. Live music is played by a trio morning and afternoon, and a classical pianist plays at lunchtime.

Café René & Le Parisien

Shires Yard, Milsom St
Tel: 01225 447147
Open: 08.00-1730 (Sun 09.00-17.00)

This was once a yard and stables for the haulage business of a certain Mr Wiltshire, who was once mayor of the city. Now dubbed as 'a little corner of France in England', it offers a good breakfast menu, both English and continental, good Lavazza coffee, crunchy filled baguettes, pastries baked on the premises and light lunches. You can also enter the yard off either Milsom Street or Broad Street, where the pavement tables under parasols lead to the café. Just off one of the main shopping streets, and among the designer shops in the arcade, it is a popular spot with shoppers and people meeting in town. Also merchandising: coffee, coffee machines, and crockery.

RSVP

5-6 Edgar Bldgs, George St
Tel: 01225 789050
Open: 08.00-23.00 (Sun 10.00-22.30)

Two converted Georgian Bath Stone houses in this elegant raised terrace north of the centre. Spacious as you'd expect, it has a rear terrace, a non-smoking area, and a separate reading room with all the newspapers. Snacks include baps and baguettes, pastries, muffins and croissants for breakfast, and there is a range of coffees and teas by the pot.

Sally Lunn's House

4 North Parade Passage
Tel: 01225 461634
Open: 10.00-22.00 (Sun from 11.00)

Claiming to be the oldest house in Bath, constructed around 1482, and home to Sally Lunn's eponymous brioche-style bun. In 1680 Sally Lunn, a Huguenot refugee, set up shop selling this confection, which is versatile enough to go with both sweet and savoury fillings/toppings. Being based on brioche, it is very light, and it's also quite large - some 7" in diameter. Candle-lit suppers. The Museum in the basement depicts how the pavement was raised one whole floor for the building of the Regency houses of the 19th century, and it shows her original kitchen.

Shades

4 Edgar Bldgs, George St
Tel: 01225 466667
Open: 11.00-23.00

A cosy wine bar in a Georgian basement, once the coal store, pantry and kitchens of the grand house, but for 20 years now a wine bar serving eight whites and eight reds by the glass, draught American Bud, bottled 1664, and Ricard, Illy coffee, and baguette sandwiches. The vaults under the pavement have some eight tables, and there's a bar, kitchen and, in the summer, a garden terrace. It has a regular clientele of people from the professions.

Brighton

One of the country's premier seaside resorts, whose early admirers included the Prince of Wales, later to become King George IV. He bought a fairly ordinary farmhouse called Brighton House and proceeded to turn it, with the architect Henry Holland, into the extraordinary Royal Pavilion that is the town's best-known landmark. The advent of the railways brought Brighton within easy reach of Londoners, and in 1863 the West Pier (long-derelict, though there are plans to restore it) was built at the western (Hove) end of the promenade. The Palace Pier, built in 1899 and apparently influenced design-wise by the Royal Pavilion, remains very much alive, a classic example of a very British institution, complete with games machines by the hundred, fairground rides and sideshows, palm-readers, bars, fish & chips, lettered rock, candy floss and silly hats. Another draw on the seafront is the Volk's Electric Railway, the first public electric railway to run in the British Isles. Built in 1883, it runs along the seafront from the pier to the marina, which, with more than 2,000 moorings and 77 acres of sheltered water, is one of the largest in Europe. Brighton boasts more than 400 eating outlets, including dozens of cafés.

Barkers Café Bar

17-18 Dukes Lane
Tel: 01273 325945
Open: 10.00-18.00 (Sat till 23.00, Sun 09.30-18.00 [till 14.30 Nov-Feb])

A daytime wining and dining venue in a part of Brighton full of interesting little shops. Barkers is decorated with a busy mural and plants, and furnished with green tables and chairs. It has live jazz guitar at the weekends. The aluminium tables and chairs outside are very popular in the warmer weather, especially as the café is in a pedestrian street which widens out at this point.

Browns

3-4 Duke St
Tel: 01273 323501
Open: 08.00-23.00 (Sat from 10.00, Sun 12.00-22.30 - restaurant from 11.00)

The original Browns, established in 1973, is one of Brighton's really trendy wine bar/cafés, with over two dozen wines on the list, many available by the glass. Baguettes and bagels and breakfasts are available weekdays from 08.00 to 10.00. It offers newspapers which you can read at the long high wooden bar-counter made of mahogany, with sturdy Victorian panels below. Plants and Edwardian lighting decorate the room, giving a warm, welcoming appeal. The good coffee, juices and cocktails are popular. The restaurant is two doors down.

Curve

45 Gardner St
Tel: 01273 603031
Open: 08.00-23.00 (Sun 11.00-22.30)
In what was formerly a bric-a-brac market, Curve is a cheerfully decorated bar and brasserie combined with a cabaret and theatre venue. Opened in September 1999, it is owned by the English family, who are renowned as the owners of one of the best seafood and oyster bar-restaurants in town. With this new venture they hope to expand and develop more outlets. Spread over two floors, Curve offers a good choice of English and Continental food, a very decent wine list (two house wines available by the glass) and excellent coffee. Management and staff are Italian, always friendly and on the ball, and this new venture looks certain to bring in the crowds.

Ha!Ha! Bar & Canteen

Pavilion Buildings
Tel: 01273 737 080
Open: 11.00-22.00 (Sat from 10.00, Sun 10.00-21.00)
One of a chain of 11 (the latest is in York), this cheerful place opened in July 1999. Bright and spacious, with a gleaming new zinc bar dominating one side, it's a very inviting spot to pause for a drink and a snack, and solos can browse through the newspapers that are laid out on a butcher's block just inside the door. There's a wide selection of wines and beers, lots of coffee and own-brand shopping of preserves, oils, vinegars and the like: get an order form from the staff and explore the shelves.

Café Puccino's (L'Anima del Caffe)

1 Bartholomew St
Tel: 01273 204656
Open: 08.00-19.00 (Fri & Sat till 23.00, Sun 09.00-22.30)
Bare boards and copper-topped round tables; a sofa in the window. Owner Jeffrey Blake offers a comfortable and relaxed atmosphere in which to enjoy a baked potato, a salad or an all-day breakfast. Three white wines and three reds, good coffees and teas as refreshments. All ages but mostly adults make up the clientele. Italian- and French-style eats are available as well, eg baguettes and panini, croques and pasta. And if you want to stay over, there's a B&B upstairs.

Zerbs Café

21 Gardner St
Tel: 01273 685248
Open: 09.30-18.00 (Sat till 17.30)
Closed: Sun
A small licensed café with round wooden tables and bentwood chairs on wooden floors. It is located in a bohemian street where the young arty types come to discuss their projects and their gigs. Lots of sandwiches in different types of bread - olive, tomato, french, granary - are for sale, and breakfast all day. Grolsch; good coffee.

Bristol

At the beginning of the 18th century Bristol, which had for centuries been a prosperous commercial city, was second in importance only to London. One of the greatest of the early passenger ships, Isambard Kingdom Brunel's *SS Great Britain*, was launched in Bristol in 1843 and now stands in its original dry dock in the Floating Harbour area. It contains a museum depicting the life of Brunel, who was also responsible for the original broad-gauge Great Western Railway and the Clifton Suspension Bridge spanning the Avon Gorge. Bristol is a major centre of the tobacco and aviation industries, and an important centre of learning and the arts, with a distinguished university and theatre company and a busy, lively café scene.

Boston Tea Party

75 Park St
Tel: 0117 929 8601
Open: 07.00-22.00 (Mon till 18.00, Sun 09.00-19.00)
On the left halfway up the hill from College Green is a popular café that's named after the famous squabble in New England in Georgian times. The ground floor of the shop displays all the goodies and has some tables and chairs. This is the non-smoking area. Upstairs is the sofa salon, where you may smoke except between 12.00 and 14.00. Past the kitchen a door leads to the four-terraced sheltered garden. They offer cooked breakfasts, but the best are on Sundays, which are very special. Popular with students, this is one of the best coffee houses in Bristol; good wines are also available, but no beers.

Browns

38 Queen's Rd, Clifton
Tel: 0117 930 4777
Open: 11.00-23.30 (Sat from 10.00, Sun from 12.00)
Built in 1783 as a copy of the Doges Palace, this exceedingly grand building was, until the Second World War took its toll, the best example of Venetian architecture outside Venice. The left hand side was almost totally destroyed, and only the last window is original. The building's life has been one of diverse occupancy: once the senior common room for the university; then the refectory, and a market on Saturdays; a gallery when the real one was burnt down, until it was restored at the end of the 19th century; and a hospital during the war. It is one of the most elegant venues to relax, entertain, or be entertained, with very friendly, attentive staff and lots to see. Long menu always available, with salmon cakes, burgers and steak, mushroom & Guinness pie among the Browns classics. Children's menu, afternoon tea, outside dining, bar terrace. Lots of bottled beers, more than a dozen wines by the glass.
UK Café of the Year 2001

Chicago Rock Café

Unit 2 The Watershed, 1 Canon's Rd
Tel: 0117 929 1361
Open: 11.30-01.00 (Fri & Sat till 02.00, Sun till 22.30)
One of 50 or so Chicago Rock Cafés around the country. It is located alongside Bordeaux Quay at the mouth of the River Frome in the centre of town. Night times are usually theme nights of one type or another. Monday is trade night when the other clubs and bars are closed or close early, Tuesday karaoke, Wednesday varies - sometimes fancy dress, Thursdays are for the banks! Weekend nights are party time. The food offered, all GM-free, ranges from elaborate sandwiches in various breads to snacks and main courses. Good wines and beers and excellent espresso.

Chicane Café

3 Christmas Steps, Lewins Mead
Tel: 0117 9149922
Open: 08.00-17.00 (Sat 10.00-16.00)
Closed: Sun
Along Lewins Mead, where traffic now races where water once did, are some old Bristol houses, leading to Christmas Steps, which in turn lead to the University. Halfway up the steep steps is Chicane Café, a popular student meeting place. It offers a short wine list, a few bottled beers, and two on draught, and good Segafredo coffee; the other speciality is exhibitions of works by local artists. A full cooked breakfast is available till noon.

Clifton Wine Bar

4 Richmond Terrace, Clifton
Tel: 0117 973 2069
Open: 11.00-23.00 (Sun till 22.30)
Probably the oldest wine bar in Bristol, located in the vaulted under-pavement of a terrace high up over the city in Clifton. At the back is a large terraced garden for the summer crowds, for this is one of the most popular venues among the gregarious young - and the not-so-young. One of the specials is the breakfast menu, available till 15.00 as is all their food - salads, baguettes, simple under-£5 main meals and blackboard offerings of the day. The main bar is flagstoned, with an elaborately carved bar counter. It's aimed at students, being near the Students Union, and there's an interactive big screen to test your skills at computer games when there isn't a match to watch. Good wines and good coffee.

Mud Dock Café

40 The Grove
Tel: 0117-934 9734
Open: 11.00-23.00 (Mon till 18.00)
A stylish, well-designed café overlooking the dock, with tables outside. The café is located above a terrific bicycle shop, and bikes hang from the ceiling in the café itself. The decor is agreeably different and so is the menu, with dishes like green apple and mixed leaf salad with roasted pistachios, or merguez and mash. A good range of beers and wines and happy, efficient service set the seal on one of Bristol's top spots for a relaxed meal. A mud dock is the earliest type of dry dock: in tidal quays such as this site boats would sink into the mud, exposing their hulls and allowing work to be carried out. A second Mud Dock, also a combination of bike shop and café, is in Exeter, in a converted warehouse on the quay by the River Exe.

Prom Music/Café/Bar

24 Promenade, Gloucester Rd, Bishopston
Tel: 0117 942 7319
Open: 11.00-23.00 (Sat from 10.00, Sun 10.00-22.30)
For some 10 years this has been a Music Café, but at the beginning of December 1999 it took over what was Bristol Coffee Company, and doubled in size. Apart from Tuesday, which is quiz night, there is live music nightly - jazz on Monday, the other nights vary from blues to folk to rock. Split level, the bar is in the right window, the musicians on the left, and the clientele on bent ply chairs at simple tables on both levels. Outside is a roped-off pavement area with aluminium terrace tables. Snacks include tapas, burgers and pasta, but for many the star of the show is the all-day breakfast.

Tantric Jazz Café Bar

39-41 St Nicholas St
Tel: 0117 940 2304
Open: 10.00-01.00 (Sun from 17.00)
There is live jazz here nightly, with Jazeera and Tony Clark as the resident musicians. The bar is located in a quiet street near the banking centre, and the food listed on the blackboard has a Moroccan slant. Newspapers are available on the big coffee table by the window. Although it has quite a low ceiling it feels spacious because it's a double-fronted property. Oilcloths cover the tables in café style, and a French waitress from St Malo serves espresso. Entry in the evening is £5 including the music and any dish on the menu, and it's well worth a visit. Sunday evenings host the weekly jam sessions.

Taverna dell' Artista

33 King St
Tel: 0117 929 7712
Open: 19.00-02.00 (restaurant 19.00-23.30, Fri & Sat till 24.00)
Closed: Sun & Mon
Owned for almost 30 years by Renato and Natalina Borgnano (who also have Trattoria da Renato across the road), this building dates back to 1640, and is the oldest in King Street. It has a restaurant upstairs and pizzeria/café with a full on-licence to 02.00 downstairs. Angela and Giorgio, the children, run this well-known café, which is frequented by casts of the productions at the nearby Old Vic, and their audiences - and, of course, the loyal regulars who have been coming here since it first opened. Always busy, it's one of the favourite meeting places in Bristol.

Hotel du Vin

The Sugar House, Narrow Lewins Mead
Tel: 0117 925 5577
Open: 07.00-21.30 (Sat & Sun 08.00-22.00)
The site, on the banks of the River Frome, was the old Sugar House (until 1831) and was subsequently put to a variety of industrial uses. Taken over by The Alternative Hotel Company, it opened in its new role in November 1999. Old the building may be, and neglected before its rescue, but it's certainly very swish inside now! You enter through a courtyard with a fountain and smart planked teak tables and chairs. From there you move into the spacious and comfortable lounge bar with leather-bound sofas and coffee tables. There's an excellent wine list, first-class coffee and meals in the restaurant. Breakfasts are available for non-residents from 07.00 to 09.30.

The Vintner Wine Bar

12 St Stephen's St
Tel: 0117 929 1222
Open: 11.00-23.00 (Sat from 18.00)
Closed: Sun
For over 15 years there's been a wine bar here in the arched, bare stone vaults of Crusader House in the banking district of the city centre. Filter coffee and a good wine list: 15 white, 15 red, 9 sparkling, with four of each of the still wines, and two of the sparkling available by the glass. There's a quiet garden for summer sipping in the shadow of St Stephen's Church next door. Under new ownership since January 2000, when a consortium of eight businessmen bought it to preserve its traditions and standards.

Watershed Café

Multimedia Centre, 1 Canon's Rd
Tel: 0117 921 4135
Open: 09.30-23.00 (Sat from 10.30, Sun till 22.30)
In what was a banana warehouse overlooking the old dock basin, an arts and entertainment centre has been developed on the newly named Bordeaux Quay, where the River Frome flows into the River Avon. Espresso (Brian Wogan coffee) with biscuit is a bargain at 80p. The café has been here since the early 1980s and serves filled baguettes, wines by the glass and lots of draught and bottled beers. The menu is interesting and wide-ranging, with the likes of coq au vin and cajun spiced salmon among the typical dishes. The company leases the whole of the upper floor of this ex-warehouse and also has a cinema and a photographic gallery, where courses on film and photography are run.

Leeds

An Anglo-Saxon township on the River Aire grew into a major cloth and weaving centre then an important player in the growth of engineering, electronics and chemical industries. Victorian arcades and a handsome town hall are worth seeing, and Leeds is a notable centre of cultural and sporting activity. The 1990s have been a period of real urban renaissance, with major explosions on the bar, café and club scenes. One of the showpieces is the Waterfront, a once neglected part of the city that has been transformed into a major residential, commercial and shopping area.... and a tourist area, too, with attractions that include the Royal Armouries and Tetley's Brewery Wharf.

Art's Café

42 Call Lane
Tel: 0113 243 8243
Open: 11.00 (12.00 for food)-23.00 (Sun 12.00-22.30)
Art's Café, one of the first of its type in the happening Calls area, pulls in the crowds with good coffee, a decent selection of wines and day-long snacking (with a full and inventive menu in the evening). This is a corner site on split levels, with lots of wood inside and lots of glass to watch what's going on outside.

Carpe Diem

Civic Court, Calverley St
Tel: 0113 243 6264
Open: 08.00-23.00 (Sat 19.00-01.00)
Closed: Sat daytime & all Sun
Carpe diem: seize the chance to visit this lively place tucked away in the basement of a local authority building, with another entrance down some wrought-iron stairs from Great George Street. Inside, the space is impressive, running right through under the building in various bars. Snacks include a good choice of sandwiches, and the café is now open early in the morning for a full choice of breakfasts. Live jazz Friday night.

Fat Cat Café

8 South Parade
Tel: 0113 245 6288
Open: 10.00-23.00 (Sun till 17.00)
This was once a bank, and after that an insurance company office - does that explain the name? It's now a successful café whose outstanding feature is the splendid original wood panelling that was uncovered during the conversion. A late breakfast starts the day but the place is busiest at lunchtime and from early evening onwards, when it serves a full selection of snacks along with many draught beers and some 20 wines.

Fourth Floor Café (Harvey Nichols)

107-111 Briggate
Tel: 0113 204 8000
Open: 10.00-18.00 (Thur & Fri till 23.00, Sat 09.00-23.00, Sun 12.00-17.00)
A smart spot for the refreshment of shoppers in central Leeds, with a modern menu for a relaxed lunch or dinner. Valet parking available in the evening.

Henry's

Greek St
Tel: 0113 245 9424
Open: 08.00-23.00 (Sat from 12.00, Sun 12.00-19.00)
A pleasant bar-café that's open early on working days for breakfast, the time for reading the mail or a newspaper; at lunchtime it's busy with snacking and chatting; the cocktail hour provides relaxation after work; and later on a full menu tempts you to make an evening of it. Sandwiches, salads and pasta are among the popular choices. Beyond the first area, which has the look of a Parisian pavement café, there's lots of stained wood (floor, bar, stools) lightened by the large ceiling light panel and a plant-filled fountain.

Café In Seine

Boar Lane
Tel: 0113 242 2436
Open: 12.00-23.00 (Thur-Sat till 24.00, Sun till 18.00)
Ultra-modern decor highlighted by a distinctive bar counter made up of backlit glazed panels. Italian-style coffees, pots of tea, sandwiches, soup, mussels, daily specials.

Milo

10-12 Call Lane
Tel: 0113 245 7101
Open: 12.00-23.30
Closed: Sun
A pop rock café at its liveliest on Friday and Saturday nights, when a DJ takes control. The Douglas fir bar has a curved plywood front, the walls are rough plaster and the ceiling is clad in stainless steel that undulates across the room. Chief offerings are Columbian coffees, lots of cocktails and snacks such as New York deli sandwiches.

Norman

36 Call Lane
Tel: 0113 234 3988
Open: 11.00-23.00 (Thur-Sat till 02.00, Sun till 22.30)
Arty and quite weird, with a design by Jam of London that includes a door full of toast and doorless lavatories - perhaps a political statement about the breaking down of the gender barrier? Norman attracts the students and young professionals who flock to the Exchange Quarter, especially in the evenings and at weekends. Food includes noodles and other Japanese-style snacks, and there's an American-style pick-up service: you ring, order and then collect in small cardboard cartons. Includes a juice bar.

Quid Pro Quo

Yorkshire House, Greek St
Tel: 0113 244 8888
Open: 10.00-23.00
Closed: Sun
Quid Pro Quo is one of many cafés and bars that occupy the ground floors of office blocks. It's large and busy, and the area immediately in front of it has been enclosed in glass as a permanent terrace. There's a good list of wines, mostly available by the glass, to accompany the sandwiches, salads, snacks and mains such as bangers 'n' mash or Thai curry.

Soho

35 Call Lane
Tel: 0113 242 9009
Open: 11.30-23.00 (Sun 12.00-22.30)
The look here is bare brick walls, a curved glass bar top with a wavy copper front, upholstered bar stools and striking coffee tables with swirls of different-coloured sand under glass panels. Snacks and more substantial meals are available in the bar and on Thursday night there's an added attraction in the shape of a 'Bossomania' Hammond organ.

Yates Wine Lodge

24-28 Boar Lane
Tel: 0113 244 8566
Open: 11.00-23.00 (Sun 12.00-22.30)
Just round the corner from Leeds City station, and a very convenient place to meet, with the pedestrian shopping streets straight ahead. Offering Italian coffee, a range of beers and a very reasonable wine list, the Lodge also does a good line in robust snacks. A popular starting point with the young before a night's clubbing.

Manchester

Linen and wool were important industries in the area as far back as the 16th century, but cotton was king in the 19th century, when the cotton exchange was the heartbeat of the industry. Part of the old exchange is now the Royal Exchange Theatre, just one of many cultural and artistic centres in the city. The Museum of Science and Industry is in Liverpool Road on the site of the world's first railway station.

Abbaye

42 Canal St
Tel: 0161-236 5566
Open: 11.30-23.00 (Thur till 01.00, Fri & Sat till 02.00, Sun till 22.30)
A Belgian-style *moules et frites* café-bar with a bar running the length of the ground floor and a restaurant above. Beer, both bottled and draught, comes in many varieties, with a special glass for each, and there's a list of about 20 wines, all available by the glass. If you don't want a full meal you can have a sandwich, a salad or some mussels in the bar.

Atlas

376 Deansgate, Castlefield
Tel: 0161-834 2124
Open: 11.00-23.00 (Sun till 22.30)
A highly successful café that broke new ground in Manchester's café culture when it opened in 1983. The design is simple, airy, bright and modern, with floor-to-ceiling windows front and back and lightweight tables and chairs. It's a popular spot with media people and musicians, who come to chat and snack on soup, ciabatta sandwiches, salad or a pasta dish. The café is built in a railway arch, and a patio at the back overlooks the canal. Atlas has its own deli across the road.

Bar 38

10 Canal St
Tel: 0161-236 6005
Open: 11.00-24.00 (Thur 11.30-01.00, Fri & Sat 11.30-02.00, Sun 12.00-22.30)
A roomy brewery-owned café-bar with an impressive glass frontage on two floors. The decor is orange and blue - look for the fish-eye mirror on the back wall - and the floors bare timber. A feature downstairs is the communal stainless-steel hand-washing fountain. There's a straightforward wine list and an interesting range of food.

Barça

Arches 8 & 9, Catalan Square, Castlefield
Tel: 0161-839 7099
Open: 11.00-23.00 (Thur-Sat till 24.00, Sun till 22.30)
Taking its name from the abbreviated Barcelona (it's in Catalan Square), this bar-restaurant in converted railway arches is *the* place for drinking and snacking in Castlefield, especially in fine weather overlooking the canal basin. Coffees and beers, daily-changing tapas-style snack menu, contemporary Mediterranean cooking in the restaurant, deli open throughout the day, guest DJs on Tuesday, Thursday, Friday and Saturday.

Lead Station

99 Beech Rd, Chorlton Green
Tel: 0161-881 5559
Open: 11.00-23.00 (Sat from 10.00, Sun 10.00-22.30)
Once a police station, now a popular café-bar. Waitress service will bring you coffee and breakfast, a glass of wine and a snack at simple wooden café tables and chairs. Especially busy at weekends, with lots of newspaper reading plus families having a break. The terrace at the back is a summer bonus.

Manto

46 Canal St
Tel: 0161-236 2667
Open: 11.00-24.00 (Sat till 01.00, Sun till 22.30)
One of the first bars to open up the Canal Street café scene (1992), Manto continues among the leaders and expanded with a restaurant floor in 1998. There's plenty of standing room by the bar, or you can take your drink to a table on the balcony, inside or out, or to a pavement table. Snacks are served until about 22.30.

Metz

3 Brazil St
Tel: 0161-237 9852
Open: 12.00-23.00 (Fri & Sat till 24.00, Sun till 22.30)
The address is misleading as Metz is really on Canal Street, on the other side of the canal, with a tiny iron bridge to take you over there. Apart from a cantilevered balcony just above water level where you can sit outside, there's also a permanently moored barge with terrace tables under a removable canopy. With no fewer than six champagnes on the list, parties here in Gay Village really fizz.

Polar Bar Café

414 Wilbraham Rd, Chorlton-cum-Hardy
Tel: 0161-881 0901
Open: 11.00-23.00 (Sun till 22.30)
An elegant Edwardian cast-iron and glass canopy fronts this popular café-bar, while inside is a spacious bar and café tables scattered around it. It's particularly busy in the evening and at weekends, when the crowds gather to enjoy the draught beer, the good coffee and the appetising snacks. Organic food and fresh juices are to the fore, and the owners have acquired the next-door premises to open a deli-café.

RSVP

64 Deansgate
Tel: 0161-839 0985
Open: 08.00-23.00 (Thur, Fri & Sat till 02.00, Sun 10.00-22.30)
Once T Hayward & Co's glass and china shop, RSVP has a preservation order inside and out, and the handsome cabinet once used to display the Hayward wares now holds some of its wines. Open early for breakfast (excellent caffè latte), they also do a two-course set lunch. Lots of bottled beers, wines by the glass (two sizes) and a variety of cocktails. Weekend is party time, with dancing till dawn and free entry till 2 o'clock in the morning.

The Temple of Convenience

100 Great Bridgewater St
Tel: 0161-288 9834
Open: 11.00-23.00 (Sun 12.00-22.30)
A lapsed public loo has surfaced as a pleasant little café serving tea, coffee, beer, wine and all-day snacks. Live jazz sessions take place on the second and fourth Thursday of every month, and acoustic music three Tuesdays each month ('The Bag in Drag' DJ on the fourth). The musicians and the crowds can make as much noise as they like as there are no neighbours to inconvenience.

Via Fossa

Canal St
Tel: 0161-236 6523
Open: 11.00-24.00 (Thur till 01.00, Fri & Sat till 02.00, Sun 12.00-22.30)
An extraordinary bar on two floors designed by Frank Ennis and making use of furniture from redundant churches in Limerick. In the bars are everything from altar screens to pulpits and pews, scarlet brocade curtains and a row of chamber pots, and you can survey the whole scene from the gallery above. Good beers, reasonable food and a guaranteed good time among a cheerful mixed crowd.

York

The northern headquarters of the Roman army occupying Britain, York later became the centre of Christianity in the north. The medieval Minster is the city's greatest glory, but the place is full of interesting things to see and do: walking along the city walls, ambling in the Shambles, seeing, hearing and even smelling Viking times recreated in the Jorvik centre, visiting one of the finest railway museums in the world and recharging the batteries in one of the city's many tea shops and cafés.

Bettys Café & Tea Rooms

6-8 St Helen's Square
Tel: 01904 659142
Open: 09.00-21.00

A legend in the North, where the original Bettys was opened in Harrogate in 1919 by Frederick Belmont, a Swiss confectioner. Bettys has made a name for itself with its excellent home baking, which runs to over 400 items both sweet and savoury, and stepping into any of the branches is a truly self-indulgent experience. Be amused by street performers in the square as you languish in luxury over a hot 'fat rascal' - oozing butter and sure to keep you satisfied for hours! Themed evenings of food and entertainment throughout the year (eg 'Winter Jazz') are a must, but be sure to book. Speciality beverages, unusual snacks, hearty meals and cakes to die for - try one and you're sure to take some home! Relaxing, comforting, with waitresses who really know how to smile - let's face it, as the locals say, if you haven't been to Bettys you haven't been to York! Other Bettys, all of them very child-friendly, are in Harrogate, Ilkley and Northallerton.
Review submitted by Jean Horsley

Café Concerto

21 High Petergate
Tel: 01904 610478
Open: 10.00-22.00

Very much in tune with the needs of locals, students and visitors to York, Café Concerto is one of the very best of its many cafés and informal eating places. Just 100 yards from the Minster, it's small, relaxed and friendly, with lots of plants in the window, and yellowing sheet music on the wall. You can enjoy an enormous cup of mocha while listening to Ella Fitzgerald and reading the newspapers provided; or choose from the excellent patés and gratins and savoury tarts, accompanied by interesting breads and salads. There's a daily 'Concerto Dauphinoise', perhaps with ham, feta, sweet cherry peppers and basil. Everything is home-made and the cakes and puddings are as great as everything else - so leave room! Reasonably priced wines are available by the glass.

Gert & Henry's

Jubbergate, The Market
Tel: 01904 621445
Open: 10.00-22.00
Closed: Sun

In a building that in parts must be 500 years old and a café-restaurant for at least the last 100, the ambience is of a cosy tea room. Teas are indeed served, along with coffees, beers, wines and full meals. The espresso is excellent, served with an amaretto biscuit. Traditional English food, substantial and very reasonably priced. The music is Ella and Broadway musicals.

Harkers Café Bar

1 St Helen's Square
Tel: 01904 672795
Open: 10.00-23.00 (Sat from 09.00)

In a spacious, once institutional building in a largely pedestrianised square, Harkers serves breakfast, lunch, dinner and a pre-theatre dinner (not Saturday). Civilised refreshment in comfortable surroundings. Happy hour from 17.00 Sunday to Tuesday, 17.00-20.00 Wednesday to Friday.

Treasurer's House Tea Rooms

Minster Yard
Tel: 01904 646757
Open: 11.00-16.30

The ancient former home of the Treasurers of York Minster, in the care of the National Trust since 1930, was restored to its original splendour between 1897 and 1930 by the Yorkshire industrialist Frank Green. Period rooms contain a fine collection of 17th and 18th century furniture, glass and china, and from the medieval hall to the old kitchen there is something to interest everyone. Admission is free to the Art Gallery and to the basement Tea Rooms, where home baking is the main attraction (Yorkshire lemon tart is a favourite from the National Trust cookbook); soup, sandwiches and filled jacket potatoes give excellent support. Children have their own section of the menu, and high chairs can be provided. House wines and three Yorkshire fruit wines, produced in the cellars of a 19th century flax mill on the banks of the River Nidd, are available by the glass or bottle. No smoking, as at all National Trust outlets. Another National Trust Tearoom in York is at Goodramgate.

Edinburgh

A city rich in history and culture, full of handsome buildings and dominated by the Castle, the birthplace of James VI and once the home of Mary Queen of Scots. The Castle looks towards Arthur's Seat, which rises over 800 feet and provides spectacular views. Edinburgh fills to bursting point in August, when the annual festival and military tattoo take place. Throughout the year there's a thriving café and bar scene.

Blue Moon Café

36 Broughton St/1 Barony St EH1
Tel: 0131-557 0911
Open: 11.00-00.30 (Fri till 01.00, Sat 09.00-01.00, Sun 09.00-00.30)

A great meeting place for the locals, and a good place for visitors to find an ideal recovery station. And if you go alone, there's a varied selection of things to read. The menu is wide-ranging (traditional, vegetarian, continental breakfasts, filled potatoes, focaccia sandwiches, burgers, lasagne, Tex-Mex), and there's a decent wine list and plenty of bottled and draught beers. It's a rabbit warren of a place - you enter through two rooms then pass the kitchen to get to a room facing on to Broughton Street. Meanwhile, downstairs, left leads to the lavatories, right to their shop. Particularly friendly and helpful staff.

City Café

19 Blair St EH1
Tel: 0131-220 0125
Open: 11.00-01.00

The hippest day/night meeting place for the city's youth, or anyone with a love of chrome, pool (two tables), beer, coffee, burgers, smoke and music. Daylight hours see quiet visits by victims of the night before, early evening sees after-workers and tourists, then it's back to the night life. Great bar, good house red, good food - nachos, fry-ups, club sandwiches, venison burgers, vegeburgers. Menu available till 22.00. A cross between art deco and 50s in style, it has a very long bar with a laminate top and an aluminium reeded front. There are four tables out on the terrace on the steep hill.

The Elephant House

21 George IV Bridge EH1
Tel: 0131-220 5355
Open: 07.30-22.00 (Sat & Sun 08.00-20.00)
A very popular and relaxed café proud of its wide selection of teas and coffees also offering a decent choice of beer and wine. Food is mostly pies and quiches and salads, but there are a few hot specials, plus an all-day Continental breakfast and lots of desserts. The walls are adorned with pictures of elephants, coffee information and shows of local and student artwork. There are also newspapers, chess sets and a board for small ads. Good view of the Castle from the back window of a typically lofty Edinburgh room in what was once a solicitor's office.

Café Grande

182 Bruntsfield Place EH10
Tel: 0131-228 1188
Open: 09.00-23.00 (Thur-Sat till 24.00, Sun 10.00-18.00)
The former La Grande Cafetière, on a busy shopping street between a butcher and a ladies' dress shop. It now regards itself as a café/bistro, but is quite happy for the morning crowd to drift along on coffee, wines (after 11.00) and newspapers, though a good range of breakfasts is served and they encourage lunchers. In the evening it becomes a simple but very pleasant bistro, where a meal ends with a choice from the impressive dessert cabinet.

Caffè Lucano

37-39 George IV Bridge
Tel: 0131-225 6690
Open: 07.00-22.00 (Sun 10.00-20.00)
Lots of cakes, salads and sandwiches: bruschetta open sandwiches served on a breadboard are a speciality. Fully licensed, but completely non-smoking. Buy six coffees, the seventh is free.

> "Yes, social friend, I love thee well,
> In learned doctors' spite;
> Thy clouds all other clouds dispel,
> And lap me in delight."
> **Charles Sprague**, *To My Cigar.*

Malmaison Brasserie & Café

1 Tower Place, Leith
Tel: 0131-555 6969
Open: Brasserie 07.00-22.00 (Sat & Sun 08.00-22.30), Café/bar 10.00-22.00 (Sun till 22.30)
The hotel is modern, the building Scottish Baronial; on one side of the entrance is the brasserie, on the other the café, French in style. Food is served all day and in summer it's very pleasant to sit outside on the cobbled quayside. Inside is a central bar surrounded by intimate booths, tables and chairs, some high at bar level, some for eating at with wicker chairs, and some coffee tables with carvers and a chesterfield. Patisserie and snacks are available throughout the day in the café, there's a good choice of wines by the glass.

Ryan's

2 Hope St, West End
Tel: 0131-226 6669
Open: 07.30-00.45
In Edinburgh's fashionable West End, occupying a strategic corner site on ground and basement floors, is this very popular meeting place. Outside, a host of aluminium tables and chairs crowds the pavement; there's a glassed-in terrace for taking coffee or breakfast on chillier days, while inside there's a warm welcome in spacious rooms under a faux-vaulted ceiling with soft lights and pretty flowers. Good wines, and the best pint of Guinness in town.

Valvona & Crolla Ltd

19 Elm Row EH7
Tel: 0131-556 6066
Open: 08.00-17.00
Closed: Sun
Italian specialist retailer, wine merchant, café, bar, baker. Sophie Grigson's favourite shop, and Antonio Carluccio has done a show here. You pass through what must be the greatest Italian deli-cum-wine shop in the UK, up some steps to the café with an atrium running its length. Wonderful coffee, ten wines by the glass (or you can buy a bottle in the shop, add £3 corkage and enjoy it in the café). Super bakery. A real must to visit when in Edinburgh.... or come just for it! No smoking. Twice a month and throughout the Festival, it's open in the evening for dinner featuring regional Italian recipes.

Glasgow

Scotland's largest city, and the third largest in Great Britain, Glasgow occupies much of the Clyde valley. It prospered successively through trade with American, cotton, textiles, coal mining, iron founding, chemicals and, most notably, shipbuilding. Few buildings of historical interest remain, though the Charles Rennie Mackintosh legacy is important and many of the old warehouses in the Merchant City district have been handsomely restored. Glasgow is also blessed with many parks and centres of education and culture, and there's a growing café scene.

Austin's

61 Miller St
Tel: 0141-221 0444
Open: 12.00-24.00

Robert Austin opened here in September 1999 after selling his place of 14 years in Hope Street. It's one large room divided into four areas: an eating area with wicker-style chairs set at wood and chrome tables; a lounge area with coffee tables and upholstered stools and a sofa; high tables and bar stools; and a marble-topped bar. The floor is partly herringbone timbered and partly crazy-paved in tiles and slate, while the ceiling is upheld by two giant pillars of a tree trunk with branches outstretched. Espresso coffee, wines by bottle or glass, snacks listed on a blackboard. Cheerful staff, and a happy 25+ clientele.

Babbity Bowster

16-18 Blackfriars
Tel: 0141-552 5055
Open: 08.00-24.00

A Robert Adam town house is home to an up-market pub/café-bar/restaurant with a hotel attached, one of the first stylish renovations in the revived Merchant City district. Breakfast is served from opening time, and at noon the full menu becomes available for the rest of the day. Barbecues on the patio in summer. The name derives from a Scottish dance, as does the name of the first-floor restaurant, Schottische. Babbity means 'bob at', Bowster is a bolster. The mind boggles! Very good wines; snacks include Italian-style panini and venison sausages & mash.

Café Gandolfi

64 Albion St
Tel: 0141-552 6813
Open: 09.00-23.30 (Sun from 12.00)

Scrubbed oak floors, mahogany-panelled walls and chunky designer furniture are distinguishing features of this bustling café in the old Merchant City district where the old fruit, cheese and furniture markets once stood. Following breakfast from 09.00 and mid-morning snacks of croissants and fruit scones, the choice widens at lunchtime with a seasonally-changing menu. There is always a wide choice of sandwiches and a good selection of cheese, and on the bar is a selection of wines available by the glass (two sizes), the whites kept in a cooler.

Café Rogano

11 Exchange Place
Tel: 0141-248 4055
Open 12.00-23.00 (Fri & Sat till 24.00)
Closed: 25, 26 Dec & 1-3 Jan

Rogano was launched in 1935, the same year as the Clyde-built *Queen Mary*, and there are echoes of the great liner in the art deco style of maple, chrome, seascape murals, ceiling fans and potted palms. The upstairs café is the less formal setting for a good variety of brasserie-style meals with an emphasis on seafood, but with plenty of light snacks also available. Espresso coffee is served with pieces of fudge-like brown sugar (which are delicious without the coffee!).

Willow Tea Rooms

217 Sauchiehall St
Tel: 0141-332 0521
Open: 09.30-16.30 (Sun from 12.00)
Closed: Some Bank Holidays

Charming and refined tea rooms set in a beautifully restored building designed at the turn of the century by Charles Rennie Mackintosh. The place seems made for the old-fashioned cream teas that are served all day, and there's also a fair selection of salads and savoury snacks. The founder, Miss Catherine Cranston, was an advocate of temperance, so this tea room is unlicensed. Perhaps she also believed in not getting into debt, as they don't take credit cards! At the newer Willow at 97 Buchanan Street (Tel: 0141-204 5242) you can enjoy a glass of wine with your food.

Madison

59-63 Botanic Avenue
Tel: 028 90 330040
Open: 07.00-24.00 (Wed-Sat till 01.00)
The roomy café-bar part of a hotel, with plenty of light coming in through the imposing glass frontage. A long bar down one side serves the open space in the centre, and beyond are tables where you can enjoy breakfast or lunch. A party atmosphere makes the place buzz in the evening.

McHugh's

29-31 Queen's Square
Tel: 028 90 247830
Open: 12.00-01.00 (Sun till 24.00)
There's live music on Thursday, Friday and Saturday at McHugh's, which retains its 18th-century front room with its low ceiling, curved bar and carved wood around the shelves behind it. The other spaces are more modern, certainly very comfortable, but less intimate. Open late every night, with a warm welcome guaranteed. The menu changes monthly.

Belfast

Beginning life as a series of forts guarding a ford across the River Farset, which now runs hidden beneath the High Street, Belfast slowly grew in importance, expanding in the 17th and 18th centuries with the growth of the textile and ship-building industries. Those areas remain powerful forces today, but the city has developed in many other directions and now enjoys a varied and thriving cultural life, with four theatres, an opera season and an Arts Festival each November. The bar and café scene is looking up, and visitors can always be sure of a warm and genuine welcome.

Café Society

3 Donegall Square East
Tel: 028 90 439525
Open: 08.30-21.00 (Thur-Sat till 22.00)
Closed: Sun
A chic Continental café and restaurant in the main square by the City Hall, on the edge of the shopping district. It opens in the morning for breakfast, offering bagels, croissants, scones and pastries to accompany a variety of coffees and delicious hot chocolate. At lunchtime it serves light snacks, and from 17.30 a bistro meal for two is available.

Monico Bars

17 Lombard St
Tel: 028 90 323211
Open: 11.00-23.00
Closed: Sun

Shoppers can take a break from the hassle and bustle in the comfortable lounge and salon areas here, sipping a coffee or a beer in one of the inviting booths. Hand-drawn real ales are the speciality. At lunchtime there's a menu of the day of traditional Irish fare.

Morrisons

21 Bedford St
Tel: 028 90 248458
Open: 12.00-24.00 (Thur-Sat till 01.00)

Like the famous Morrissey's in Abbeyleix, Morrisons is modelled on a Victorian grocer's shop. The provisions are not for sale, and the counter where food would have been sliced and weighed and served now acts as a servery for meals. Business people come here at lunchtime and after work, and in the evening all ages gather to enjoy the company and the traditional surroundings.

Bar Twelve (Metro)

12 Lower Crescent
Tel: 028 90 323349
Open: 11.00-01.00 (Sun 17.00-23.00)

On the corner of Lower Crescent and Botanic Avenue is a grand town house called The Crescent incorporating a hotel, a brasserie and this café-bar, comfortably appointed in Gothic style. Chef Tony O'Neill produces an inventive menu of excellent dishes such as goat's cheese frittata or sweet chili chicken with fried rice and black sesame seed sauce.

Vincents

78/80 Botanic Avenue
Tel: 028 90 434546
Open: 09.00-23.00 (Sun from 10.00)

Modern in style, with wooden-seated wrought-iron chairs set at light wooden tables, Vincents matches the mood of its setting in the cosmopolitan area south of the centre. In the morning good coffee and breakfast is served to business people or anyone wanting to relax with a newspaper, while the main choice of food ranges far and wide, from France to America and Morocco to Mexico.